Pg 33   LESSON 8. NUMERALS

Or Fracker   test in numerals.

Test on ? of 8 lessons

Dec ?

etc.

Lesson 9 [37·38 -39

Lesson 9 complete to 41 (both
write übung & übersetzung

12/13/46 Pg 41 written übun über
42 to Bottom 43 Transl.

12/16/46 Pg. 42 to übersetzung written

(B)

VOCab

| übersit Pg 91 & 96 |
| Translate lesson 19 & 20 |

1. He gave my sister this book
2. she will give it to her brother
3. Yesterday I had no money   (Gestern)   } See
4. I did not have it yesterday (Gestern) } book
5. speak louder with me (to one child)
6. Speak louder with us, children
7. Speak louder with him
8. Hold your glass, Karl
9. Hold your glasses
10. Hold your glass (formal)
11. The germans live in Germany
12. Some germans live in America
13. A good acquaintance of mine (Bekannte)
14. has bought a new book   (von mir)
14. I have been the city for three weeks
15. Since when have you been my friend
16. At what time does our German lesson begin
17. At what time does it end (when is it at end)

| Imperatives of sein, haben, werde)

CONCISE
GERMAN GRAMMAR

By

B. J. VOS
Professor Emeritus
Indiana University

With

Readings, Exercises and Supplementary Exercises

by

HEDWIG G. LESER
Indiana University

NEW YORK
HENRY HOLT AND COMPANY

PREFACE

In the *Concise German Grammar*, as indicated by its name, the grammatical sections have been curtailed. All facts essential for a beginner have, however, been treated. Minor items are relegated to the Notes on the text. Wherever feasible, the example precedes the rule and, in accordance with the same principle, the Lesson Vocabularies have been placed after the German texts.

A wholly new set of Readings and Exercises has been provided. These are the work of Professor H. G. Leser, who has also elsewhere acted as critic and adviser. In particular, the luminous chapter on Indirect Discourse is entirely hers.

In Part I, the German text presents scenes from life, whether they be of an everyday character or constitute a pleasant break in the routine of the year. As examples may be cited: a family dinner, marketing, a film, a birthday party, a ball, Christmas and New Year celebrations, a betrothal, a wedding. These are all of an authentic character and will give actuality and a touch of color to the work of the classroom. Part II retells, in simple language, Carl Schurz' thrilling account of the escape of Kinkel from Spandau. In both parts there has been a conscious effort to avoid text-book German and to use throughout the language that is actually spoken and read by educated Germans.

The English Exercises (übersetzung) are frankly based on the principle of imitation, the fundamental principle of all language acquisition. The best preparation for them is a close study of the original, rather than a thumbing of the English-German Vocabulary.

Los Angeles, May, 1941.   B. J. Vos.

CONTENTS

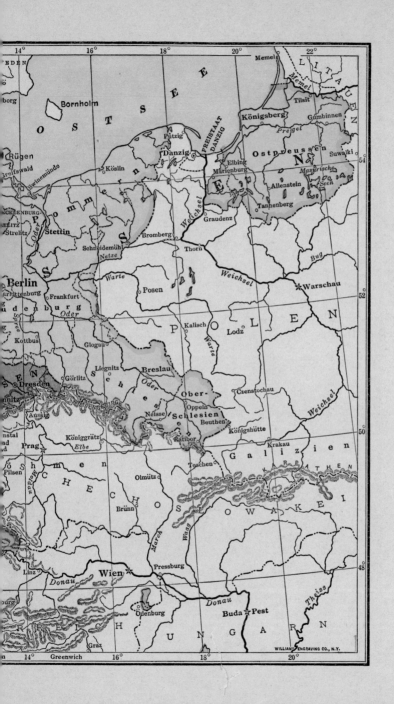

CONCISE GERMAN GRAMMAR

INTRODUCTION

ALPHABET

1. **Alphabet.** The German characters, more especially the capitals, differ considerably from the English forms.

German Form	German Name	Roman Form	German Form	German Name	Roman Form
𝔄 𝔞	ah	a	𝔑 𝔫	enn	n
𝔅 𝔟	bay	b	𝔒 𝔬	oh	o
ℭ 𝔠	tsay	c	𝔓 𝔭	pay	p
𝔇 𝔡	day	d	𝔔 𝔮	koo	q
𝔈 𝔢	ay	e	𝔑 𝔯	er (as in error)	r
𝔉 𝔣	eff	f	𝔖 𝔰	ess	s
𝔊 𝔤	gay	g	𝔗 𝔱	tay	t
𝔥 𝔥	hah	h	𝔘 𝔲	oo	u
𝔍 𝔦	ee	i	𝔙 𝔳	fow	v
𝔍 𝔧	yot	j	𝔚 𝔴	vay	w
𝔎 𝔨	kah	k	𝔛 𝔵	ix	x
𝔏 𝔩	ell	l	𝔜 𝔶	üpsilon	y
𝔐 𝔪	emm	m	𝔷 𝔷	tset	z

(a) Do not confuse f and ſ, n and u.

(b) For the German script see the Appendix.

2. Note that capital *I* and *J* have the same form: Italien, *Italy;* Jahr, *year.*

3. *s* has two forms ſ and ß. At the end of a word or syllable ß

ix

is used, elsewhere ſ: ſagen, *to say;* leſen (le=ſen), *to read;* Hauŝ, *house;* zu Hauſe (Hau=ſe), *at home;* Hauŝfrau, *housewife.*

4. Double *s* is written ß or ſſ. Both are pronounced as *ss* in *glass.*

    (a) At the end of a word or syllable, and before a t, ß is used: Fuß, *foot;* Fußball, *football;* er haßt, *he hates.*

    (b) Between vowels ſſ stands after a short vowel, ß after a long vowel: Wäſſer, *water;* Stråße, *street;* häſſen, *to hate.*

In Roman type, used in nearly all German scientific books, *ss* represent ſſ, while for ß a special type is used: Wasser, Straße. In English script, the two are distinguished as *ss* and *sz*, or the distinction is disregarded, by writing *ss* for both.

The student is advised to get the pronunciation of German words through imitating the teacher. A fairly complete treatment of German pronunciation is found in the Appendix.

CONCISE GERMAN GRAMMAR

PART ONE

LESSON I

GENDER

1 Gender. Nouns are masculine, feminine, or neuter. All names of objects, living and lifeless alike, have gender.

With living beings, the sex ordinarily fixes the gender. Thus Bater, *father*, is masculine; Mutter, *mother*, feminine. In a few cases, however, gender and sex differ. Thus Weib, *woman*, Mädchen, *girl*, Fräulein, *young lady*, are all neuter.

In English, the name of a lifeless object is regularly neuter, and the pronoun *it* is used in speaking of it. In German, lifeless objects are as frequently masculine or feminine as neuter.

2 Definite Article. For the English *the*, German has the three forms: der (masc.), die (fem.) das (neut.). The gender of the German word determines the form used.

der Bater the father	die Mutter the mother	das Kind the child
der Tisch the table	die Schule the school	das Buch the book

Article and noun must be associated from the start. It is not enough to know that *table* is Tisch. The word must be learned as der Tisch, *the table*.

3

3 **Er, sie, es.** Of a masculine noun, whether denoting a person or a thing, one uses **er,** *he;* of a feminine noun, **sie,** *she;* of a neuter noun, **es,** *it.* Thus, of der **Bleistift,** *the pencil,* one says **Er liegt auf dem Tisch,** *It lies on the table;* of die **Feder,** *the pen,* **Sie liegt auf dem Tisch;** of das **Buch,** *the book,* **Es liegt auf dem Tisch.**

Never use **es** of masculine or feminine nouns.

Notice the correspondence: **der : er; die : sie; das : es.**

4 **Nouns** begin with a capital letter.

SONNTAG

Es ist Sonntag. Die Kinder besuchen (*visit*) **die Eltern.**
„Guten Tag, Vater und Mutter!" sagen sie.
„Ach, wie schön, daß ihr kommt!" sagen Vater und Mutter.
Die vier Kinder, zwei Söhne und zwei Töchter, sind schon groß
5 (*grown-up*).
Hans (*Jack*) **ist noch zu Hause, er geht noch zur Schule.**
Paul ist Kaufmann[1]**; Martha ist Lehrerin.**
Marie ist verheiratet (*married*), **sie kommt mit Mann und Kind.**
Das Haus ist warm, und das Essen ist fertig.
10 **Die Familie geht zu Tisch.**

VOKABELN

die Eltern parents	**das Kind** child; **Kinder** children
das Essen dinner, food	**die Lehrerin**[1] (woman) teacher
die Fami'lie (pron. *familye*) family	**der Mann** man, husband
das Haus house	**die Mutter** mother
der Kaufmann business man	**die Schule** school

[1] A noun of vocation in the predicate, if without adjective, stands without the indefinite article.
[2] A 'man teacher' is **Lehrer;** the **=in** makes the word feminine.

der Sohn son; Söhne sons
der Sonntag Sunday
der Tag day
der Tisch table
die Tochter daughter; Töchter daughters
der Vater father
geht goes
ihr kommt you come; sie kommt she comes; sie kommen, they come
sie sagen they say
ach oh

alle all
fertig ready
groß large; klein small
gut good
mit *w. dative* with
nicht not
noch still, yet
schon already
schön beautiful, nice
warm warm
wie how, how?
zu to; zur to the

ist is; sind are; hat has
und and; daß that; ja yes; nein no
wer? who? was? what? zwei two; vier four

REDEWENDUNGEN (IDIOMS)

guten [1] Tag! how do you do?
zu Hause at home

zur Schule to school
zu Tisch to dinner

FRAGEN

1. Was sagen die Kinder zu Vater und Mutter? 2. Sind alle vier Kinder noch zu Hause? 3. Wer geht noch zur Schule? 4. Was ist Paul? 5. Ist Martha verheiratet? Was ist sie? 6. Ist Marie verheiratet? 7. Wer kommt mit Marie? 8. Wie ist das Haus? 9. Ist das Essen fertig? 10. Wer geht zu Tisch?

ÜBERSETZUNG

1. The children say how do you do to father and mother. 2. The children are already grown. 3. Jack is still at home; he goes to school. 4. Paul is a business man. 5. Martha is not married; she is a teacher. 6. Marie

[1] At present also used for *good-bye*.

has a (eine) family. **7.** Is the food still warm? **8.** Is the family small? — No, it is not small. **9.** Is the table large? — Yes, it is large. **10.** How nice that the children come.

LESSON TWO

THE DEFINITE ARTICLE

5 **Cases.** German has four cases, the nominative, genitive, dative, and accusative.

6 **der, die, das** is declined as follows:

	Singular			Plural
	Masc.	Fem.	Neut.	M. F. N.
Nom.	der	die	das	die
Gen.	des	der	des	der
Dat.	dem	der	dem	den
Acc.	den	die	das	die

The plural forms are the same for all genders. This is true of the plural forms of all adjectives and pronouns.

7 **Use of Cases.**
Nominative. Der Enfel ist jung, *The grandson is young.* The nominative, the English subjective, is the case of the subject. It is also used in the predicate after such verbs as *to be, to become:* Ich bin der Enfel, *I am the grandson.*

Genitive.

(*a*) des Vaters Buch, *the father's book.*

(*b*) das Buch des Vaters, *the book of the father.*

The genitive expresses the owner, des Vaters being the equivalent of both 'the father's' and 'of the father,' Either (*a*) or (*b*) is correct. If the word for the owner is feminine, as in das Buch der Mutter, the second order is preferred in the spoken language. If the 'owner' is a lifeless thing, as in das Papier des Buches, the second order alone is used, as in English, where one would not say 'the book's paper' but only 'the paper of the book.'

Dative.

(*a*) Ich gebe dem Vater das Buch, *I give the father the book* or *I give the book to the father.* The dative is the case of the indirect object. In English 'to' is omitted whenever the indirect object comes before the direct. In German all indirect objects are put in the dative.

(*b*) Nach dem Essen, *After the dinner.*

The dative is also used after certain prepositions.

Accusative.

(*a*) Der Vater liest den Brief, *The father reads the letter.*

The accusative (objective) is the case of the direct object.

(*b*) Das Buch ist für den Vater, *The book is for the father.*

The accusative is also used after certain prepositions.

8 **Feminine Nouns** do not change in the singular: Nom. die Mutter, Gen. der Mutter, Dat. der Mutter, Acc. die Mutter.

9 **Genitive.** The masculine and neuter nouns of the Vocabularies on pages 4 f. and 9 all have a genitive singular in =s or =es: der Vater, des Vaters. The Vocabularies of subsequent lessons indicate such genitives singular.

10 Present Indicative of fein, *to be*.

ich bin, I am
du bift, thou art, you are
er (fie, es) ift, he (she, it) is
    Sie find, you are

wir find, we are
ihr feid, you are
fie find, they are

CAUTION. Pronounce the b of find and feid as t. App., p. 202.

11 du, ihr, Sie.

du. The pronoun du, *thou, you*, is used:

(*a*) toward intimate friends, members of one's family, and young children;

(*b*) toward animals;

(*c*) like the English *thou*, toward God.

ihr is the plural of du and is used, for example, in speaking to two or more young children.

Sie. In all other cases *you* = Sie. It is always written with a capital. Like the English *you*, it is used for singular and plural alike. The verb form is the same as that for fie, *they*. Thus fie find, *they are*, but Sie find, *you are*. Use Sie when you know of no particular ground for using du or ihr. Sie is polite and conventional.

BEI TISCH

„Seid ihr hungrig?" fragt der Vater. „Ja, wir find fehr hung= rig," antworten alle. Die Mutter ruft Anna, die Köchin des Haufes, und Anna bringt die Suppe. Die Mutter gibt dem Vater, den Kindern (dat. *children*) und dem Enkel einen (*a*)
5 Teller Suppe. Nach der Suppe kommt der Braten (*roast*). Der Vater fchneidet den Braten und gibt der Mutter das größte Stück. „Das Stück ift zu groß," fagt die Mutter und lacht. Anna geht wieder in die Küche und holt die Kartoffeln, das Gemüfe und den Salat.

„Ich will den Spinat nicht,“ sagt Peter, Maries Söhnchen, und 10
weint. Ernst, der Vater des Kindes, ist sehr böse und sagt: „Du
bist unartig, Peter, und du bekommst keine Speise.“ Peter ißt nun
ein bißchen Spinat und bekommt auch Speise.

Der Vater, Paul und Ernst, der Schwiegersohn (*son-in-law*),
rauchen nach dem Essen. „Die Zigarre ist gut,“ sagt Ernst. „Ja, 15
sie ist auch teuer,“ sagt der Vater.

Martha lobt Anna und sagt: „Sie sind eine (*a*) sehr gute
Köchin.“ Das freut das Mädchen sehr.

VOKABELN

der Enkel grandson
das Gemü'se (green) vegetable
die Kartof'feln potatoes
die Köchin cook
die Küche kitchen
das Mädchen girl
das Söhnchen little son
die Speise dessert, food
das Stück piece
der Teller plate
die Zigar're cigar
bekom'men to get
bringen to bring, take
freuen to please
gibt gives
holen to fetch, go and get
ißt eats
loben to praise

rauchen to smoke
rufen to call, call out
schneiden to cut
ich will I want
auch also, too
ein bißchen a little
böse angry
das that (demonstr.)
zu groß too large; das größte the
   largest
hungrig hungry
kein no; none
nach w. *dative* after, to
nun now
sehr very; very much
teuer dear, expensive
unartig naughty
wieder again

der Salat' salad; der Spinat' spinach; die Suppe soup
fragen ask; antworten answer; lachen laugh; weinen cry
wessen? whose? wem to whom? wen? whom? in in

REDEWENDUNGEN

bei Tisch at table, at dinner   ein Teller Suppe a plate of soup

FRAGEN

1. Wer ist Anna? 2. Wem gibt die Mutter Suppe? 3. Was bringt die Köchin nach der Suppe? 4. Was schneidet der Vater? 5. Wessen Stück ist das größte? 6. Was holt Anna nun? 7. Was will Peter nicht? 8. Wer ist Ernst? 9. Wen lobt Martha?

10. (a) Wie sagt die Mutter zu den Kindern? } In each case, give
    (b) Wie sagt der Vater zu dem Enkel? } the pronoun of address: du, ihr,
    (c) Wie sagt Martha zu der Köchin? } or Sie.

ÜBERSETZUNG

1. Children, you are naughty. 2. Ernest, are you at dinner? 3. Anna, are you in the (der, dative) kitchen? 4. The father's piece is not large. 5. Is the child's father angry? 6. He eats the spinach and the salad. 7. The father gives the son-in-law the cigar. 8. She fetches the plate. 9. Ernest is the husband of the daughter. 10. Who are you? I am the cook.

LESSON THREE

DEMONSTRATIVES

12 Dieser. Dieser, *this*, is declined as follows:

	Singular			Plural
	Masc.	*Fem.*	*Neut.*	*M. F. N.*
Nom.	dieser	diese	dieses, dies	diese
Gen.	dieses	dieser	dieses	dieser
Dat.	diesem	dieser	diesem	diesen
Acc.	diesen	diese	dieses, dies	diese

Diese Familie ist groß.
Ich bin der Sohn dieses Mannes.
Das Gemüse ist in diesem Garten.
Anna bringt diesen Teller.

The endings are practically the same as those of der. Dieser and words declined like it are called the der-words.

13 Pronominal Use. In the above sentences dieser is a demonstrative adjective. Dieser may also be used as a demonstrative pronoun: dieser (of a masculine noun), *this one, the latter;* diese (of a feminine noun), *this one;* dieses, dies (neuter), *this thing, this.* Notice this use of *one* in English and its absence in German. Similarly with other der-words: jener, *that* or *that one, the former;* welcher? *which* or *which one?* mancher, *many a* or *many a one.*

14 dies, das, es. The shorter neuter form dies is in common use as the indefinite subject of forms of sein, *to be,* when identity is to be established:

Dies ist mein Vater, *This is my father.*

So also, different from English, with a plural verb:

Dies sind meine Eltern, *These* (lit. *this*) *are my parents.*

Das and es are similarly used:

Das sind meine Zimmer, *Those* (lit. *that*) *are my rooms.*
Es sind meine Brüder, *They are my brothers.*

Where it is not a question of identity, but where there is a definite reference to a previously mentioned noun, the regular form of the personal pronoun is used:

Wo ist der Kuchen (*cake*)? Er ist nicht auf dem Tisch.

15 Other der-Words. Like dieser are declined jeder (singular only), *each, every;* jener, *that;* mancher, *many a;* solcher, *such, such a;* welcher? *which, which one?*

EXAMPLES: jeder Vater, jede Mutter, jedes Kind; jeder, *every one;* solche Tinte, *such ink;* in welchem Zimmer? *in which room?* Die Feder? Welche? *The pen? Which one?*

Do not confuse jeder and jener: jenes Haus, *that house.*[1]

NOTE. Mancher is chiefly used in the singular. *Many* in the plural is regularly viele. Manche in the plural is a stressed *some* (Übersetzung, sentence 2).

16 welcher, was. Was can only be used by itself. *What* modifying a noun is welcher, not was.

What is that? Was ist das?
What child is that? Welches Kind ist das?

17 Present Indicative of haben, *to have.*

ich habe, I have	wir haben, we have
du hast, you have	ihr habt, you have
er (sie, es) hat, he (she, it) has	sie haben, they have
	(Sie haben, you have)

CAUTION. Pronounce the b of habt as p (App., p. 202.).

DER GARTEN

Das Haus dieser Familie hat einen Garten. In diesem wachsen [2] Bäume, Sträucher und Blumen. „Wir gehen (*are going*) jetzt in den Garten, nicht wahr, Großvater?" bittet das Kind nach dem Essen.

5 „Welche Blumen habt ihr denn [3] jetzt in Blüte (*bloom*)?" fragt Marie. „Wir haben diese Woche Veilchen, Maiglöckchen (*lilies of the valley*) und Tulpen (*tulips*) in jedem Beet (*bed*) auf dieser Seite des Hauses. Kommt [4] und seht nur diese Farben! Auf jener Seite ist es zu kühl, solche Blumen brauchen mehr Sonne." —
10 „Großmutter, was ist das auf dem Strauch dort?" — „Das ist Flieder (*lilac*), mein Kind." — „Ach, wie schön dieser Flieder

[1] § 129 gives another way of expressing *that* in German.
[2] Pronounce chs as *ks*.
[3] Common in German questions. Render: *Well, what flowers have you* . . .
[4] Kommt and seht are imperatives.

riecht!" Manche Leute lieben Flieder und Tulpen mehr als Rosen.

Hinter dem Haus ist der Obstgarten des Vaters. Er hat in diesem vier Obstbäume. Das Obst auf diesen Bäumen ist noch nicht reif, aber jeder Baum blüht wunderschön. Hinter diesem 15 Haus steht auch ein Lindenbaum. Unter diesem sind Tische und Stühle. Das ist gemüt'lich (*cozy, comfortable*); hier trinkt die Familie jeden Nachmittag [1] Kaffee. Dort kommt schon Anna mit dem Kaffee und der Milch für Peter. „Anna, haben Sie auch Kuchen? Heute ist Sonntag." 20

Nach dem Kaffee danken die Kinder den Eltern für diesen Tag und fahren nach Hause.

VOKABELN

Self-explanatory compounds are omitted in the lesson Vocabularies.

der Baum, –es, *plur.* Bäume tree
die Blume, *plur.* Blumen flower
die Farbe, *plur.* Farben color
der Garten, –s garden
der Kaffee, –s coffee
der Kuchen, –s cake
die Leute, *plur.* people
der Lindenbaum linden tree
die Milch milk
der Nachmittag, –s afternoon
das Obst, –es fruit
die Rose, *plur.* Rosen rose
die Seite side, page
die Sonne sun
der Strauch, –es, *pl.* Sträucher shrub
der Stuhl, –es, *plur.* Stühle chair
das Veilchen, –s, *pl.* Veilchen violet
die Woche week
bitten (er bittet) to beg
blühen to bloom

brauchen to need
danken *w. dative* to thank
fahren to go, travel, drive
lieben to love
riechen to smell
sehen to see
stehen to stand
trinken to drink
sie wachsen they grow
aber but, however
an on, at, to; auf on, upon, to
für *w. accus.* for
genug' enough
hinter behind
kühl cool
mehr more; mehr als more than
mein my, mine
reif ripe
unter under
wunderschön wonderful

hier here; dort there; heute today; jetzt now
Großvater grandfather; Großmutter grandmother

[1] Accusative of definite time. Diese Woche above is also accusative.

REDEWENDUNGEN

nach $\mathfrak{H}$ause (toward) home; nicht wahr (true)? not so? aren't we?
nicht mehr no longer; noch nicht not yet

FRAGEN

1. Haben Sie zu Hause einen Garten? 2. Welche Blumen blühen jetzt in diesem Garten? 3. Welcher Garten ist hinter dem Haus? 4. Ist das Obst auf jenen Bäumen schon reif? 5. Was steht unter jenem Lindenbaum?

6. (a) Wie sagt die Mutter zu der Tochter? (Hast du Kuchen?)

(b) Wie sagt die Mutter zu der Köchin?

(c) Wie sagt die Mutter zu den Kindern?

ÜBERSETZUNG

1. That garden; which side? every shrub; what house? many a child. 2. The fruit on this tree; on each chair; with these children (Kindern); some people. 3. They have the lilac on this side of the house. 4. Have you the salad on each plate, mother? 5. The family drinks the coffee under that tree. 6. This flower is a (ein) violet, that one is a (eine) tulip. 7. These are roses. 8. Which vegetable does he eat? 9. In that bed grow lilies of the valley. 10. This is enough for this day.

LESSON FOUR

INDEFINITE ARTICLE. POSSESSIVES

18 ein, *a, an*, has no plural and is declined as follows:

	Masc.	*Fem.*	*Neut.*
Nom.	ein (Mann)	eine (Frau)	ein (Kind)
Gen.	eines (Mannes)	einer (Frau)	eines (Kindes)
Dat.	einem (Manne)	einer (Frau)	einem (Kinde)
Acc.	einen (Mann)	eine (Frau)	ein (Kind)

The cases differing from those of dieſer are underlined.

NOTE 1. An accented ein before a noun means *one*.

NOTE 2. As before noted, a noun of vocation in the predicate without adjective has no ein: Er iſt Lehrer, *He is a teacher.* So, usually, with words of nationality: Er iſt Franzoſe, *He is a Frenchman.*

19 Kein. **Possessive Adjectives.** Like ein are declined kein, *no, not any*, and the possessives. The possessives correspond to the personal pronouns as follows:

ich: mein, my   ſie: ihr, her   ihr: euer, your
du: dein, thy, your   es: ſein, its   ſie: ihr, their
er: ſein, his   wir: unſer, our   Sie: Ihr, your

Notice the three forms for *your:* dein, euer, Ihr. With du use dein; with ihr use euer; with Sie use Ihr.

20 Agreement. In ich habe mein Buch, the mein agrees with Buch in number, gender, and case (sing., neut., acc.). With Bleiſtift, *pencil*, and Feder, *pen*, the forms would be: Ich habe meinen Bleiſtift; ich habe meine Feder. Similarly, *the hand and its fingers* = die Hand und ihre Finger, lit. *her fingers. My father and mother* = mein

Vater und meine Mutter; the possessive must be repeated because the forms differ.

21 Examples of declension are:

	Singular			*Plural*
	Masc.	*Fem.*	*Neut.*	*M. F. N.*
Nom.	kein	keine	kein	keine
Gen.	keines	keiner	keines	keiner
Dat.	keinem	keiner	keinem	keinen
Acc.	keinen	keine	kein	keine
Nom.	euer	eure	euer	eure
Gen.	eures	eurer	eures	eurer
Dat.	eurem	eurer	eurem	euren
Acc.	euren	eure	euer	eure

NOTE. In euer the e before =r of the stem is commonly dropped wherever a case-ending follows the =r. With unser the e of either the stem or the case-ending may be dropped: unseres, unsres, or unsers.

22 **Ein-Words.** Ein, kein, and the possessives are, for short, called the **ein**-words. Their inflection differs from that of the der-words in the three underlined forms only, in which the ein-words have no ending. The =er of unser and euer is, of course, part of the stem (cf. English *our, your*):

dies|er	Tisch	dies|e	Feder	dies|es	Zimmer
ein|	Tisch	ein|e	Feder	ein|	Zimmer
unser|	Tisch	unser|e	Feder	unser|	Zimmer

23 **kein, nein.** Do not confuse kein and nein. *No, I have no pen* = Nein, ich habe keine Feder. Often kein = *not a, not any: No, I do not have any pen.*

24 **Pronouns and Possessive Adjectives.** In *This is my pen* the word 'my' is used adjectively and is called a possessive adjective. In *The pen is mine* 'mine' stands for "my pen" and is called a possessive pronoun. In German the same words are used as pronouns and as adjectives.

Hier ist dein Stuhl, dort ist meiner.
Hier ist dein Zimmer (*room*), dort ist mein(e)s.

When used as pronouns the ein-words have the inflection of the der-words, i.e., they have an =er in the nom. masc. sing., and an =es or, more commonly, =s in the nom. and accus. neuter sing., the three cases underlined in § 21.

25 Article for Possessive. Er hat das Buch in der Hand. Ich habe Geld in der Tasche, *I have money in my pocket.* Instead of a possessive, German frequently uses the definite article whenever the possessor is evident from the context. This is especially true of parts of the body and of clothing.

26 Past Indicative of sein, *to be*, and haben, *to have*.

ich wär, I was	ich hatte, I had
du wärst, thou wert, you were	du hattest, thou hadst, you had
er wär, he was	er hatte, he had
wir waren, we were	wir hatten, we had
ihr wärt, you were	ihr hattet, you had
sie waren, they were	sie hatten, they had
(Sie waren, you were)	(Sie hatten, you had)

DAS HAUS

Die Eltern, Herr und Frau Neumann, und ihr Sohn Hans wohnen auf dem Lande. Marie und Ernst Linke, Martha und Paul wohnen in einer Stadt. Martha hat ein Zimmer bei einer Freundin, Paul hatte eins bei einem Freund, aber dieser hat jetzt keinen Platz mehr. Seine Schwiegermutter (*mother-in-law*) 5 wohnt jetzt in Pauls Zimmer. Paul, der Kaufmann, hat eine

Buchhandlung (*bookshop*) und wohnt in einem Zimmer hinter dieser. Marie und Ernst hatten früher eine Mietswohnung (*rented apartment*), diese war aber zu klein. Jetzt haben sie ein
10 Haus, und ihr Haus ist ganz neu.

„Wollt ihr nicht unser Haus sehen?" fragt Ernst seinen Schwager (*brother-in-law*) und seine Schwägerin (*sister-in-law*), „oder habt ihr keine Zeit?" Paul und Martha hatten Zeit, es war ja [1] Sonntag.

15 „Willkommen in unserm Heim!" ruft Marie. „Eine Veran'da (*porch*) vorn (*in front*) ist nicht mehr modern, wir haben also keine. Geht nur durch die Vorhalle in unsre Wohnstube!" — Wie gemütlich war es in dieser Wohnstube! — „Wie findet ihr den Blick (*view*) aus dem Fenster auf jene Berge? In einer
20 Stadt hat man solch einen Blick nicht oft. Aber kommt in die Eßstube und die Küche! Diese ist ganz modern."

„Warum sagt ihr denn Wohnstube, Eßstube usw.?" fragt Martha, „euer Haus ist groß und modern genug, ihr könnt doch ‚Zimmer' sagen." — „Ach, wir sind bescheiden, und ‚Stube'
25 klingt gemütlicher (*cozier*)."

„Wollt ihr auch unsre Schlafstuben (*bedrooms*) sehen?" — „Nein, heute nicht, wir müssen jetzt nach Hause," sagt Paul und hat den Hut schon in der Hand. Martha hatte noch Arbeit, sie ist ja [1] Lehrerin, und Paul — nun, das ist ein Geheimnis (*secret*).

VOKABELN

die **Arbeit** work	der **Hut**, –es hat
der **Berg**, –es mountain	der **Platz**, –es place, room, space
die **Eßstube** dining room	die **Stadt** city, town
das **Fenster**, –s window	die **Vorhalle** front hall
die **Frau** woman, wife, Mrs.	die **Wohnstube** or das **Wohnzimmer**,
das **Heim**, –s home	–s living room
der **Herr**, –n, *plur.* **Herren** gentle-	die **Zeit** time
man, Mr., master	das **Zimmer**, –s room

[1] Render ja by *you see*.

klingen to sound
wohnen to live, dwell
also therefore, so then
aus *w. dative* out of; from; over
bescheiden modest
doch after all
durch *w. accus.* through
früher formerly
ganz entire(ly); quite

man one, people, they
neu new
nun well; now
nur only, just
oder or
oft often
usw. = und so weiter, etc.
warum' why
willkom'men welcome

Words alike in German and English: die Hand hand; modern' modern;
der Freund, –es friend; die Freundin (woman) friend; finden to find.
wollen will, want; müssen must; können can.

REDEWENDUNGEN

auf dem Lande in the country
wir müssen nach Hause we must go home

wie findet ihr? how do you like?
bei einem Freund at a friend's

FRAGEN

Answer all questions with Warum with simple sentences:
Seine Schwiegermutter wohnt jetzt in seinem Zimmer (Question 2).

1. Bei wem wohnt Martha? 2. Warum wohnt Paul nicht mehr bei seinem Freund? 3. Warum wohnen Linkes nicht mehr in der Mietswohnung? 4. Warum haben Linkes vorn keine Veranda? 5. Wo wohnen Linkes jetzt? 6. Was hat man in einer Stadt nicht oft?

Answer Questions 7–9 by substituting *one* or *none* for the noun object: Yes, we have one (No, we have none).

7. Haben Sie zu Hause eine Vorhalle? 8. Haben Sie in der Küche einen Kühlschrank (*refrigerator*)? 9. Haben Sie ein Haus? 10. Warum sagt Marie ‚Wohnstube‘ und nicht ‚Wohnzimmer‘?

ÜBERSETZUNG

1. My room; her home; his brother-in-law; your room, Peter; your friend, Mr. Neumann; your house, father and mother; their kitchen; no space. 2. In a city; at my friend's; through our garden; for your (three ways) cook; his son's wife; the hand of our mother. 3. This room? No, that one. — My child? Yes, yours. — One piece? Yes, one. — No friend? No, none. 4. She had her hat in her hand. 5. Paul was a business man. 6. Here are two plates (Teller). Which is mine?

LESSON FIVE

DECLENSION OF NOUNS

27 **Declensions.** There are two noun declensions in German, the strong (ſtark) and the weak (ſchwach). The strong is taken up first.

 Remember that feminine nouns do not change in the singular. — In compound nouns the last element is the one declined.

28 **Strong Declension.** Strong nouns, always excepting feminine nouns, form the genitive singular in =ß or =eß. Class 1 has no plural ending: der Lehrer, gen. sg. des Lehrers, nom. pl. die Lehrer. The nominative, genitive, and accusative plural of all nouns are identical. **The dative plural of all nouns ends in** =n.

STRONG DECLENSION. CLASS I

29 **Umlaut.** Some nouns of this class modify the stem vowel in the plural, others do not.

Paradigms: der Bäcker, *the baker;* der Bruder, *the brother;* die Tochter; das Gemüse. *Mutter & Tochter only fems. in class*

	Singular			
N.	der Bäcker	der Bruder	die Tochter	das Gemüse
G.	des Bäckers	des Bruders	der Tochter	des Gemüses
D.	dem Bäcker	dem Bruder	der Tochter	dem Gemüse
A.	den Bäcker	den Bruder	die Tochter	das Gemüse
	Plural			
N.	die Bäcker	die Brüder	die Töchter	die Gemüse
G.	der Bäcker	der Brüder	der Töchter	der Gemüse
D.	den Bäckern	den Brüdern	den Töchtern	den Gemüsen
A.	die Bäcker	die Brüder	die Töchter	die Gemüse

30 The most common nouns with umlaut in the plural are:

der Apfel, apple	die Mutter	der Vater
der Garten	der Ofen, stove	der Vogel, bird

31 Of the more common nouns of this class the following have previously occurred: der Enkel, das Fenster, der Garten, der Kuchen, das Mädchen, die Mutter, der Teller, das Zimmer.

32 **Key-Forms.** The key-forms of a German noun are the nominative and genitive sing., and the nomin. plural. In all subsequent vocabularies of this book these forms are given as follows:

der Vogel, –s, ‟, = der Vogel, des Vogels, die Vögel.

For feminine nouns only the nom. sing. and plural are given.

33 Membership. Class 1 comprises:

1. Practically all masculine and neuter nouns ending in =el, =er, and =en.
2. All diminutives in =chen and =lein.
3. Neuter nouns with the prefix Ge= and the ending =e.
4. The feminines Mutter and Tochter.

No words of one syllable belong to this class.

34 Diminutives. Diminutives ending in =chen (English –*kin* in *manikin, gherkin*) and =lein are always neuter. They express affection as well as smallness: das Söhnchen, *the little son;* das Brüderchen, *the little brother;* das Fräulein, *the young lady, Miss.* An a, o, u, au of the stem takes umlaut. The usual ending is =chen.

AUF DEM MARKT

An einem Vormittag nach dem Frühstück bringt Frau Linke ihr Söhnchen in den Kindergarten und geht mit ihrem Dienstmädchen (*servant-girl*) auf den Markt.

Sie geht zuerst zu einem der Gemüsehändler. „Haben Sie Ge= 5 müse der ersten Klasse der starken Deklination[1]?" fragt Frau Linke. „Nein, gnädige Frau, unfre sind meistens schwach, nur die Radies'chen (*radishes*) sind stark." — „Das ist schade. Unfre Schüler sind Amerikaner, Engländer, Franzosen usw. Sie lernen die schwache Deklination später. Auf Wiedersehen!"

10 Beim (bei dem) Bäcker ist es besser. Er hat nicht nur Brot, er hat auch Brötchen und Kuchen. „Sind die Plätzchen dort in dem Kasten frisch?" — „Jawohl, meine Dame, sie sind eben aus dem Ofen." — „Schön, also bitte ein Dutzend Brötchen, für eine Mark Plätzchen und drei Apfelkuchen."

15 Auf jener Seite des Marktes stehen die Gärtner. Es ist noch nicht Sommer, aber ihre Blumen sind wunderschön. „Schöne Veilchen,

[1] For the pronunciation see page 206 under t.

Maiglöckchen, Tulpen heute, meine Dame?" — „Nein, wir brauchen keine, sie wachsen im Garten meiner Mutter. Aber ich brauche zwei Kästen mit Blumen für die Fenster meines Wohn= zimmers." Frau Linke kauft sie (*them*) bei diesem Gärtner und 20 sagt, wo sie wohnt.

„Nun gehen wir zum (zu dem) Fleischer und kaufen Fleisch für morgen zum Abendessen. Meine Brüder kommen und wollen Schinken essen."

VOKABELN

(Words used in paradigms are not repeated in Vocabularies.)

das Abendessen, –s supper	der Vormittag, –s, –e forenoon
der Apfelkuchen, –s, — apple tart	essen to eat
das Brot, –es, –e bread; das Bröt= chen, –s, — roll	kaufen to buy
	besser better
die Dame, –n lady	bitte please
das Dutzend, –s, — *or* –e dozen	drei three
das Frühstück, –s breakfast	eben just now
der Kasten, –s, ‒ box	erst first
die Klasse, –n class, classroom	frisch fresh
die Mark, — mark (coin worth 40 cents)	jawohl' yes (indeed)
	meistens mostly
der Ofen, –s, ‒ stove, oven	morgen to-morrow
das Plätzchen, –s, — cooky	später later
der Schinken, –s, — ham	von *w. dative* of, from
der Schüler, –s, — pupil	wo where
der Sommer, –s, — summer	zuerst' (at) first

Ame'rika, Amerika'ner; England, Engländer; Franzose Frenchman; das Fleisch meat, Fleischer butcher; Garten, Gärtner gardener; Gemüse= händler dealer in Gemüse; der Markt, –es, ‒e market; lernen to learn

REDEWENDUNGEN

Auf Wiedersehen goodbye	schön! very well, all right
auf den Markt to market	gnädige (gracious) Frau madam
das ist schade that is too bad	für eine Mark a mark's worth

FRAGEN

1. Wo ist Peter, während (*while*) seine Mutter auf dem Markt ist? 2. Wer geht mit Frau Linke auf den Markt? 3. Welche Deklination lernen Sie jetzt? 4. Was kauft Frau Linke beim Bäcker? 5. Welche Blumen haben die Gärtner heute? 6. Warum braucht Frau Linke keine Blumen? 7. Was kauft sie beim Gärtner? 8. Was kauft man beim Fleischer? 9. Warum kauft Frau Linke Schinken? 10. Ein Mann aus Amerika ist ein . . . . Ein Mann aus England ist ein . . . .

ÜBERSETZUNG

1. Out of the windows; two cookies; with my brothers; at the vegetable dealer's; at the baker's; in his ovens; three marks; from (von) these Americans. 2. He goes to the market with his pupils. 3. Are two hams enough for these people? 4. We had boxes with flowers on (auf, w. dative) the veranda. 5. Please bring (bring) my mother these violets. 6. Our meat was always (immer) in the refrigerator (dative). 7. Children, how do you like (finden) these gardens? 8. Their cook buys two marks worth of fruit and vegetables. 9. Goodbye, madam, we are going (gehen) home now (arrange *now home*). 10. I have two brothers-in-law (Schwäger).

LESSON SIX

STRONG DECLENSION. CLASS 2

35 **Class 2.** The second class forms its plural by adding
=e. The plural usually has umlaut (§ 39).

Paradigms: der Hund, *dog;* der Abend, *evening;* die Braut [1];
das Geheim'nis, *secret.*

	Singular			
N.	der Hund	der Abend	die Braut	das Geheimnis
G.	des Hundes	des Abends	der Braut	des Geheimnisses
D.	dem Hunde	dem Abend	der Braut	dem Geheimnis
A.	den Hund	den Abend	die Braut	das Geheimnis
	Plural			
N.	die Hunde	die Abende	die Bräute	die Geheimnisse
G.	der Hunde	der Abende	der Bräute	der Geheimnisse
D.	den Hunden	den Abenden	den Bräuten	den Geheimnissen
A.	die Hunde	die Abende	die Bräute	die Geheimnisse

36 **Genitive and Dative.** Words of one syllable commonly have =es in the genitive sing.; other words
regularly have =s. But words in an s-sound (Milchglas)
always have =es.

In the dative, words of one syllable often have =e; other
words are without ending.

37 Nouns in =nis double the final s before an ending.

38 **Membership.** The bulk of strong nouns belong here.
It is mainly the class of monosyllabic masculines.

---

[1] Braut is *fiancée* or the bride on her wedding day; das Brautpaar, *engaged*
or *bridal couple.*

39 Umlaut in the Plural. 1. The masculine mono-syllables generally have umlaut. Without umlaut are:

der Arm: die Arme	der Schuh: die Schuhe
der Hund: die Hunde	der Tag: die Tage

2. All feminine monosyllables have umlaut: die Hand, die Hände; die Nacht, die Nächte.

3. The neuter monosyllables never have umlaut: das Jahr, die Jahre; das Paar, die Paare.

Words of more than one syllable rarely have umlaut.

40 Common nouns of Class 2 from previous Lessons are: der Baum (äu), der Berg, das Brot, der Freund, der Hut (ü), der Markt (ä), der Platz (ä), der Tag, der Tisch.

41 Present and Past Indicative of wērden, *to become, turn, get.*

ich wērde, I become, am	ich wurde, I became, etc.
du wirst [getting, etc.	du wurdest
er wird	er wurde
wir werden	wir wurden
ihr werdet	ihr wurdet
sie werden	sie wurden

The d in wird is pronounced as t (Appendix p. 202). Notice lack of d in wirst.

42 Phrases with *do* and *am.* German has nothing corresponding to the English forms with *do* and *am.* *I have, I am having, I do have* are all ich habe.

I had, was having, did have = ich hatte.
I become, am becoming (getting), do become = ich werde.
I became, was becoming (getting), did become = ich wurde.
Er hat keinen Bruder, *He doesn't have any brother.*
Hat er Geld? *Does he have money?*
Singt er? *Does he sing?*

DAS GEHEIMNIS

Am (an dem) nächsten Abend ist die Familie bei Linkes zum Abendessen. „Paul, du bist ja[1] so still und lächelst immerzu. Was ist denn los?" fragt die Mutter. „Mütter sehen alles," antwortet Paul und wird ganz rot, „ja, es ist wahr, ich habe ein Geheimnis." — „Keine Geheimnisse hier, bitte," ruft sein Schwager Ernst, 5 „heraus mit der Sprache!" — „Nun," stammelt (*stammers*) Paul, „ihr bekommt bald eine Schwiegertochter (*daughter-in-law*) und Schwägerin, und Peter bekommt eine neue Tante!" Alle stehen von den Stühlen auf (*up*), großer Jubel (*jubilation*) herrscht (*prevails*), Karo, der Hund, bellt, alle rufen durch= 10 einander[2]: „Wer ist es? Wie heißt sie? Wo wohnt sie? Ist sie hübsch? Was für Haar hat sie? Ist sie reich?" Paul erzählt. Vor einem Jahr war eine Stelle in seinem Geschäft frei. Fräulein Charlotte Arnold wurde seine Buchhalterin (*bookkeeper*) und bald seine Braut. „Wann zeigst du uns denn deine Braut?" 15 fragt seine Schwester Martha. Paul geht ans (= an das) Telephon. „Lottchen, wir wollen dich (*you*) hier haben!" ruft er, stürzt (*rushes*) aus dem Haus in Ernsts Wagen, und fort ist er.

Ernst geht in den Keller und holt Wein. „Das müssen wir be= gießen (*drink to*)," sagt er, „Marie, setz die Gläser auf den Tisch!" 20

Bald kommt Paul wieder und bringt seine Braut. Lotte ist lieb und herzlich, jung und hübsch und wird schnell der Liebling (*favorite*) der Familie.

„Ein dreifaches Hoch dem Brautpaar!" ruft der Vater und erhebt (*raises*) sein Glas. Alle haben ein Glas Wein in der Hand und 25 trinken auf das Wohl des jungen Paares.

[1] *Why, you are so'...*
[2] *at the same time, in confusion.*

VOKABELN

das Fräulein, -s, — Miss, young lady

das Geschäft', -s, -e business, affair, shop

das Glas, -es, -er glass

das Haar, -es, -e hair

das Jahr, -es, -e year

der Keller, -s, — cellar

das Paar, -es, -e pair, couple

der Schuh, -es, -e shoe

die Schwester, -n sister

die Sprache, -n speech, language

die Stelle, -n position

die Tante, -n aunt

das Telephon', -s, -e telephone

der Wagen wagon, carriage, car

der Wein, -es, -e wine

das Wohl, -es health, welfare

bellen to bark

erzäh'len to relate

lächeln to smile

setzen set, place

zeigen to show

alles everything

bald soon

fort away

frei free, vacant

herzlich cordial

hübsch pretty

immerzu' all the time

lieb dear, sweet

rot red

schnell quick(ly), fast

uns us

wann? when?

Words like English: so; still; jung young; reich rich; nächst next

REDEWENDUNGEN

los sein to be going on, be doing

wie heißt sie what is her name

ein dreifaches Hoch three cheers

heraus' mit der Sprache out with it

vor einem Jahr a year ago

FRAGEN

1. Warum ist Paul beim Abendessen so still? 2. Was ist sein Geheimnis? 3. Was wurde Charlotte zuerst? 4. Was wurde sie später? 5. Ist sie reich? 6. Wie bringt Paul jetzt Charlotte zu seiner Familie? 7. Was holt Ernst aus dem Keller? 8. Woraus (out of what) trinkt man Wein? 9. Was sagt man, wenn (when) man auf das Wohl eines Brautpaars trinkt?

ÜBUNG

1. In these years; which secrets? no shops; from their shops; with these wines; for my hands. 2. Do you have a position? She does not have a position. I did not have a position. 3. She is getting pretty. He was getting rich. 4. She goes and gets a chair. 5. Paul became very quiet. 6. He had a secret.

ÜBERSETZUNG

1. Here comes your little son with his shoes in his hand. 2. Under the trees is room for tables and chairs. 3. Our servant-girl goes to the market. 4. The apples in my father's orchard are getting ripe. 5. Did they have two dogs or only one? 6. Who was the young lady in the shop? 7. The mother had her child on her arm. 8. They had their cars already a year ago. 9. His hair was fast turning grey (grau). 10. Paul and Lotte soon became an engaged couple.

LESSON SEVEN

STRONG DECLENSION. CLASS 3

43 **Class 3.** The third class forms its plural by adding ⸗er. The stem vowel, if capable of it, invariably has umlaut. It is preëminently the class of neuter nouns of one syllable.

Paradigms: das Dorf, *village;* das Huhn, *chicken;* der Wald, *forest;* der Reichtum, *wealth, riches.*

		Singular		
N.	das Dorf	das Huhn	der Wald	der Reichtum
G.	des Dorfes	des Huhnes	des Waldes	des Reichtums
D.	dem Dorf(e)	dem Huhn(e)	dem Wald(e)	dem Reichtum
A.	das Dorf	das Huhn	den Wald	den Reichtum
		Plural		
N.	die Dörfer	die Hühner	die Wälder	die Reichtümer
G.	der Dörfer	der Hühner	der Wälder	der Reichtümer
D.	den Dörfern	den Hühnern	den Wäldern	den Reichtümern
A.	die Dörfer	die Hühner	die Wälder	die Reichtümer

44 Membership. Only neuters and masculines belong to Class 3. It is composed of:

1. A large number of neuter monosyllables. Some of the most common words of the language belong here.

2. All nouns in =tum (*–dom* as in *kingdom*) whether neuter or masculine. In the plural =tum becomes =tümer.

3. Some ten masculines, the more common of which are: der Geist, *the spirit;* der Mann; der Wald.

45 Nouns from previous Lessons belonging to this class are: das Buch, das Glas, das Haus, das Kind, der Mann, der Strauch.

46 Present Indicative. The present indicative of a regular verb is conjugated as follows:

ich frag|e	wir frag|en
du frag|st	ihr frag|t
er frag|t	sie frag|en

EIN AUSFLUG AUFS LAND

Marie bekommt oft Briefe von Freunden auf dem Lande. Diese wohnen auf einem der Güter im Tal, von Wäldern umgeben (*surrounded*). „Es ist jetzt wunderschön hier,“ schreibt die Freundin. „Die Felder sind grün, Sträucher und Bäume blühen, und die Vögel singen. Du liebst doch [1] unser Dorf und die Berge 5 mit den alten Schlössern. Also bring deine Familie, auch deinen Bruder und seine Braut, und bleibt (*stay*) über Nacht! Wir haben keine Reichtümer — aber Platz für alle.“

„Ernst, was sagst du, machen wir den Ausflug?“ — Die Ein= ladung (*invitation*) freut Ernst sehr, denn in der Stadt wird es 10 später Frühling als auf dem Lande. Aber am glücklichsten ist Peter. Er weiß, auf dem Gute sind Pferde und andere Tiere.

Ernsts Geschäft schließt Sonnabendmittag. Auf dem Weg nach Hause kauft er Benzin' (*gasoline*) an einer Tankstelle (*filling station*), holt Lotte und Paul und seine Familie, und nun geht es 15 hinaus aufs Land! Das Wetter ist schön, und die Landstraße hat nur wenige Löcher. „Seht ihr die roten Dächer dort? Das sind schon die ersten Bauernhäuser [2] im Dorfe.“ Bald sehen sie das Haus der Freunde, und davor' (*in front of it*) stehen diese und winken (*wave*). 20

Die Zeit vergeht' (*passes*) nur zu schnell. Die Männer reiten am Nachmittag durch die Felder. Die Frauen fahren später auf Rädern ins (in das) Dorf, wo die Landleute am Abend in den Wirtshäusern (*inns*) tanzen und Lieder singen. Die Kinder gehen mit Peter in die Ställe und zeigen ihm (*him*) die Pferde, 25 Kälber, Hühner und die anderen Tiere. Er findet zwei Nester mit Eiern.

Am Sonntagmorgen sagt die Mutter: „Kinder, macht schnell, wir gehen in die Kirche!“ Dort predigt der Pfarrer, und die Dorfleute sind alle in ihren Sonntagskleidern. 30

Nach dem Essen machen sie noch einen Spaziergang durch den Wald, und dann geht es zurück in die Stadt.

[1] Here *don't you.*
[2] The peasants live together in a village.

VOKABELN

der Ausflug, –s, ⸚e excursion, trip
das Bauernhaus, –es, ⸚er peasant's house
der Brief, –es, –e letter
das Dach, –es, ⸚er roof
das Ei, –s, –er egg
das Feld, –es, –er field
der Frühling, –s, –e spring
das Gut, –es, ⸚er estate
das Kalb, –es, ⸚er calf
die Kirche, –n church
die Landstraße, –n highway
das Lied, –es, –er song
das Loch, –es, ⸚er hole
die Nacht, ⸚e night; über N. overnight
das Nest, –es, –er nest
der Pfarrer, –s, — parson
das Pferd, –es, –e horse
das Rad, –es, ⸚er wheel, bicycle
das Schloß, –es, ⸚er castle
der Sonnabendmittag, –s, –e Saturday noon

der Sonntagmorgen, –s, — Sunday morning
das Sonntagskleid, –s, –er Sunday dress
der Stall, –es, ⸚e stable, barn
das Tal, –es, ⸚er valley
das Tier, –es, –e animal
der Weg, –es, –e road, way
das Wetter, –s weather *no plural*
predigen to preach
reiten to ride
schließen to close, conclude
schreiben to write
singen to sing
tanzen to dance
er weiß he knows
alt old
ander other
denn for
am glücklichsten happiest
grün green
wenige few
zurück back

REDEWENDUNGEN

mach (macht) schnell! hurry up   hinaus' aufs Land! out into the country
einen Spazier'gang (Ausflug) machen to take a walk (trip)

FRAGEN

1. Wo wohnen Maries Freunde? 2. Wann schließt Ernsts Geschäft? 3. Welche Tiere zeigen die Kinder Peter? 4. Was findet Peter? 5. Was machen die Männer am Sonnabend? 6. Was machen die Frauen? 7. Was machen die Landleute am Sonnabendabend? 8. Was sagt die Mutter zu den Kindern am Sonntagmorgen? 9. Was ist ein Sonntagskleid? 10. Wo ist die Familie am Sonntagmorgen?

ÜBUNG

Translate: **1.** The birds in the woods. **2.** The nests with the eggs. **3.** The horses, calves, and chickens on the estates. **4.** The people in the country. **5.** The country people in the taverns.

ÜBERSETZUNG

1. Are (there) [1] holes in our roof? **2.** These eggs were in the nests. **3.** One does not get rich overnight. **4.** The country people are dancing and singing in the tavern. **5.** The friends stand on the road and are waving. **6.** What do they see on the mountains? **7.** They see castles on the mountains. **8.** The children sing songs in [the] [1] school. **9.** Such estates are often very large. **10.** They make the trip in their car.

LESSON EIGHT

NUMERALS

47 The cardinal numbers are

1	eins	8	acht
2	zwei	9	neun
3	drei	10	zehn
4	vier	11	elf
5	fünf	12	zwölf
6	sechs	13	dreizehn
7	sieben	14	vierzehn

[1] Parentheses mean "Omit in German," square brackets "Render in German."

15 fünfzehn	90 neunzig
16 sechzehn	100 hundert
17 siebzehn	101 hundertundeins
18 achtzehn	121 hunderteinundzwanzig
19 neunzehn	200 zweihundert
20 zwanzig	1000 tausend
21 einundzwanzig	1871 achtzehnhundert einund=
30 dreißig	siebzig
40 vierzig	2000 zweitausend
50 fünfzig	1 000 000 eine Million'
60 sechzig	1 000 000 000 eine Milliar'de,
70 siebzig	*a billion*
80 achtzig	0 null

1. Examine carefully the forms in bold type.
2. In sechs pronounce chs as ks.
3. In vierzehn and vierzig pronounce the ie as short i.
4. Pronounce dreißig as spelled, with the ß of heißen.
5. The u of null is the *u* of *pull*.

NOTE 1. The form eins is used in counting when no other numeral follows (eins, zwei, drei; hundertundeins) and in designating time. The numeral ein, *one*, is inflected like the indefinite article ein. It is sometimes spaced (ein) or printed with a capital to distinguish it from the article.

NOTE 2. Our *billion* is in German eine Milliar'de: the German Billiōn' means a *million millions*. These nouns form plurals in =n or =en.

NOTE 3. As nouns, that is, as names of figures, the cardinal numbers are feminine: eine Null, *a zero;* die Fünf, *the (figure) 5.*

48 =mal. For the English *once, twice,* etc., German has compounds with mal (*time, times*): einmal, *once;* zweimal, *twice;* diesmal, *this time;* manchmal, *many a time, sometimes.*

49 Addition, Subtraction, etc. The signs of addition, etc., are read as follows in German:

2 + 4 = 6, zwei plus vier ist sechs; 8 — 5 = 3, acht weniger (*less*) fünf ist drei; 6 × 7 = 42, sechsmal sieben ist zweiund= vierzig; 18 ÷ 2 = 9, achtzehn geteilt durch zwei ist neun.

dividiert = divided

EINE RECHENSTUNDE

Fräulein Martha Neumann, die Lehrerin, kommt um 11 in ihre
Klasse zur Rechenstunde. Kinder, wir haben heute zuerst Kopfrech=
nen. Wieviel ist 16 weniger 4? Frieda! — „12." — Richtig.
Wieviel ist 31 plus 25? Erna! — „46." — Falsch! Dora,
wieviel ist es? — „56." — Richtig! Wieviel ist fünfmal 12?
Ella! — „60." — Richtig. Wieviel ist 70 geteilt durch 5?
Nun, Erna? — „14." — Diesmal richtig. Grete, sage jetzt das
Einmaleins mit der 7! — Grete: „1 × 7 = 7
2 × 7 = 14 usw." —

Nun paßt auf! Herr Braun kauft ein Haus für 20 000 Mark. 10
Er hat aber nur 8 600 Mark. Wieviel muß er borgen? Eva! —
„Er muß 11 400 Mark borgen." — Das ist gut.

Berlin' hatte 1933 4 190 000 Einwohner. Ist das mehr oder
weniger als New York? Lisbeth! — „Ich weiß nicht, Fräulein
Neumann." — Weißt du es, Luise? — „Ja, New York hat mehr, 15
es hat mehr als 7 000 000 Einwohner."

3 Pfund Fleisch kosten 2 Mark 40 Pfennig (ℳ2,40), was kosten
4 Pfund? — „4 Pfund kosten ℳ3,20," antwortet die Klasse.

Anna, komm an die Tafel und rechne schriftlich: 266 + 1835 +
3954. Anna rechnet richtig, es ist 6055. 20

Käthe, komm jetzt an die Tafel! Wieviel Tage haben Januar,
Februar, März, April', Mai und Juni zusammen? — „181." —
Richtig! Gertrud, wieviel Tage haben Ju'li, August', September,
Oktober, November und Dezember zusammen? — „184." —
Das war gut, Kinder. Ihr dürft jetzt nach Hause gehen, die 25
Rechenstunde ist aus.

VOKABELN

das Einmaleins' multiplication table

der Einwohner, –s — inhabitant
das Geld, –es, –er money

das Kopfrechnen, –s mental arithmetic
die Kuh, ̈e cow
der Monat, –s, –e month
der Pfennig, –s, — or –e penny,
1/100 of a mark
das Pfund, –es, — or –e pound
die Rechenstunde, –n arithmetic
lesson
das Schaltjahr, –s, –e leap-year
die Tafel, –n blackboard
die Tasche, –n pocket
der Weltkrieg, –s world war
borgen to borrow

ihr dürft you may
kosten to cost
er muß he must
paßt . . . auf' pay attention, look
out
rechnen to reckon, figure
du weißt you know
falsch wrong
richtig correct
schriftlich in writing
um at
wieviel', wie viele how much, how
many
zusam'men together

FRAGEN

1. Wie alt sind Sie? 2. Welches Jahr haben wir jetzt?
3. Wann war der erste Weltkrieg? 4. Wieviel Tage hat dieser
Monat? 5. Hat jeder Monat 31 Tage? (Nein, manche . . .)
6. Wieviel Tage hat dieses Jahr? 7. Wieviel Tage hat ein
Schaltjahr? 8. Was kostet [1] ein Ford=Wagen?

ÜBERSETZUNG

1. In our family (there) are five children and nine grand-
children. 2. Their friends on the estate had six horses,
five cows, seven calves, and a hundred and fifty chickens.
3. How much money did Paul have in his pocket? 4. He
had only eleven marks and twenty pfennig. 5. This town
has 100,000 inhabitants. 6. How many inhabitants has
your home town (Heimatstadt)? 7. My home town has
— inhabitants. 8. We raise our glasses and call Hoch
three-times.[2]

[1] There is no plural ending in Dollar.
[2] Arrange " three-times Hoch."

LESSON NINE

COMPOUND TENSES. NORMAL ORDER

50 **Future Tense.** The auxiliary of the future is the present of werden.

haben	fein	werden
ich werde haben,	ich werde fein,	ich werde werden,
I shall have	I shall be	I shall become
du wirst haben	du wirst fein	du wirst werden
er wird haben, etc.	er wird fein, etc.	er wird werden, etc.

On this model the future of any verb can be constructed: ich werde fragen, du wirst antworten.

NOTE. Like English, and to an even greater extent, German uses the present for the future when the general context clearly shows the meaning to be future: Morgen ist keine Schule, *There is no school to-morrow.*

51 **werden.** Note the difference in meaning between werden as verb and its use as auxiliary: Es wird kalt, *It is getting cold.* Es wird kalt sein, *It will be cold.*

52 **Other Compound Tenses of haben, fein, werden.** The past participles are gehabt, *had;* gewesen, *been;* geworden, *become.*

(*a*) For haben German and English agree exactly: ich habe gehabt, *I have had;* ich hatte gehabt, *I had had.*

(*b*) For the English *I have been* German says ich bin gewesen. So with werden: ich bin geworden, *I have become* (older English ' I am become '). In other words, the auxiliary for fein and werden is, in German, fein; in English it is *have*.

haben	sein	werden

Present Perfect

id) habe gehabt, I have had du haft gehabt, etc.	id) bin gewesen, I have been du bift gewesen, etc.	id) bin geworden, I have become du bift geworden, etc.

Past Perfect

id) hatte gehabt, I had had du hatteft gehabt, etc.	id) war gewesen, I had been du warft gewesen, etc.	id) war geworden, I had become du warft geworden, etc.

53 **Future Perfect.** The tense in its literal sense is little used in either English or German. The German tense differs in three respects from the English.

1. The past participle is put before the infinitive: id) werde gehabt haben, *I shall have had.*

2. As stated, haben uses haben as auxiliary, sein and werden use sein.

Future Perfect

id) werde gehabt haben, I shall have had du wirft gehabt haben, etc.	id) werde gewesen sein, I shall have been du wirft gewesen sein, etc.	id) werde geworden sein, I shall have become du wirft geworden sein, etc.

3. In German the tense *is* used, idiomatically, to denote past probability, just as the future denotes present probability. If Charles is absent the teacher may say „Karl wird frank sein," *Charles is probably ill.* If Charles was absent yesterday, the teacher may today similarly say „Karl wird frank gewesen sein," *Charles was probably ill.*

54 **Normal Order.** In the normal order, the subject stands first, the verb second. It is used, under normal conditions, in direct statements (declarative sentences). In the compound tenses, the infinitive or participle stands last and its modifiers are put between it and the auxiliary.

Predicate adjective: Er ist reich geworden.
Direct object: Er hat kein Glück gehabt, *He has had no luck*.
Time precedes predicate adjective: Es ist heute kühl gewesen.
Time precedes noun objects: Ich habe jetzt kein Geld.
Time precedes place: Wir werden morgen nicht zu Hause sein.

55 **Nicht and nie.** 1. In the simple tenses, nicht and nie, *never*, stand at the end of their clauses: Er antwortet nie, *He never answers*. Ich habe das Buch nicht. In the compound tenses, they precede infinitive and participle, as in English: Er wird nicht antworten. Er hat nie geschrieben, *He has never written*.

2. As in English, they precede a predicate adjective, adverb, noun, or phrase: Er ist nie krank. Er ist nicht hier. Er ist nicht Arzt. Wir sind nicht in der Stadt gewesen.

3. When modifying a particular word or phrase, nicht stands immediately before this word or phrase: Nicht er ist krank, sondern sein Bruder, *Not he but his brother is ill*. So in such a sentence as Ich habe nicht viele Freunde, the nicht is felt as applying to viele Freunde rather than habe.

DIE FERIENREISE

Der Frühling wird bald vorbei sein. Die Monate Mai und Juni sind kühl gewesen, manche Tage sogar kalt, aber jetzt wird es schnell Sommer werden. Martha, die Lehrerin, wird dann Ferien haben. Sie hatte dieses Jahr viel zu tun und war ziemlich müde geworden. Auch Marie war viele Monate sehr fleißig gewesen. Sie und ihr 5 Mann hatten viel Arbeit mit dem Umzug gehabt.

„Ernst, wann wirst du diesen Sommer Ferien haben?" fragt Marie. „Ich weiß noch nicht," antwortet Ernst, „wir werden Anfang Juli im Kaufhaus sehr beschäftigt sein." — „Aber das wird Ende Juli weniger werden, nicht wahr?" — „Ja, das ist richtig; die Frage 10

ist nur: werden wir noch Geld zu einer Ferienreise haben? Das
neue Haus ist sehr teuer gewesen." — „Ach, Ernst, wir leben nur
einmal. Es wird bald sehr heiß hier in der Stadt. Wie schön
wird es für uns alle an der See sein! Du wirst ein ganz andrer
15 Mensch werden."

Martha hatte auch Pläne für die Ferien und war später an diesem
Abend bei Linkes gewesen. Martha, Marie und Peter werden am
Anfang der Ferien mit der Eisenbahn an die See reisen und dort
ein Sommerhäuschen mieten. Ernst wird später mit seinem
20 Wagen kommen.

(Fortsetzung folgt.)

VOKABELN

der Abend, –s, –e evening	bleiben to stay, remain
der Anfang, –s, ⁅e beginning	folgen *w. dative* to follow
die Eisenbahn, –en railway	leben to live
das Ende, –s, –n end	mieten to rent
die Ferien *plur.* vacation	reisen to travel
die Ferienreise, –n vacation trip	spielen to play
die Fortsetzung, –en continuation	tun to do
die Frage, –n question	er will he wishes, desires
das Kaufhaus, –es, ⁅er department store	beschäftigt busy
der Mensch, –en, –en man, human being	dann then
der Plan, –es, ⁅e plan; map	fleißig industrious
die See, –n sea, seaside	heiß hot
das Sommerhäuschen, –s, — summer cottage	kalt cold
die Sommerreise, –n summer trip	müde tired
der Umzug, –s, ⁅e the moving	sogar' even
	vorbei' past
	ziemlich fairly, rather
	zu for

REDEWENDUNGEN

Anfang (Ende) Juli at the beginning (end) of July
mit der Eisenbahn by train, by rail(way)

FRAGEN

1. Welche Monate waren kühl gewesen? 2. Wann wird Martha Sommerferien haben? 3. Wo hatte sie viel zu tun gehabt? 4. Womit (*with what*) war ihre Schwester beschäftigt gewesen? 5. Wann wird im Kaufhaus weniger Arbeit sein? 6. Warum will Ernst keine Sommerreise machen? 7. Wie wird es im Sommer in der Stadt? 8. Wer wird bald an die See reisen? 9. Was werden sie dort mieten? 10. Wird Ernst auch mit der Eisenbahn fahren?

ÜBUNG

1. I am getting tired; they will be beautiful; you will get rich. 2. It was hot; it was getting hot; it had been hot. 3. Peter, you will play; they will learn; children, will you travel? 4. They have become ripe; they had not become ripe on the tree; where has she been? 5. Our cook has been to (auf dem) market three times this week. 6. Have you never been on (auf) his estate?

ÜBERSETZUNG

1. Spring will be past in two weeks. 2. Martha has had much work this year. 3. Martha and Marie have been very busy. 4. Marie asks Ernest: Will you have no vacation this entire (ganzen) summer? 5. Ernest will not be so busy at the end of July. 6. Ernest says: I shall not have money enough for a summer trip. 7. Ernest will stay at home and come later. 8. He is like (wie) many men. Vacation at home is (sind) for them (sie) the best (besten) vacation.

LESSON TEN

WEAK DECLENSION

56 **Weak Declension.** It is called the weak declension because in both singular and plural only one ending is used, ⸗n or ⸗en. Compare the following:

Strong	*Weak*
das Buch des Schülers	das Buch des Studenten
zwei Tage; zwei Monate	zwei Stunden; zwei Wochen

57 **Gender and Endings.** Weak nouns are masculine or feminine. There are no neuters. Weak nouns never add umlaut in the plural. Nouns in ⸗e, ⸗el, ⸗er, add ⸗n, all others ⸗en. Feminine nouns remain unchanged in the singular.

Paradigms: der Neffe, *nephew;* die Straße, *street;* die Fahrt, *trip, excursion;* die Freundin.

der Neffe	die Straße	die Fahrt	die Freundin
des Neffen	der Straße	der Fahrt	der Freundin
dem Neffen	der Straße	der Fahrt	der Freundin
den Neffen	die Straße	die Fahrt	die Freundin
die Neffen	die Straßen	die Fahrten	die Freundinnen
der Neffen	der Straßen	der Fahrten	der Freundinnen
den Neffen	den Straßen	den Fahrten	den Freundinnen
die Neffen	die Straßen	die Fahrten	die Freundinnen

NOTE. Herr, Frau, Fräulein are often prefixed to nouns of relationship and to titles: Ihre Frau Mutter, *your mother;* der Herr Professor, *the professor.* But in speaking of one's own relations, meine Schwester, not mein Fräulein Schwester; meine Mutter, not meine Frau Mutter.

58 ⸗in. As noted, the suffix ⸗in forms feminine nouns. The stem vowel regularly takes umlaut. In the plural the n is doubled.

> der Koch: die Köchin, plur., Köchinnen, *cook*
> der Lehrer: die Lehrerin

But Amerikanerin, Nachbarin, *neighbor*, Malerin, *painter*, Studentin, without umlaut.

59 **Membership.** More than one third of all nouns belong to the weak declension. Most feminines belong here.

Feminines

1. All feminines of more than one syllable, except Mutter and Tochter, and except those in ⸗nis and ⸗sal.

2. Many feminines of one syllable, namely all those not belonging to Class 2, Strong.

Masculines

1. Some twenty, in part very common, masculines of one syllable: der Mensch.

2. Masculines of more than one syllable, ending in ⸗e and denoting living beings: der Neffe.

3. Some foreign nouns: der Student.

NOTE. Class 2, Strong, and the Weak Declension are the two most important classes, embracing the great majority of all nouns.

60 The importance of this declension is shown by the large number of previous occurrences, the more common of which are: die Blume, die Dame, die Familie, die Farbe, die Feder, der Franzose, die Frau, die Kartoffel, die Kirche, die Küche, der Mensch, die Rose, die Schule, die Schwester, die Seite, die Speise, die Sprache, die Stunde, die Woche, die Zeit.

DIE FERIENREISE (FORTSETZUNG)

Auf dem Bahnhof sind viele Menschen. Manche haben Reise=
taschen, andre kommen mit Blumen und sagen ihren Familien
oder Freunden Lebewohl. Man hört von allen Seiten: „Glück=
liche Reise, Herr Professor! Gute Erholung, Frau Doktor!
5 Auf Wiedersehen! Grüßen Sie Ihr Fräulein Tante! Schreibt
Ansichtskarten!"

In dem Zuge sind drei Klassen. Linkes fahren dritter Klasse.
In ihrem Abteil (*compartment*) sind noch zwei Damen, Ameri=
kanerinnen, und zwei Studenten der Universität. Diese sind lustig
10 und erzählen Geschichten. So vergehen die fünf Stunden Fahrt
schnell. Der Zug hält auf dem Bahnhof des Seebads, und die
Leute steigen aus. Marie und Martha nehmen einen Wagen und
fahren durch die Straßen. Sie sehen bald ein hübsches Sommer=
häuschen und mieten es.

15 Nun beginnen herrliche Zeiten für alle. Man macht Spazier=
gänge in den Dünen und durch die Straßen der Fischerdörfer.
Man liegt viele Stunden am Strande und badet in dem klaren
Wasser, wenn die Wellen nicht zu hoch gehen. Peter macht Burgen
und Schlösser aus Sand und hat viele Spielkameraden.

20 Nach drei Wochen kommt auch Ernst und findet alle lustig, gesund
und ganz braun. Er macht oft mit andren Herren Fahrten in
einem Segelboot und fährt mit den Fischern hinaus auf die See.
Das liebt er mehr als baden und im Sande liegen.

Die Ferien sind leider bald zu Ende, und die Familie muß zurück
25 an die Arbeit.

VOKABELN

die Ansichtskarte, –n picture post
   card
der Bahnhof, –s, ⸗e railway station

die Burg, –en, citadel, castle
die Düne, –n dune, down
der Fischer, –s, — fisherman

die Geſchich'te, –n story, history	begin'nen to begin
Lebewohl ſagen to say farewell	fahren to go, drive; *3d pers.*, fährt
der Profeſ'ſor, –s, –o'ren professor	hält stops
die Reiſe, –n journey	hören to hear
die Reiſetaſche, –n traveling bag	liegen to lie
der Sand, –es sand	nehmen to take
das Seebad, –s, ‥er seaside resort	ſteigen . . . aus' get out, alight
das Segelboot, –s, –e sailboat	verge'hen to pass
der Spiel'kamerad', –en, –en play-	braun brown, tanned
mate	dritt third
der Strand, –es, –e beach	geſund' healthy
der Student', –en, –en student	herrlich glorious, splendid
die Stunde, –n hour, lesson	hoch high
die Univerſität', –en university	klar clear
das Waſſer, –s, — water	leider unfortunately
die Welle, –n wave	luſtig jolly, merry
der Zug, –es, ‥e train	wenn whenever
baden to bathe	

REDEWENDUNGEN

gute Erho'lung! have a good rest	noch zwei Damen two more ladies
grüßen Sie remember me to	er muß zurück he must go back
ſind zu Ende are over	fahren dritter (gen.) Klaſſe travel
	third class

FRAGEN

1. Werden alle Menſchen auf dem Bahnhof mit dieſem Zuge fahren? 2. Fährt man in Amerika auch dritter Klaſſe? 3. Wer iſt in dem Abteil? 4. Warum vergeht die Zeit ſo ſchnell? 5. Wo ſteigen die Leute aus? 6. Was macht man in einem Seebad? 7. Baden Sie, wenn die Wellen hoch gehen? 8. Nach wieviel Wochen kommt Ernſt? 9. Wie findet er ſeine Familie? 10. Was macht er in dem Seebad?

ÜBUNGEN

1. Put all the nouns in the plural: Die Blume auf der Wieſe; meine Freundin, die Engländerin; die Köchin in der Küche; der Menſch in der Stadt.

2. Change the following masculines to feminines: (*a*) without umlaut, der Student; der Herr (*master*); der Schüler; der Buchhalter; der Spanier; der Enkel; der Gemüsehändler. (*b*) with umlaut, der Schwager; der Koch; der Hund.

ÜBERSETZUNG

1. I have had two picture postal cards in (an) one day.
2. They will be at (in) the seaside resort four weeks.
3. You have become quite tanned. 4. Please, remember me to your mother (formal address). 5. Peter will soon have a playmate. 6. Ernest had been at home only two days. 7. It will get cool in the dunes today. 8. The husbands with their wives and children were all at the station.

LESSON ELEVEN

INVERSION

61 **Inverted Word Order.** Compare:

(*a*) Ich habe heute keine Zeit.
(*b*) Heute habe ich keine Zeit.

In (*b*) heute is put first for emphasis. An adverb, direct or indirect object, a predicate adjective, or any other suitable part of the predicate may thus be put first. The verb keeps its second place but the subject is thrown into the third place. This is called inverted word order. English has traces of a similar inversion: Here are the stamps. — Now is the time.

Other Examples

Ĳn bem Buge find brei Klaffen.
So vergehen bie vier Stunben Fahrt ſchnell.
Das liebt er mehr als baden unb im Sande liegen.

In all of these examples the verb keeps the second position.

CAUTION 1. Only one part of the predicate may precede the verb: Yesterday unfortunately I was not at home = Geſtern war ich leiber nicht zu Hauſe. — In such a sentence as Die Bilber in bieſem Buche finde ich ſehr ſchön, the phrase in bieſem Buche modifies Bilber.

CAUTION 2. In normal order no part of the predicate must be put between subject and verb: They now lie many hours in the sand = Sie liegen nun viele Stunben im Sande. He soon became rich = Er wurde balb reich.

62 Questions and Commands. Compare:

Werben alle Menſchen mit bem Buge fahren?
Grüßen Sie Ihr Fräulein Tante!

As in English, the verb stands first in questions and commands (imperative).

GEBURTSTAG

Heute hat Peter Geburtstag. Früh am Morgen kommt bie Mutter an ſein Bett unb gibt ihm einen Kuß. Er war ſchon wach, denn ein Geburtstag iſt wichtig. Schon am Abenb vorher war er aufgeregt geweſen unb wollte nicht zu Bett gehen.

„Jetzt biſt bu ſechs Jahre alt, Peter," ſagt ſein Vater, „balb gehſt 5
bu zur Schule!" Schnell ſpringt Peter aus bem Bett unb läuft
in bie Wohnſtube. Da ſteht ber Geburtstagstiſch mit ben Ge=
ſchenken von ben Eltern unb Großeltern! Mit ber Poſt bekommt
er brei Pakete, eins von Onkel Hans, eins von Tante Martha
unb eins von Onkel Paul. In bieſem findet er zwei ſchöne Bücher. 10
Leſen kann er noch nicht, aber balb geht er ja [1] zur Schule, bann
wirb er bie Bücher leſen.

[1] *You see.*

Am Nachmittag hat das Geburtstagskind Gäste. Um drei kommen seine Freunde und Freundinnen und spielen lustig in Haus und
15 Garten. Um vier ruft die Mutter die Kinder, denn nun gibt es Schokolade mit Schlagsahne und Geburtstagskuchen. „Iß nicht zuviel Kuchen!" hatte manche Mutter zu ihrem Kind gesagt (*said*), „sonst wirst du krank!" Aber das ist alles vergessen.

Um fünf holen die Mütter ihre Jungen und Mädchen und danken
20 Frau Linke für die Einladung. „Habt ihr dem Geburtstagskind Glück gewünscht?" fragt eine Dame. „Ach nein, das haben wir vergessen. Herzliche Glückwünsche zum Geburtstag, Peter!"

VOKABELN

das Bett, –es, –en bed; zu Bett gehen to go to bed

der Gast, –es, ⸚e guest

der Geburts'tag, –s, –e birthday

das Geschenk', –s, –e present

das Glück, –es happiness, good fortune

die Großeltern *plur.* grandparents

der Junge, –n, –n boy

der Kuß, –es, ⸚e kiss

der Morgen, –s, — morning

der Onkel, –s, — uncle

das Paket', –s, –e package

die Post, –en post, mail, post office

die Schlagsahne whipped cream

die Schokola'de chocolate

iß eat; *imper. of* essen

er kann he can

laufen; er läuft he runs

lesen to read

springen to spring, jump

verges'sen to forget; verges'sen forgotten

er wollte he would

aufgeregt excited

früh early

krank ill, sick

sonst else, otherwise

vorher before, beforehand

wach awake

wichtig important

zuviel' too much

REDEWENDUNGEN

mit der Post by mail

herzliche Glückwünsche zum Geburtstag! many happy returns

es gibt there is (are), they have

FRAGEN

1. Wessen Geburtstag ist heute? 2. Wie alt wird der Junge heute? Heute . . . 3. Wo steht der Geburtstagstisch? 4. Was

liegt auf dem Geburtstagstisch? **5.** Von wem sind diese Geschenke?
6. Was kommt mit der Post? **7.** Wer kommt am Nachmittag?
8. Was machen die Gäste zuerst? Zuerst... **9.** Was gibt es
zu trinken und zu essen? **10.** Was wünscht man einem Ge=
burtstagskind? Einem Geburtstagskind...

ÜBUNGEN

A. In the following sentences make the inverted order
necessary by placing the underlined element before the
subject: 1. Ich war um sechs wach. 2. Es wird bald sehr heiß.
3. Der Geburtstag ist für ein Kind wichtig. 4. Ich kann das
nicht lesen.

B. In the story „Geburtstag," change all the sentences
having inverted order to normal order.

ÜBERSETZUNG

1. Today we drive to the country. 2. In the country it is
wonderful now. 3. In the arithmetic lesson the class had
the multiplication table of 6 yesterday. 4. At twelve
father comes home. 5. On Sunday morning the families
were at (= in the) church. 6. Don't you want to go to
bed now?

LESSON TWELVE

TIME. PROPER NOUNS

63 **Time.**   Time is designated as follows:

Wieviel Uhr ift es? *What time is it?*
Es ift eins (or ein Uhr), *It is one (o'clock).*
Um zwei Uhr, *at two o'clock.*
Ein Viertel [1] auf fünf, ¼ 5, *a quarter past four.*
Drei Viertel [1] auf fünf, ¾ 5, *a quarter to five.*
Halb drei,[1] ½ 3, *half past two.*
Zehn Minu'ten nach eins, *ten minutes after one.*
Zehn Minu'ten vor drei, *ten minutes before three.*

Speaking of trains one would say Mein Zug geht um sieben Uhr dreißig, *My train leaves at 7:30.* However, in modern Germany railway time tables give time of arrival and departure according to the 24-hour dial, in which 24 = midnight, 20 = 8 p.m., 13 = 1 p.m.

Theaters announce performances similarly: Anfang, 20 Uhr, *Performance begins at 8 p.m.* Note that Uhr means either *o'clock* or *timepiece* (watch, clock). It does *not* mean *hour* (= Stunde).

NOTE. The names of the days are: Sonntag, Montag, Dienstag, Mittwoch, Donnerstag, Freitag, Sonnabend (Samstag). *all masculine*

[1] The meaning is that the time has advanced one quarter of the distance towards five. So with drei Viertel auf fünf: *three-quarters (from four) towards five,* i.e., a quarter to five. In conversation, the auf is usually omitted: drei Viertel fünf. One can also say ein Viertel nach vier (4¼) and ein Viertel vor fünf. The same idea underlies the designation of the half-hour: halb drei, *half way towards three.*

64 **Phrases with heute, geſtern.** The English *this* in *this morning*, etc., is heute: heute morgen; heute vormittag, *this forenoon;* heute mittag, *this noon;* heute nachmittag, *this afternoon;* heute abend, *to-night;* heute nacht, *this night.*

The nouns Morgen, etc., of these phrases are felt as adverbs and are not capitalized.

Similar phrases with geſtern are: geſtern morgen, *yesterday morning;* geſtern abend, *last night;* morgen nachmittag, *to-morrow afternoon;* morgen abend, *to-morrow evening.* But *to-morrow morning* = morgen früh.

Nacht is not used in the sense of *evening; to-night* = heute abend.

am morgen but in der nacht

65 **Names of Persons.** Names of persons have a genitive in ⹀s, but no other inflection: Karl, *Charles*, gen. Karls; Anna, Annas. No apostrophe is used.

Names ending in an s-sound either use an apostrophe or form a genitive in ⹀ens: Schurz' Erinnerungen, *Schurz' Memoirs.* Hans, Hanſens.

Feminine names in ⹀e form a genitive in ⹀ns or ⹀s: Mariens, Maries, *Mary's.*

An article may precede the genitive of a name. If so, the noun remains unchanged, the case being already sufficiently indicated: das Buch der Marie; der Hut des Fritz.

66 **Names of Places.** All names of towns, and most names of countries are neuter. These follow the rules for names of persons, except that names ending in an s-sound use von instead of the genitive. They take the definite article when modified by an adjective: die Straßen Berlins'; die Straßen von Paris'; die Straßen des alten (*ancient*) Rom.

A few names of countries are feminine. Like other feminine nouns in the singular, these are invariable. To show the case, these feminine names always have the definite article: die Schweiz (gen. der Schweiz), *Switzerland;* die Türkei', *Turkey.*

CAUTION. German says die Stadt Hamburg, *the city of Hamburg;* der Freistaat Sachsen, *the State of Saxony.* In *the king of,* von is used: der König von Frankreich.

67 Adjectives in =er. Names of places form adjectives in =er. Such adjectives are indeclinable and are capitalized: das Heidelberger Schloß, *the Heidelberg castle;* eine Frankfurter Familie, *a Frankfurt family;* die Londoner Brücke, *London Bridge;* Wiener Wurst, *Vienna sausage* (' Wienie '). **Names of places cannot, as in English, be used adjectively in their original form.**

Speaking of universities, one can say either die Berliner Universität or die Universität Berlin.

IN DER BUCHHANDLUNG

Pauls Buchhandlung ist in der Nürnberger Straße an der Ecke der Schillerstraße. Jeden Morgen um acht Uhr macht er sein Geschäft auf. Am Sonnabend schließt er schon um zwölf. Sonst schließt er um halb sechs, manchmal um drei Viertel sechs.

5 Vor dem Schaufenster stehen heute mittag Hans Neumann, Pauls Bruder, und Hansens Freund Franz. „Du,[1] da sehe ich einen Plan der Stadt Dresden und da ein Bild des Kölner (*Cologne*) Doms," sagt Franz, „die möchte (*should like*) ich haben." Die Jungen gehen in die Buchhandlung, wo mehrere Käufer
10 (*customers*) schon warten. Eine Dame sucht Bilder der neusten Pariser Moden, ein Knabe kauft Bleistifte und Federn, ein junger Mann möchte Heines Buch der Lieder haben, ein Herr kauft eine

[1] *Look here,* or *Say.*

Füllfeder und eine Karte des Königreichs Italien mit einem
Bild des Königs von Italien, ein Dienstmädchen fragt nach
(*for*) einem spannenden Liebesroman. Auf Bücherbrettern 15
stehen Goethes, Schillers, Lessings, Shakespeares Werke und viele
andre, teuer und billig. Auf Tischen liegen die neusten Bücher, an
den Wänden hängen die Bilder berühmter Männer und Frauen.

„Hier ist ein Buch für euch (*you*) Jungen," sagt Paul, „Carl
Schurz' Lebenserinnerungen (*memoirs*), das muß jeder Deutsche 20
lesen. Ich leihe es euch (*dative*)." Die Jungen danken ihm, und
Franz macht seine Einkäufe. „O weh (*O dear*), es ist schon zehn
Minuten vor eins (dreizehn) dort auf der Wanduhr. Wir müssen
zurück in die Schule, und ich muß noch zum Uhrmacher. Gestern
abend sind beide Zeiger, der Stundenzeiger und der Minutenzeiger, 25
meiner Armbanduhr zerbrochen. Bitte warte eine Sekunde, gleich
bin ich wieder da."

VOKABELN

die Armbanduhr, –en wrist watch
das Bild, –es, –er picture
der Bleistift, –s, –e lead-pencil
das Bücherbrett, –s, –er book shelf
der Deutsche, –n, –n German
der Dom, –s, –e cathedral
die Ecke, –n corner
der Einkauf, –s, –̈e purchase
die Feder, –n pen
die Füllfeder, –n fountain pen
(das) Ita'lien, –s Italy
die Karte, –n map
der Knabe, –n, –n boy
der König, –s, –e king
das Königreich, –s, –e kingdom
der Lie'besroman', –s, –e 'love
   novel', love story
die Mode, –n fashion
das Schaufenster, –s, — shop
   (show) window
die Sekun'de, –n second

die Uhr –en clock; watch; o'clock
der Uhrmacher, –s, — watchmaker
die Wand, –̈e wall
das Werk, –es, –e work
der Zeiger, –s, — hand (of timepiece)
da there; bin wieder da am back
   again
hängen hang
leihen to lend
macht . . . auf' opens
suchen to seek, look for
warten (auf *w. accus.*) to wait (for)
beide both
berühmt' famous
billig cheap
gleich in a moment
mehrere several
neust newest, most recent
spannend exciting
sind . . . zerbro'chen broke

FRAGEN

1. In welcher Straße ist Pauls Buchhandlung? 2. In welcher Straße wohnen Sie? 3. Wohnen Sie in der Stadt oder auf dem Lande? 4. Um wieviel Uhr beginnt die Schule am Morgen? 5. Ist 15 Uhr am Morgen, am Nachmittag oder am Abend? 6. Wann gehen Sie zu Bett? 7. Wieviel Zeiger hat Ihre Uhr? 8. Wo sind Sie heute vormittag gewesen? 9. Wessen Werke haben Sie zu Hause? 10. Wer ist Franz?

ÜBUNG

The Frankfurt station; the houses of Paris; the streets of Berlin; Vienna cake; the cities of Germany; the city of Nuremberg; the king of England; the university of Heidelberg (express in two ways).

ÜBERSETZUNG

1. Hans would like a map of the city of Berlin. 2. Here is a picture of a village in Switzerland. 3. Are New York fashions now better than Paris fashions? 4. A clock on the wall is a —, a clock on the tower (der Turm) is a —. 5. On Monday, Wednesday, and Friday, our school closes at half past three in the afternoon. 6. Was Mr. Schulz' watch ready? 7. Smyrna is a city in Turkey. 8. The cook is in the kitchen until (bis) half past seven.

LESSON THIRTEEN

IRREGULAR NOUNS

68 **Mixed Declension.** A number of masculine and neuter nouns are strong in the singular and weak in the plural. The plural has no umlaut.

Paradigms: der Bauer, *peasant;* der Nerv,[1] *nerve;* der Doktor; das Auge, *eye.*

	Singular		
N. der Bauer	der Nerv	der Doktor	das Auge
G. des Bauers	des Nervs	des Doktors	des Auges
D. dem Bauer	dem Nerv	dem Doktor	dem Auge
A. den Bauer	den Nerv	den Doktor	das Auge
	Plural (all cases)		
Bauern	Nerven	Dokto'ren	Augen

Other nouns belonging here are:

Masculines: Muskel, *muscle;* Nachbar, *neighbor;* Schmerz, *pain;* See, *lake;* Staat, *state;* Strahl, *ray;* Vetter, *cousin;* Professor, and other nouns in =or.

Neuters: Bett; Ende; Hemd, *shirt;* Ohr, *ear.*

Notice the shifting of accent in the plural of nouns in =or.

69 **Irregular Masculine Nouns.** A number of masculine nouns have a nom. sing. in both =e and =en. Starting from the nominative in =en, these nouns are wholly regular (Strong Decl., Class 1).

One neuter noun, Herz, *heart,* is similarly declined but has no ending in the nom. and accus. singular.

---

[1] Final v is pronounced *f.* App., p. 202.

Paradigms: Name (Namen) *name;* Herz, *heart.*

der Name (–n), des Namens, dem Namen, den Namen; *pl.* Namen.

das Herz, des Herzens, dem Herzen, das Herz; *pl.* Herzen.

Some others are: der Gedanke(n), *thought;* der Glaube(n), *faith;* der Haufe(n), *heap.*

70 **Foreign Nouns.** (*a*) Foreign nouns in =um form a genitive singular in =ums and in the plural substitute =en for =um. They are all neuter: das Studium, *study,* des Studiums, die Studien; das Gymna'sium,[1] die Gymnasien; das Amphi'bium, die Amphi'bien.

(*b*) Neuter foreign nouns in =al and =il form a genitive singular in =s and a plural in =e or =ien: das Mineral, des Minerals, die Mineralien; das Reptil', die Reptile or Reptilien.

NOTE. The ending =ien in these plurals is pronounced as English –*yen,* Studien = *Stu-dyen.*

BESUCH VOM LANDE

Herrn Neumanns Vorfahren waren meistens Bauern. Einer seiner Vettern, Gottlieb Krause, ist jetzt noch Bauer. Gottliebs Frau ist (*has been*) schon mehrere Monate krank und kommt mit ihrem Mann in die Stadt, denn auf dem Lande gibt es nicht so gute
5 Doktoren wie in der Großstadt.[2] Vetter Gottlieb und Kusine Augus'te wohnen bei Linkes, denn diese haben ja ein Gastzimmer mit zwei Betten.

„Was fehlt dir denn, Tante[3] Auguste?" fragt Marie teilnahms= voll (*sympathetically*). „Ach, ich habe immer Schmerzen in
10 allen Muskeln und kann keine Arbeit mehr tun. Ja, liebe Nichte,

---

[1] Not our *gymnasium* (Turnhalle), but a secondary classical school.
[2] A Großstadt is a city of 100,000 or more inhabitants.
[3] It is the custom in Germany that cousins of the parents are called aunt and uncle by the children.

man wird alt und schwach!" — „Aber Tante, solche Gedanken! Du bist doch noch nicht sechzig Jahre alt."

Der Arzt untersucht [1] Frau Krauses Augen, Ohren, Nase, Hals und Lungen, sogar die Zähne in ihrem Munde. Zur Untersuchung des Herzens hat er einen Apparat' (*apparatus*), und er durch= [15] leuchtet sie mit Röntgenstrahlen. „Es sind Ihre Nerven, Frau Krause. Sie arbeiten zuviel und machen sich Sorgen. Tun [2] Sie das nicht, dann werden Sie wieder ganz gesund werden. Bleiben [2] Sie eine Woche im Bett! Ihr Mann wird die Hühner füttern und Butter und Käse machen. 50 M bitte!" — „Eine [20] Bäuerin und Nerven, wie dumm!" sagt Tante Auguste auf dem Heimweg.

Ernst fährt inzwischen den Onkel durch die Hauptstraßen der Stadt. Dann trinken sie ein Glas Bier im Ratskeller. [3] „Willst du jetzt ins Muse'um gehen?" fragt Ernst. „Nein, lieber Neffe, [25] Museen interessieren mich nicht. Ich möchte im Aqua'rium die Repti'lien und Amphi'bien sehen." Die Krokodi'le amüsieren ihn sehr. „Solche gibt es nicht in unsrem See," sagt er lachend (*laughing*).

VOKABELN

der Arzt, -es, ⸚e physician, doctor	das Krokodil', -s, -e crocodile
der Besuch', -s, -e visit, company	die Kusi'ne, -n (female) cousin
das Bier, -s, -e beer	die Lunge, -n lung
die Butter butter	der Mund, -es mouth
das Gastzimmer, -s, — guest-room	die Nase, -n nose
der Hals, -es, ⸚e throat, neck	die Nichte, -n niece
die Hauptstraße, -n main street	das Reptil', -s, -e or -ien reptile
der Heimweg, -s way home	der Vorfahr, -en, -en ancestor
der Käse, -s, — cheese	der Zahn, -s, ⸚e tooth

die Base N
der Vetter, s N

[1] Notice how =ung forms nouns from verbs: untersu'chen, *to examine;* die Untersuchung, *examination;* such nouns are feminine and weak.
[2] Tun and bleiben are imperatives.
[3] Ratskeller, the (formerly municipal) restaurant in the basement of the city hall.

amüſie′ren to amuse
arbeiten to work
füttern to feed
intereſſie′ren to interest
√ willſt du will you, do you want to
dumm stupid
immer always

inzwi′ſchen meanwhile
mehr more, any longer
√ ſich him-, her-, yourself; themselves
ſo = ſolche such
wie as, how

REDEWENDUNGEN

was fehlt dir? what is the matter with you?
mit Röntgenſtrahlen (*rays*) durchleuch′ten (*illumine*) to X-ray
ſich (dative) Sorgen (*care*) machen to worry

FRAGEN

1. Warum kommt der Vetter Gottlieb in die Stadt? 2. Wer
ist Auguste? 3. Warum wohnen ſie bei Linkes? 4. Was fehlt
der Tante? 5. Was brauchen die Doktoren jetzt bei Unter-
ſuchungen? 6. Was findet die Tante dumm? 7. Welche
Arbeiten machen Bäuerinnen? 8. Wo ist Onkel Gottlieb
inzwiſchen? 9. Erzählen [1] Sie, was Onkel Gottlieb ſieht (*sees*)!
10. Wie viele Vettern haben Sie?

ÜBUNGEN

(*a*) Put the nouns in the plural: der Direktor des Muſeums;
der Hund meines Neffen; der Gedanke des Vetters.

(*b*) Change to the singular: die Namen der Profeſſoren;
Schmerzen in den Ohren; an den Enden; die Seen in den
Staaten.

ÜBERSETZUNG

1. An examination with X-rays costs much money.
2. Will Mrs. Krause get quite well again? 3. She must

[1] Imperative.

remain in bed a week. 4. In the country there are often very good (gute) doctors. 5. Are there gymnasia in America? 6. My uncle's sons are my cousins. 7. The sons of my brothers and sisters are my nephews, their daughters are my nieces. 8. We shall have company to-morrow evening.

LESSON FOURTEEN

WEAK CONJUGATION. AUXILIARIES

71 Weak and Strong Verbs. A verb like *I praise, I praised, I have praised*, is called weak (regular). A verb like *I sing, I sang, I have sung*, is called strong (irregular).

A German weak verb forms its past by adding =te, and its past participle by adding =t, to the present stem. The past participle has the prefix ge=.

> loben, to praise   ich lobte   ich habe gelobt

A strong verb forms its past and past participle by a change in the stem vowel:

> singen, to sing   ich sang   ich habe gesungen

NOTE. Vocabularies mark weak verbs *wk*. Of strong verbs the principal parts are given.

72 Principal Parts. The principal parts (Grundformen) of a verb are the infinitive, the third person singular of the past, and the past participle. All other forms may be developed from these.

73 **Weak Conjugation.** The conjugation of the weak verb loben, *to praise*, is in part as follows:

INDICATIVE

PRESENT	**PAST**
ich lobe, I praise, I do praise, I am praising	ich lobte, I praised, I did praise, I was praising
du lobst	du lobtest
er lobt	er lobte
wir loben	wir lobten
ihr lobt	ihr lobtet
sie loben	sie lobten

PRESENT PERFECT	**PAST PERFECT**
ich habe gelobt, I have praised	ich hatte gelobt, I had praised
du hast gelobt, etc.	du hattest gelobt, etc.

FUTURE	**FUTURE PERFECT**
ich werde loben, I shall praise	ich werde gelobt haben, I shall have praised
du wirst loben, you will praise	du wirst gelobt haben, etc.

IMPERATIVE	**INFINITIVE**	**PARTICIPLES**
Sing. lobe, praise	loben	*Present* lobend, praising
Plur. lobt		*Past* gelobt, praised
loben Sie (formal)		

CAUTION. Pronounce the b in lobst, lobt, lobte, gelobt as p (App., p. 202). The o remains long throughout (App., p. 200).

74 **Imperative.** 1. In the imperative, pronouns follow the verb. Du and ihr are used only when the pronoun is to be emphasized. Sie cannot be omitted.

Karl, frage den Lehrer! Charles, ask the teacher.
Karl, frage du' den Lehrer! Charles, *you* ask the teacher.
Leben Sie wohl! Farewell!

2. The ending ‿e of the singular is often omitted. An apostrophe may, but need not, indicate such an omission: Spiel im Garten! *Play in the garden.*

3. Imperatives regularly have the exclamation point.

75 **Tense Auxiliaries.** As stated before, verbs use either haben or fein to form the perfect tenses.

76 **Verbs using fein.** 1. Intransitive verbs denoting change of place or of condition use fein. The most common of these are: werden; gehen; kommen; fahren, *to drive, go;* laufen, *to run;* fallen, *to fall;* folgen, *to follow:* Er ist zu spät gekommen. — Das Kind ist gefallen, *The child has fallen.*

2. The intransitives fein; bleiben, *remain;* geschehen, *happen:* Was ist geschehen? *What has happened?* — Er ist zu Hause geblieben.

77 **Verbs using haben.** All other verbs use haben, viz.:

1. All transitive verbs, including reflexives.

2. All intransitives not covered by § 76.

3. All modal auxiliaries.

NOTE. A verb is transitive if it can take an accusative as its object, intransitive if it cannot take such an accusative. Thus folgen takes the dative, and is regarded as an intransitive verb.

78 **The Compound Tenses of folgen** are accordingly:

Pres. Perfect.   ich bin gefolgt, I have followed
Past Perfect.   ich war gefolgt, I had followed
Fut. Perfect.   ich werde gefolgt sein, I shall have followed

79 *Am-* and *Do-*Forms. Attention is again called to the fact that German does not have *am* and *do-*forms, and that no distinction is made among *I praise, I am praising,* and *I do praise.* All three are ich lobe. Similarly, *I praised, I was praising,* and *I did praise* are all ich lobte, and *I have praised him* and *I have been praising him* are both ich habe ihn gelobt. In phrases like *What does your teacher say? I did not praise him,* and *Don't praise him,* the German order

is what it would be in English if English used the forms
What says your teacher? I praised him not, and *Praise him
not.*

EIN BALL

An einem Abend im Herbst führte Paul seine Braut auf einen Ball
im Hotel' Deutsches Haus. Beide liebten den Tanz und hatten
schon lange nicht getanzt. Lotte brauchte ein Ballkleid und kaufte
sich eins für diesen Abend. Es war aus grüner Seide und paßte
5 schön zu ihrem blonden Haar und ihrer schlanken (*slender*)
Gestalt. „Werde ich einen Frack (*dress suit*) brauchen?" hatte
Paul gefragt. Wie so vielen Herren war ihm der Frack unbequem
(*uncomfortable*), der Kragen zu hoch, das Hemd zu steif, die
Lackschuhe drückten immer. „Und mein Frack ist mir (*for me*)
10 auch viel zu eng geworden." — „Nun, dann borge einen!" hatte
Lotte gesagt, „kein Mensch wird ohne Frack zu diesem Ball
gehen."

Ein Freund und seine Frau holten Lotte und Paul in ihrem Wagen.
Im Hotel folgten sie einem Diener, dieser zeigte den Gästen den
15 Weg nach dem Ballsaal (*ball room*). Von weitem schon hörte
man die Musik; die Musikanten spielten einen Wiener Walzer,
„die schöne, blaue Donau (*Danube*)". „Macht schnell," sagte
Paul, „und legt die Mäntel ab! Diesen Walzer müssen wir
tanzen. — Gnädiges Fräulein, darf ich um diesen Tanz bitten?"
20 scherzte (*jested*) Paul mit einer tiefen Verbeugung (*bow*). Lotte
machte einen Knicks, und sie tanzten, die Melodie' summend
(*humming*) und sich im Takte der Musik wiegend (*swaying*).
Dann kam eine Polka, und nach dieser winkte Paul dem Kellner
(*waiter*). „Herr Ober,[1] bringen Sie zwei Glas Wein für die
25 Herren und zweimal Eis für die Damen!"

Paul war dem Rat Lottes gefolgt, und das war gut,[2] denn alle

---

[1] Shortened from Oberkellner, *head waiter*, any waiter being called that by
courtesy.
[2] Here *that was a good thing.*

Herren waren elegant gekleidet. In den Nebenzimmern rauchten die Gäste zwischen den Tänzen, manche spielten auch Karten. Alle waren lustig, grüßten ihre Freunde, scherzten und lachten. „Wirst du mich heute noch nach Hause bringen," fragte Lotte. „Nein, heute nicht mehr, erst morgen." Und richtig! Es wurde schon Morgen, als der Ball zu Ende war. 30

VOKABELN

der Ball, –es, ⸚e ball
der Diener, –s, — servant
die Gestalt', –en form, figure
das Hemd, –es, –en shirt
der Herbst, –es, –e autumn
das Kleid, –es, –er clothing, dress
der Knicks, –es, –e curtsy
der Kragen, –s, — collar
der Lackschuh, –s, –e patent leather shoe
der Mantel, –s, ⸚ cloak
der Musikant', –en, –en musician
das Nebenzimmer, –s, — adjoining room
der Rat, –s advice
die Seide silk
der Takt, –es, –e rhythm

der Tanz, –es, ⸚e dance
der Walzer, –s, — waltz
darf ich may I
drücken wk. to press, pinch
führen wk. to lead, take
kleiden wk. to dress
legt . . . ab' take off
passen wk. to fit, suit
als when
blau blue
eng tight, small
erst not until; first
lange adv. a long time
ohne w. accus. without
steif stiff
tief deep
zwischen between

Eis ice-cream; das Hotel' (plur. Hotels'); die Musik'; die Melodie'; blond; elegant'

REDEWENDUNGEN

von weitem from afar
zwei Glas Wein two glasses of wine

zweimal Eis two servings of ice-cream
paßte zu went well with

FRAGEN

1. Wo war der Ball? 2. Was für ein Kleid hat Lotte gekauft? 3. Warum will Paul keinen Frack tragen (*wear*)? 4. Welchen Rat gibt Lotte dem Paul? 5. Ist Paul diesem Rat gefolgt? 6. Wer hat das Paar geholt? 7. Von wem ist der Walzer

„die schöne, blaue Donau"? 8. Für wen war der Wein, und für wen war das Eis? 9. Was machten die Gäste in den Nebenzimmern? 10. Um wieviel Uhr war der Ball zu Ende?

ÜBUNG

Give synopses [1] of the following sentences: Ich mache eine Verbeugung. — Paßt der Frack? — Sie tanzen einen Walzer. — Du folgst dem Diener. — Spielt ihr nicht Karten?

ÜBERSETZUNG

1. Buy a coat of silk and patent leather shoes, Lotte. 2. Paul, why do you not call the waiter? 3. He will take his fiancée home soon. 4. The ball was on an evening in (im) October. 5. We laid off our coats first. 6. The gentlemen had followed the ladies. 7. "Please, play a waltz now!" said the guests to the musician. 8. The friend had a car, and that was a-good-thing.

LESSON FIFTEEN

WEAK VERBS IN –T, –D, ETC.

80 **Lengthened Forms.** The reasons for the use of longer endings (-est, -et, -ete) in the forms below will be obvious. Compare du lobst, er lobt, er lobte, er hat gelobt with:

(a) Stems in -t and -d

du wartest	er wartet	er wartete	er hat gewartet
du redest,	er redet	er redete	er hat geredet
you talk			

[1] That is, put each sentence in each of the tenses, but only in the person and number of the original. Omit the future perfect.

(b) Stems in ⸗n and ⸗m

du öffnest, you open	er öffnet	er öffnete	er hat geöffnet
du atmest, you breathe	er atmet	er atmete	er hat geatmet

(c) Stems in an ⸗s-sound

du grüßest   du reisest, you travel

(a) The use of the longer endings prevents the coalescing of stem and ending in three of the forms.

(b) Forms like öffnst, atmst, etc., are difficult to pronounce.

(c) ⸗est keeps the ⸗s-sound of the stem intact. However, the shorter forms grüßt, etc., are common in conversation.

NOTE. Stems in ⸗el and ⸗er show shorter forms of stem or ending: lächeln, *to smile;* ich lächle, wir lächeln, sie lächeln. Imper., lächle.

81 Conjugation of warten, *to wait.*

INDICATIVE

PRESENT	PAST
ich warte, I wait, etc.	ich wartete, I waited, etc.
du wartest	du wartetest
er wartet	er wartete
wir warten	wir warteten
ihr wartet	ihr wartetet
sie warten	sie warteten

PRES. PERFECT: ich habe gewartet
PAST PERFECT: ich hatte gewartet
FUTURE: ich werde warten
FUT. PERFECT: ich werde gewartet haben

IMPERATIVE

warte, wartet, warten Sie

INFINITIVE	PARTICIPLES
warten	*Present* wartend
	Past gewartet

Pg 70 →

82 Imperative of haben, sein, and werden:

Singular	habe, have	sei, be	werde, become
Plural	habt	seid	werdet
	haben Sie	seien Sie	werden Sie

83 **Use of Present Perfect.** Of an isolated past fact German uses the present perfect, instead of the past. Thus: Gestern hab' ich mit Karl gespielt, *Yesterday I played with Charles.* The narrative past tense, stating events in their connection, is, however, the past, in both German and English: Gestern spielte ich mit Karl, da kam dein Vater und sagte . . . , *Yesterday I was playing with Charles, then your father came and said* . . . (Colloquial German often uses the present perfect in the narrative as well.)

84 **Special Use of Present and Past.** *I have been here three months now* is in German Ich bin schon drei Monate hier, i.e., of an action that has been, and is still going on, German uses the present tense, English the present perfect. Similarly, Ich war schon drei Monate hier, *I had been here three months*, where the German past corresponds to the English past perfect; schon regularly accompanies this use of the two tenses.

This use of the present for the present perfect, etc., does not apply to such a sentence as: Sie sind immer mein Freund gewesen, *You have always been my friend*, i.e., a time when the action began must be mentioned or referred to in a question: Seit wann seid ihr schon Freunde? *How long have you been friends?*

EIN UNFALL

Hans und sein Schulkamerad Franz sind nach einem kleinen See eine Meile [1] von Neumanns Haus gewandert, haben ein Boot gemietet und wollen angeln.

[1] die Meile, –n, is the German *mile*, 4½ English miles.

„Neulich haft du gerudert, und ich habe geangelt, heute rudre ich, und du angelst, ja?"[1] sagt Franz. „Schön, ich angle, und du paßt auf (*watch*), daß das Boot nicht umkippt," antwortet Hans. „Haft du genug Würmer gekauft?" — „Gekauft? Ich habe sie gestern abend im Garten ausgegraben (*dug up*). Ich sage dir, ich habe gearbeitet, ich war nicht faul."

Drei Stunden sitzen die beiden Jungen nun schon und warten auf die Fische. Keiner redet ein Wort. Endlich reißt etwas sehr stark an der Angel, so stark, daß das Boot umkippt. Beide Jungen fallen ins Wasser, aber nur Hans kann schwimmen.

Der Besitzer des Bootes wartete schon lange auf die Jungen. Endlich hört er Hansens Hilferufe, stürzt in ein Boot und rettet Franz. Hans war ans Ufer geschwommen, er konnte Franz nicht retten. „Ist er tot?" fragt er den Mann angstvoll. „Nein, diesmal nicht; er atmet, und jetzt öffnet er die Augen."

„Wo ist mein großer Fisch?" ruft Franz. Hans tröstet ihn: „Nächstes Mal werden wir mehr Glück haben." Mit nassen Kleidern wandern sie nach Hause. Hoffentlich sind sie nicht krank geworden.

VOKABELN

die Angel, –n fishing pole and line
der Besi'tzer, –s, — owner
das Boot, –es, –e boat
der Fisch, –es, –e fish
der Hilferuf, –s, –e call for help
das Mal, –s, –e time (succession)
der Schul'kamerad', –en, –en school-mate, school-chum
das Ufer, –s, — bank, shore
der Unfall, –s, ⸚e accident
das Wort, –es, ⸚er *or* –e word
der Wurm, –es, ⸚er worm

angeln *wk.* to angle, still-fish
fallen *aux.* sein to fall
er konnte he could
reden *wk.* to talk
reißen to pull
retten *wk.* to save
rudern *wk.* to row
schwimmen to swim; war geschwom= men had swum
sitzen to sit
trösten *wk.* to console
um'kippen *aux. sein* to tip over

[1] *won't you.*

wandern *wk.*, *aux.* sein to wander	faul lazy
sie wollen they wish to, intend	naß wet
angstvoll fearful	neulich recently, the other day
endlich finally, at last	tot dead
etwas something	

REDEWENDUNG

Hoffentlich sind sie nicht . . . , I hope they did not . . .

FRAGEN

1. Wo war der kleine See? 2. Was wollten Hans und Franz dort? 3. Was braucht man zum Angeln? 4. Hatten die Jungen die Würmer gekauft? 5. Wie lange angelten sie schon, als das Boot umkippte? 6. Wie lange können Sie schon schwimmen? 7. Wer hat Hansens Hilferufe gehört? 8. Hat Hans seinen Freund gerettet? 9. Wie konnte man sehen, daß Franz noch lebte? 10. Haben Sie oft beim Angeln Glück gehabt?

ÜBUNGEN

(*a*) Give synopses of the following sentences: 1. Ich öffne den Kasten. 2. Du mietest ein Haus. 3. Er atmet wieder.

(*b*) Give the first person singular present of: füttern, wandern, angeln, lächeln, stammeln.

(*c*) Give the three forms of the imperative of the verbs under (*a*) and (*b*).

(*d*) Give the second person singular present of: reisen, stürzen, setzen, tanzen, passen, scherzen, grüßen.

ÜBERSETZUNG

(In sentences 1, 3, 7, 10, the present perfect is to be used.)

1. Did the boys rent a boat? 2. Who was rowing when the boat capsized? 3. Their clothes became wet. 4. Franz

was still breathing. **5.** They had already been on the water two days. **6.** You have been smoking (for) an hour. **7.** Did I show you the picture of my cousin? **8.** Marie was working in the kitchen. **9.** Do you (ðu) dance this polka with your wife? **10.** You talked too long.

REVIEW LESSON

I. Supply the lacking endings:

1. Marie ſetzt d– Gläſ– auf d– Tiſch. **2.** Peter iſt d– Enkel dieſ– Leute. **3.** Ich tanzt– ein– Walzer auf d– Ball. **4.** Warum rauch– du dein– Zigarre nicht? **5.** In unſer– Garten wachſen viel– Blume– und Obſtbäum–, aber kein– Gemüſe. **6.** Er gibt ſein– Schüler jed– Tag ein– Rechenſtunde. **7.** D– Familie wohn– dieſ– Sommer in ein– Seebad. **8.** Kauf– ihr ein– Plan dieſ– Stadt? **9.** Jen– Gärtner kommt in d– Haus d– Dame mit ein– Kaſten für d– Fenſter. **10.** Bei welch– Arzt war dein– Mutter zur Unterſuchung ihr– Herz–?

II. (*a*) Give the key forms of fifteen nouns denoting family relationship.

(*b*) Give the key forms of fifteen nouns denoting articles of food.

III. Was iſt das Gegenteil (*opposite*) von alt, klein, dumm, falſch, billig, kühl, reich, ſtark, geſund, kalt?

IV. Give in simple German sentences the meaning of the following compound nouns (Example, Eine Kinderſtube iſt eine Stube für die Kinder): Kinderſtube, Vaterhaus, Apfelbaum, Weinglas, Eierkuchen, Kartoffelfeld, Suppenteller, Halsſchmerzen, Morgenpoſt, Bücherſchrank.

V. Make simple German sentences with the following idiomatic phrases: zur Schule; zu Hauſe; nach Hauſe; bei Tiſch; zu Tiſch; auf den Markt; zum Abendeſſen; beim Bäcker; mit der Poſt; jeden Nachmittag; von weitem; am Morgen; am Abend; für eine Mark Kuchen.

VI. Translate the following idioms: **1.** Hoffentlich ist das Wetter gut. **2.** Macht schnell, Kinder! **3.** Grüßen Sie Ihre Frau Mutter! **4.** Glückliche Reise und gute Erholung! **5.** Auf Wiedersehen! **6.** Wie heißt er? **7.** Heraus mit der Sprache! **8.** Das ist schade. **9.** Was ist denn los? **10.** Die Rechenstunde ist aus.

VII. Translate: **1.** We were living. **2.** She is smiling. **3.** He was still breathing. **4.** They have rented it. **5.** Children, open the door. **6.** You (du) dance well. **7.** Were you (ihr) smoking? **8.** He has rushed out of the house. **9.** They had wandered into the country.

VIII. Antworten Sie auf deutsch: **1.** Haben Sie gestern Tennis gespielt? **2.** Wie lange haben Sie Ihren Hut schon? **3.** Um wieviel Uhr sind Sie gestern abend zu Hause gewesen? **4.** Wie lange sind Sie schon Student?

LESSON SIXTEEN

ADJECTIVES. STRONG DECLENSION

85 Predicate Adjective. In Das Kind ist arm, *The child is poor*, the word arm is a predicate adjective. So with werden: Du wirst reich, *You are getting rich*. A predicate adjective is not inflected.

In Wir sind arme Leute, *We are poor people*, arm is inflected. It modifies a noun and is an attributive adjective.

86 Attributive Adjective. The declension of an attributive adjective is either strong or weak.

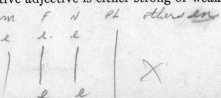

It is strong, if the adjective stands alone before the noun, i.e., is not preceded by a der- or ein-word.

It is weak, if a der-word precedes. For the adjective after an ein-word see § 95.

Participles when used as adjectives follow the same rules of inflection as adjectives: gekochte Eier, *boiled eggs.*

87 **Strong Declension.** Observe:

dieser Mann	diese Frau	dieses Kind
Lieber Mann!	Liebe Frau!	Liebes Kind!

Notice that lieb here has the same endings as dieser. Except for the two unimportant forms blocked below, the strong adjective endings are identical with the endings of dieser.

SINGULAR

	MASC.	FEM.	NEUT.
Nom.	armer Mann	arme Frau	armes Kind
Gen.	armen Mannes	armer Frau	armen Kindes
Dat.	armem Manne	armer Frau	armem Kinde
Acc.	armen Mann	arme Frau	armes Kind

PLURAL

Nom.	arme Männer, Frauen, Kinder
Gen.	armer Männer, Frauen, Kinder
Dat.	armen Männern, Frauen, Kindern.
Acc.	arme Männer, Frauen, Kinder

The plural is the same for all genders.

NOTE. Adjectives in -el, -er, -en shorten their inflected forms by dropping an e: offen, *open,* offne Fenster, *open windows.*

88 **hoch.** The adjective hoch, *high,* in all inflected forms, changes its ch into h. This h is not pronounced: hohe (pron. ho-e) Berge, *high mountains.*

89 (a) Whether **one or more adjectives** modify a noun, their inflection remains the same: guter, alter Wein, *good old wine;* lange, kalte Winter, *long, cold winters.*

(b) **Omission of the noun** does not affect the form of the adjective: große Städte und kleine, *large cities and small* (ones). *German uses no word corresponding to this English* ' *one, ones.*'

90 Numerals and indeclinable words, such as mehr, *more,* genug, *enough,* etwas, *some, a little,* do not influence the ending of the adjective: vier kurze Sätze, *four short sentences;* mehr schlechtes Wetter, *more bad weather.*

91 etwas Neues. Neuter adjectives expressing a substantive idea, when used after viel, *much,* manch, *many a,* etwas, *something,* and nichts, *nothing,* are written with a capital: etwas Neues, *something new;* viel Interessan'tes, *much (that is) interesting.*

92 Adjectives as Adverbs. Any adjective may be used as an adverb in its uninflected form. Thus gut = *well* in Er redet gut and Er schreibt gut. Die Sonne scheint hell, *The sun shines brightly.*

WEIHNACHTSEINKÄUFE

„Ernst, in vier kurzen Wochen ist Weihnachten!" sagte Marie eines Abends Ende November zu ihrem Mann. „Ja, liebes Kind, das ist doch nichts Neues!" — „Aber wir müssen bald Weihnachts= einkäufe machen!" Ernst hörte eben schöne Rundfunkmusik, rauchte guten Tabak und war in gemütlicher Stimmung. „Nun, 5 da (*then*) komm nur bald ins Kaufhaus, sonst wirst du dort zu große Mengen Leute finden, junge und alte, arme und reiche. Viele wollen nur schauen, andre möchten etwas Hübsches kaufen, aber nicht zu hohen Preisen. Wir haben sehr schöne Sachen, und jetzt ist noch reiche Auswahl (*choice*). Aber bitte, schenke mir 10

dem Wahren, Schönen, Guten

nichts Praktisches!" — „Wieviel darf ich denn ausgeben?" — „Na (*O well*), nicht zuviel!" — „Darf ich es anschreiben lassen (*have it charged*), lieber Schatz?" — „Meinetwegen!" (Kluge Geschöpfe, diese Frauen!)

15 Glitzernder Schnee liegt auf Bäumen und Sträuchern, auf Türmen und Dächern, und knirscht (*crunches*) unter den Füßen fröhlicher Menschen. „Guten Tag! Sie machen wohl Einkäufe? Herrliches Weihnachtswetter, nicht wahr? Hoffentlich bleibt es so," hört man von allen Seiten. Ganze Wälder grüner Tannenbäume
20 stehen überall auf den Straßen und Plätzen (*squares*), wunderschöne Schaufenster locken (*lure, entice*) groß und klein, arm und reich. Auch unsre Freunde kommen mit großen Paketen nach Hause; jeder hat interessante Geheimnisse.

Mitte Dezember, ungefähr vierzehn Tage vor Weihnachten, beginnt
25 das Backen bei Frau Neumann. Was für süße Gerüche steigen in die Nase! Aber niemand darf in die Küche, bei verschlossenen Türen bäckt das Christkind schöne, braune Lebkuchen (*honey cakes*) und Pfeffernüsse (*spiced cookies*), allerlei köstliche Süßigkeiten für glückliche Menschen.

VOKABELN

das Christkind, –s Christ child
(das) Deutschland, –s Germany
der Fuß, –es, ̈e foot
der Geruch', –s, ̈e odor
das Geschöpf', –s, –e creature
die Menge, –n crowd, quantity
die Mitte middle, center
der Preis, –es, –e price
der Rundfunk, –s, –e radio
die Sache, –n thing
der Schatz, –es, ̈e treasure, sweetheart
der Schnee, –s snow
die Stimmung, –en mood, atmosphere

die Süßigkeit, –en sweets
der Ta'bak, –s tobacco
der Tannenbaum, –s, ̈e spruce
die Tür, –en door
der Turm, –es, ̈e tower
Weihnachten (plur. but sing. verb) Christmas
aus'geben to spend
backen (bäckt) to bake; das Backen baking
glitzern *wk.* to glitter
schauen *wk.* to see, look
schenken *wk.* to give (as present)
allerlei' all kinds of
fröhlich joyous, happy

interessant' interesting
klug clever, wise
köstlich delicious
kurz short(ly); in short
meinetwegen for all I care
niemand, –s nobody

praktisch practical
reich rich
süß sweet
überall' everywhere
vielleicht' perhaps
wohl probably

REDEWENDUNGEN

vierzehn Tage two weeks
bei verschlossenen Türen behind locked doors

Weihnachtseinkäufe machen do Christmas shopping
steigen (rise) in die Nase meet one

FRAGEN

1. Was macht man in den Wochen vor Weihnachten? 2. Was für Musik hört man oft im Rundfunk? 3. Was für Leute kommen oft in das Kaufhaus? 4. Wollen sie viel Geld ausgeben? 5. Warum sagt Marie zu ihrem Mann: „lieber Schatz"? 6. Was für Wetter ist es? 7. Was sieht man überall auf Straßen und Plätzen und in den Schaufenstern? 8. Was beginnt bei Frau Neumann vierzehn Tage vor Weihnachten? 9. Riecht es vor Weihnachten in Ihrer Küche zu Hause auch gut? 10. Was gibt es zu Weihnachten in Deutschland zu essen?

ÜBUNGEN

(a) Decline in the singular: beautiful music; red wine; splendid weather.

(b) Translate: 1. Something good; nothing small; much (that is) cheap. 2. From rich parents; in hot water; with blond hair; three small children. 3. Good evening [1]; good morning; good night.

---

[1] Such greetings are put in the accusative, " I wish you " being understood.

ÜBERSETZUNG

1. Have you perhaps bought something pretty today?
2. One evening Ernest and Marie were hearing good radio
music. **3.** Young and old, poor and rich people will soon
do their Christmas shopping. **4.** Women are clever
See 74 creatures, are they not? **5.** Buy no presents for (zu)
high prices, Marie. **6.** How do you do? Here are three
large packages. **7.** Sweet odors lured the children into the
kitchen two weeks before Christmas. **8.** Will they not get
sick from all kinds of delicious sweets?

LESSON SEVENTEEN

WEAK DECLENSION OF ADJECTIVES

93 **Weak Declension.** Adjectives follow the weak declension if preceded by a ber-word, which itself has
endings corresponding to those of the strong adjective.
Compare:

armer Mann	armes Kind
der arme Mann	das arme Kind

SINGULAR

	MASC.	FEM.	NEUT.
N.	der arme Mann	die arme Frau	das arme Kind
G.	des armen Mannes	der armen Frau	des armen Kindes
D.	dem armen Manne	der armen Frau	dem armen Kinde
A.	den armen Mann	die arme Frau	das arme Kind

PLURAL

N. die armen Männer, Frauen, Kinder
G. der armen Männer, Frauen, Kinder
D. den armen Männern, Frauen, Kindern
A. die armen Männer, Frauen, Kinder

The endings are =e in the five blocked forms, and =en everywhere else. In the same way are declined dieser arme Mann, jeder arme Mann, jener arme Mann, welcher arme Mann?

94 The words viele, wenige, andere, einige, *some,* mehrere, solche, are in the nom. and accus. plural regularly followed by adjectives with strong endings. But after alle, the weak adjective is used: viele neue Bücher, alle großen Städte.

NOTE. wenig Geld, das wenige Geld. Viel and wenig may remain uninflected when not preceded by the definite article or a pronominal adjective. Otherwise they are always inflected. The phrase ein wenig, *a little,* is invariable.

95 **Adjectives after ein-words.** When used after an ein-word the adjective takes the strong endings wherever the ein-word is itself without ending, i.e., in the three forms blocked below. Elsewhere it has the weak ending.

SINGULAR

MASC.	FEM.	NEUT.
ein armer Mann	eine arme Frau	ein armes Kind
eines armen Mannes	einer armen Frau	eines armen Kindes
einem armen Manne	einer armen Frau	einem armen Kinde
einen armen Mann	eine arme Frau	ein armes Kind

PLURAL

keine armen Männer, Frauen, Kinder
keiner armen Männer, Frauen, Kinder
keinen armen Männern, Frauen, Kindern
keine armen Männer, Frauen, Kinder

CAUTION. Do not mistake the =er of unser and euer for a declensional ending. Unser and euer are ein-words and the adjective following them has the same endings as after ein, mein: ein schöner Garten, unser schöner Garten.

NOTE 1. *such a* has three equivalents: 1. ſolch (uninflected) ein; 2. ein ſolcher; 3. ſo ein. In all three ein has its usual inflection.

NOTE 2. In derſelbe, *the same*, both der and ſelb are inflected and the two are written as one word: derſelbe Name, dasſelbe Buch.

NOTE 3. In conversational language welch (*some*) is much used in the place of einig: Haſt du noch Geld? Ja, ich habe noch welches.

96 **Adjectives used as nouns** retain their regular adjective inflection: fremd, *strange:* ein Fremder, *a stranger;* der Fremde, *the stranger;* die Fremden, *the strangers;* bekannt', *acquainted:* ein Bekannter, *an acquaintance;* der Bekannte, *the acquaintance;* deutſch: ein Deutſcher, *a German;* der Deutſche, *the German;* jeder Deutſche, *every German;* die Deutſchen, *the Germans.*

FRÖHLICHE WEIHNACHTEN

„Ihr kommt doch am Heiligen Abend zu uns?" hatte Frau Neumann ihre Kinder gefragt. Das war aber eine unnötige Frage, denn ſo war es ſeit Jahren geweſen. Am Nachmittag ſtellten der Vater und Hans den Weihnachtsbaum in die gute Stube auf den

5 Fußboden. „Mutter, haben wir noch bunte Glaskugeln (*glass balls*) und vergoldete (*gilded*) Nüſſe vom vorigen Jahr?" fragte Martha. „Ja, oben im Schrank ſind welche." Und nun ſchmückten Martha und Hans den Baum mit den bunten Glaskugeln, vergoldeten Nüſſen und allerlei glitzerndem Tand (*tinsel*). Oben an

10 der Spitze war ein goldner Stern; viele blaue, grüne und rote Glühbirnen (*electric bulbs*) waren überall angebracht (*fastened*). Frau Neumann wollte lange keine elektriſchen Lichter auf ihrem Baum. Die lieben, alten Wachskerzen, meinte ſie, machten eine viel ſchönere Stimmung. Einmal aber hatten ſie beinahe ein

15 großes Feuer, und ſeitdem war ſie mit den modernen Lichtern zufrieden.

Auf den großen, runden Tiſch in der guten Stube legte man nun alle geheimnisvollen Pakete. An jeden Platz ſtellte Frau Neumann

auch einen großen Teller mit Obst, Nüssen, Lebkuchen und Mar=
zipan. Die gute, treue Köchin war natürlich nicht vergessen. 20

Inzwischen war es Abend geworden. Linkes, Paul und Lotte
waren angekommen und warteten ungeduldig, besonders der kleine
Peter. Endlich hörte man aus der guten Stube die Melodie des
schönen Liedes: O Tannenbaum![1] Der Vater öffnete die Tür,
da glänzte der wunderschöne Baum! Martha spielte Klavier, und 25
die ganze Familie sang nun in feierlicher Stimmung das schönste
Weihnachtslied der Deutschen: Stille Nacht, heilige Nacht![1]

(Fortsetzung folgt.)

O Tannenbaum

O Tannenbaum, o Tannenbaum,
Wie treu sind deine Blätter![2]
Du grünst[3] nicht nur zur Sommerzeit,
Nein, auch im Winter, wenn es schneit.[4]
O Tannenbaum, o Tannenbaum,
Wie treu sind deine Blätter!

Stille Nacht

Stille Nacht, heilige Nacht!
Alles[5] schläft, einsam[6] wacht
Nur das traute[7] hochheilige[8] Paar.
Holder[9] Knabe im lockigen[10] Haar,
Schlaf in himmlischer[11] Ruh'!

---

[1] The first stanza will be found below.
[2] *leaves.* [3] *are green.* [4] *it snows.*
[5] Here *every one.* [6] *lonely.* [7] *beloved.* [8] *most holy.* [9] *sweet.* [10] *curly.*
[11] *heavenly rest.*

VOKABELN

das Feuer, -s, — fire
der Fußboden, -s, ⸚ floor
das Klavier', -s, -e piano
das Licht, -es, -er candle, light
der Marzipan', -s almond paste,
  marzipan
die Nuß, ⸚e nut
der Schrank, -es, ⸚e cupboard
die Spitze, -n top, summit
der Stern, -es, -e star
die Wachskerze, -n wax candle
waren an'gekommen had arrived
glänzen *wk.* to shine, gleam
was heißt what is called
legen *wk.* to lay, put
meinen *wk.* to mean, say, think
schmücken *wk.* to adorn, trim
singen; sang sang
stellen *wk.* to place, put

beinahe almost
beson'ders especially
bunt motley, gay-colored
elek'trisch electric
feierlich solemn, festive
geheim'nisvoll mysterious
golden golden, gold
heilig holy
natür'lich of course
oben *adv.* above, on top
rund round
schöner, schönste more, most beautiful
seit since; seitdem' since then
treu faithful
ungeduldig impatient(ly)
unnötig unnecessary
vorig last, past, former
zufrie'den content, satisfied

REDEWENDUNGEN

auf deutsch in German
die gute Stube (old-fashioned) parlor

der Heilige Abend Christmas Eve
seit Jahren for years

FRAGEN

1. Was heißt auf deutsch „Christmas Eve"? 2. Wo war die ganze Familie immer an diesem Abend? 3. In welcher Stube war der Weihnachtsbaum? 4. Womit schmückten Martha und Hans den Baum? 5. Was für Lichter hatte man früher am Weihnachtsbaum? 6. Was für Lichter hat man jetzt? 7. Was für ein Tisch war in der guten Stube? 8. Wer war nicht vergessen? 9. Was für eine Stimmung herrschte im Haus? 10. Nennen (*name*) Sie zwei schöne, deutsche Weihnachtslieder!

ÜBUNGEN

(a) Decline in the singular and plural the German equivalent of: this golden star; no big fire.

(b) Decline in the plural the German equivalent of: some brown cakes; all red apples.

(c) Translate: our electric light; an unnecessary table; the poor (man); the poor (woman); the poor; the German (man); a German (man); a German (woman); the Germans; many Germans.

ÜBERSETZUNG

1. On Christmas Eve no stranger was at (the) Neumanns.
2. They have trimmed the Christmas tree with the glittering tinsel of last year. 3. They have also fastened a golden star at the top. 4. Have you had many big fires in the city this year? 5. The mysterious package is lying on the round table in our little dining room. 6. It will become evening very early today. 7. Merry Christmas, my dear brothers and sisters! 8. The Germans have several beautiful Christmas songs. 9. Mother gives her faithful cook something practical for (зu) Christmas. 10. [The] poor little Peter was waiting impatiently.

Karl, laufe (nach Hause) heim / bleibe daheim zu Hause

Ich gab dir dem Buch

Ich " euch euer "

" " Ihren Ihr "

Pg 9

LESSON EIGHTEEN

COMPARISON OF ADJECTIVES

Der Dezember ist kalt.
Der Januar ist kälter als der Dezember.
Der Februar ist der kälteste Monat.
Der Februar ist am kältesten.

97 Comparison. The comparison of adjectives does not greatly differ from that in English. As in English, the comparative adds =er; but the superlative has =st, not =est: klein, kleiner, der kleinste. The English *than* is als.

98 Umlaut. The more common adjectives of one syllable modify an a, o, u of the stem: jung, jünger, der jüngste. An au is not modified: Sprechen Sie lauter! *Speak louder.*

Excepting blank, bunt, falsch, klar, schlank, all monosyllabic adjectives with a, o, u previously used modify the vowel of the stem.

99 more, most. German does not, like English, use ' *more* ' (mehr) and ' *most* ' (meist) in comparison: *more beautiful* = schöner; das schönste Mädchen.

100 Declension. Comparatives and superlatives are declined in the same way as positive adjectives:

| warmes Wasser | ein junger Sohn | das kleine Kind |
| warmeres Wasser | ein jüngerer Sohn | das kleinste Kind |

1. Adjectives in =e drop the e in the comparative: weise, *wise*, weiser.

2. Adjectives in =el, =er, =en drop the e in the comparative but keep it in the superlative: dunkel, *dark*, dunkler, der dunkelste.

more & most cannot be used

101 =ſt and =eſt. The superlative ending is =ſt, but after an
s-sound and after a d or t, the ending is =eſt: das
heißeſte Waſſer; der älteſte Sohn. But groß has größt.

102 Irregular Comparison. The following are irregular:

gut, beſſer, der beſte   nah, näher, der nächſte
hoch, höher, der höchſte   viel, mehr, der meiſte

103 mehr, meiſt. The comparative mehr is not inflected:
Berlin hat mehr Einwohner als Paris.

Most people = die meiſten Leute. *Most dictionaries* = die
meiſten Wörterbücher, i.e., meiſt is always preceded by the
definite article.

104 immer ſchneller. For the English double comparative,
German uses immer + the single comparative. Er
geht immer ſchneller, *He is going faster and faster.*

105 Use of the Superlative. German never uses the
superlative without an article (*a*) in the predicate, or
(*b*) as an adverb, as does English in (*a*) *Heidelberg is
loveliest in spring* and (*b*) *William writes best.*

(*a*) Im Frühling iſt Heidelberg am ſchönſten.
(*b*) Wilhelm ſchreibt am beſten.

The phrases am ſchönſten and am beſten in (*a*) and (*b*) mean
' *at the loveliest,*' ' *at the best.*'

On the other hand, in such a sentence as:

Dieſes Gebäude iſt das ſchönſte in der Stadt,

German and English idioms do not differ. Here das ſchönſte
modifies an unexpressed noun: Dieſes Gebäude iſt das ſchönſte
(Gebäude) der Stadt. So, Welche Tage ſind die längſten im Jahr?

The rule is, accordingly: For a superlative that follows a
verb, use the phrase with am unless you can supply a noun.

106 Absolute Superlative.

(a) If I say " She sang most beautifully," I am not making a comparison but merely mean " She sang very beautifully." This is called the Absolute Superlative. The German equivalent is: Sie sang aufs schönste, in which aufs = auf das.

(b) When ' most ' is followed by an adjective ('a most happy beginning'), höchst (*highest*, *highly*), äußerst (*extremest*, *extremely*), or sehr are used: ein höchst glücklicher Anfang.

FRÖHLICHE WEIHNACHTEN (FORTSETZUNG)

Das Lied war zu Ende, die Eltern umarm'ten (*embraced*) die Kinder, und alle wünschten einander aufs herzlichste „Fröhliche Weihnachten!"

„Nun kommt aber das Wichtigste, nicht wahr, Peter?" sagte 5 Onkel Hans. Peters Augen wurden immer größer. Schönere Geschenke hatte er noch nie gehabt. Da waren Schlittschuhe, viel besser und blanker als die alten, die neusten (*latest*) Bücher von Onkel Paul und Tante Lotte, und — ja, was ist denn das? Eine Eisenbahn? „Ich habe doch [1] schon eine!" — „Aber sieh nur 10 mal,[2] diese fährt viel schneller," sagte sein Vater, schaltete den elektrischen Strom ein, und fort sauste der Zug, zu Peters und seines Vaters größtem Vergnügen. Inzwischen hatten auch die andern einander ihre Geschenke gezeigt, und des Dankens, Küssens und Lachens war kein Ende. „Am besten gefällt mir dieser rote 15 Schlips," sagte Vater Neumann, „einen hübscheren konnte ich mir nicht wünschen."

Ernst und Paul brauten einen köstlichen Weihnachtspunsch (*Christmas punch*), man knackte Nüsse und knabberte (*nibbled*) Süßigkeiten, und es wurde höchst gemütlich. „Morgen kommt ihr

[1] *Why, I already have one.*
[2] mal = einmal, with imperatives, *just.*

Vocab Test
74-80

alle zu uns zu Tisch, nicht wahr?" fragte Marie, „wir haben die 20
größte Gans auf dem ganzen Markt gekauft." — „Das brauchst
du uns nicht zweimal zu sagen," antwortete der Vater, „denn eine
gute gebratene Gans [1] und ein guter Gur'kensalat' (*cucumber
salad*) sind eine gute Gabe Gottes! sagt Schiller."

Draußen war es immer kälter geworden. Der Mond stand voll 25
am Himmel, es war die kälteste aber schönste Nacht seit Wochen.
Langsamer als sonst lenkte Ernst auf dem Heimweg den Wagen
durch die weihnachtliche Landschaft und die feierlich stillen Straßen.
In den Fenstern der Reichsten sowie der Ärmsten glänzten freund=
liche Lichter. Die Menschen feierten die Geburt des Friedens= 30
fürsten (*Prince of Peace*).

VOKABELN

die Gabe, –n gift
die Gans, ⁼e goose
die Geburt', –en birth
Gott, –es, ⁼er God
der Himmel, –s, — sky, heaven
die Landschaft, –en landscape, scen-
    ery
das Mittagessen, –s, — dinner
der Mond, –es, –e moon
der Schlips, –es, –e necktie
der Schlittschuh, –s, –e skate
der Strom, –s, ⁼e stream, current
das Vergnü'gen, –s, — pleasure,
    delight
er bekam' he received
brauen *wk.* to brew
feiern *wk.* to celebrate
gefal'len; gefällt pleases
knacken *wk.* to crack

küssen *wk.* to kiss
lenken *wk.* to guide, steer
sausen *wk.* ist gesaust to rush
schaltete . . . ein' connected
sehen (er sieht; *imper.* sieh) to see,
    look
blank shiny
draußen outside
dunkel dark
einan'der each other
freundlich friendly
gebra'ten roast
langsam slow(ly)
sonst usually
verlobt' engaged; die Verlob'te, *adj.*
    infl. fiancée; *plur.* engaged
    couple
voll full
weihnachtlich *adj.* Christmas

---

[1] „Eine gute gebratene Gans ist eine gute Gabe Gottes" with g pronounced as y
is frequently used to parody Berlin pronunciation.

FRAGEN

1. Was wünschen die Menschen einander am Heiligen Abend?
2. Was war das Wichtigste für den kleinen Jungen? 3. Was für eine Eisenbahn bekam er? 4. Was schenkt man den Männern immer? 5. Was haben Ernst und Paul gebraut? 6. Bei wem wird das Mittagessen am Weihnachtstag sein? 7. Was hat Marie gekauft? 8. Warum fährt Ernst langsamer als sonst nach Hause? 9. Was sieht man überall in den Häusern? 10. Wie feiert man den Heiligen Abend in Amerika?

ÜBUNGEN

(a) Compare: süß, bunt, alt, teuer; mein hübscher Schlips, die gute Gabe, das nahe Dorf; er fährt langsam.

(b) Decline in the singular and plural the German equivalent of: the darker night, our strongest man.

ÜBERSETZUNG

1. We wished each other most cordially a Merry Christmas.
2. They are giving their smallest nephew the latest book.
3. Father and son had the greatest pleasure with the new electric train. 4. Which present pleases his fianceé most (= best). 5. Isn't it cozier here than outdoors? 6. The young men will brew the Christmas punch fastest. 7. Last (vorig=) year it was colder on (am) Christmas Eve. 8. The cook makes a better cucumber salad than I. 9. Which goose cost most? 10. The richest and the poorest are celebrating Christmas.

write 2, 3, 4, 5, 7, 10

LESSON NINETEEN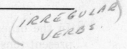

STRONG CONJUGATION

107 **Vowel-Change in Present Tense.** A verb like ɧelfen, *to help*, has:

ich ɧelfe, du ɧilfſt, er ɧilft; Imper. ɧilf!

That is, strong verbs change an e of the stem to i or ie in the 2d and 3d persons sing. of the present indicative and in the sing. of the imperative. Short e becomes i; long e usually becomes ie.

A verb like ɧalten, *to hold*, has:

ich ɧalte, du ɧältſt, er ɧält; Imper. ɧalte!

That is, verbs whose present vowel is a, umlaut this a in the second and third persons, but the imperative retains a.

ich ɧelfe nicht	was ſeɧe ich?	ich ɧalte ſtill
du ɧilfſt nicht	was ſieɧſt du?	du ɧältſt ſtill
er ɧilft nicht	was ſieɧt er?	er ɧält ſtill
Mutter, ɧilf!	Mutter, ſieɧ!	ɧalte ſtill!

108 **Personal Endings.** The personal endings in the present are the same as for weak verbs. So verbs in ꞏd and ꞏt have ꞏeſt and ꞏet in the singular: du findeſt, er findet. This does not hold good, however, for strong verbs that show a change of vowel in these forms. Compare er wartet with er ɧält.

Similarly, the sing. imper. is without ending if the stem vowel changes: thus, geben, *to give*, has gib, while ɧalten has ɧalte.

109 **Past Tense.** The first and third persons singular have no personal ending:

ich ſaɧ, er ſaɧ; ich gab, er gab; ich ɧalf, er ɧalf

In the other persons, the endings are the same as for the present tense.

110 **Principal Parts.** Principal parts of strong verbs are indicated in the lesson vocabularies, ſprechen (i), a, o, meaning ſprechen, er ſpricht, er ſprach, er hat geſprochen.

For giving principal parts orally, the above model is recommended; or, better still, with some modifier of the verb:

ſprechen, er ſpricht laut, er ſprach laut, er hat laut geſprochen

111 **Conjugation of: geben; halten; bleiben** (*aux.* ſein)

INDICATIVE
PRESENT

ich gebe	ich halte	ich bleibe
du gibſt	du hältſt	du bleibſt
er gibt	er hält	er bleibt
wir geben	wir halten	wir bleiben
ihr gebt	ihr haltet	ihr bleibt
ſie geben	ſie halten	ſie bleiben

PAST

ich gab	ich hielt	ich blieb
du gabſt	du hielteſt	du bliebſt
er gab	er hielt	er blieb
wir gaben	wir hielten	wir blieben
ihr gabt	ihr hieltet	ihr bliebt
ſie gaben	ſie hielten	ſie blieben

PRESENT PERFECT

ich habe gegeben	ich habe gehalten	ich bin geblieben

PAST PERFECT

ich hatte gegeben	ich hatte gehalten	ich war geblieben

FUTURE

ich werde geben	ich werde halten	ich werde bleiben

FUTURE PERFECT

| ich werde gegeben haben | ich werde gehalten haben | ich werde geblieben sein |

IMPERATIVE

| gib | halte | bleibe |
| gebt, geben Sie | haltet, halten Sie | bleibt, bleiben Sie |

INFINITIVE

| geben | halten | bleiben |

PARTICIPLES

| Pres. gebend | haltend | bleibend |
| Past gegeben | gehalten | geblieben |

Translate

SILVESTERABEND

„Komm und hilf Silvester [1] feiern!" hatte Paul an einen alten Schulkameraden geschrieben, der Lehrer an einem Gymnasium in einer Kleinstadt war. „Meine Braut und ich wollen mit meiner älteren Schwester und ihrem Mann und meiner jüngeren Schwester am letzten Abend des Jahres einen Bummel machen und das neue 5 Jahr begrüßen." — „Deine Einladung, liebster Paul, kam wie vom Himmel gefallen!" schrieb Bernd Förster als Antwort, „hier in der Kleinstadt wird nichts los sein; bei euch sieht man doch etwas am Silvesterabend."

Bernd kam und schien ein äußerst netter, junger Mann zu sein. 10 Man sprach und lachte über die alten Zeiten. „Wie geht es denn deinen Eltern?" fragte Bernd. „Sehr gut, danke! Heute abend sind sie zu Hause geblieben. Sie wollen um Mitternacht Blei gießen [2] und in die Zukunft (future) sehen."

Um elf ging (went) die kleine Gesellschaft in die Stadt, wo am 15 meisten los war. Ein immer regeres Leben herrschte auf den

[1] The thirty-first of December is St. Silvester's Day in the Roman Catholic calendar. Silvester was pope in the fourth century.
[2] Casting lead in water and thus 'forecasting' the future from the forms that result is a common practice at 'Silvester.'

Karl, gib mir dein Buch
Kinder, gebt mir euer Buch
Herr Müller, geben sie mir Ihr Buch

Straßen und in den Gaststätten. Überall sah man lustige Men=
schen, nur die Alten und Kranken schienen zu Hause geblieben zu
sein. Die Herren gaben den Damen den Arm, denn das Gedränge
20 (*crowding*) wurde immer schlimmer. Kurz vor Mitternacht
kamen sie in Pauls Stammlokal, dort hatte der Kellner einen
Tisch freigehalten. „Bringen Sie uns einen guten Silvesterpunsch
und die üblichen (*customary*) Berliner Pfannkuchen!" bestellte
Paul. „Siehst du dort in der Ecke das fidele Kleeblatt?" fragte
25 Ernst seine Schwägerin, „die haben schon einen über den Durst
getrunken!" — „Sprich nicht so laut, Ernst," sagte Martha,
„sonst kommen sie und halten uns eine Rede."

Plötzlich ertönte draußen lautes Rufen, die Turmuhren schlugen
zwölf, die Glocken läuteten, das Neue Jahr war da! Alle erhoben
30 die Gläser, stießen an (*touched glasses*) und stimmten ein in den
Ruf der Tausende draußen: „Prosit Neujahr!"

VOKABELN

die Antwort, –en answer
der Arm, –es, –e arm
das Blei, –s lead
die Gaststätte, –n hotel, restaurant
die Gesell'schaft, –en company, party
die Glocke, –n bell
das Kleeblatt, –s, ⸚er clover-leaf, trio
das Leben, –s life
die Mitternacht, ⸚e midnight
das Neujahr, –s New Year
der Pfannkuchen, –s, — cruller, pancake
der Ruf, –s, –e call
der Silve'ster, –s, — New Year's Eve
das Stamm'lokal', –s, –e tavern or inn frequented by a person
begrü'ßen *wk.* to greet
bestel'len *wk.* to order
erho'ben (they) raised

ertö'nen *wk.* to resound
freihalten, *past part.* freigehalten to reserve
gießen, o, o to pour, cast
kam, kamen came
läuten *wk.* to ring
rufen, ie, u to call; R. shouting
scheinen, ie, ie to seem
schlagen (ä), u, a to strike
schreiben, ie, ie to write
sprechen (i), a, o to speak
stimmten ein' joined in
trinken, a, u to drink
fidel' hilarious, jolly
laut aloud, loud(ly)
letzt last
nett pleasant, nice
plötzlich suddenly
rege lively, gay
schlimm bad
über (*w. accus.*) across, about

REDEWENDUNGEN

einen Bummel machen to 'step out'   Wie geht es dir? How are you?
eine Rede halten to make a speech   Prosit Neujahr! Happy New Year.
einen über den Durst (thirst) trinken to get tipsy.

FRAGEN

1. Wie heißt in Deutschland der letzte Abend des Jahres? 2. An wen hatte Paul geschrieben? 3. Welche Antwort bekam er? 4. Was für ein Mann war Bernd? 5. Was erzählt Paul von seinen Eltern? 6. Wann beginnt das Leben auf den Straßen am Silvesterabend? 7. Was für Leute sah man überall? 8. Wo war unsre Gesellschaft kurz vor Mitternacht? 9. Was ißt und trinkt man am Silvesterabend? 10. Was ruft man, wenn das Neue Jahr beginnt?

ÜBUNGEN

(a) Give synopses of the German of the following sentences: 1. He gives the lady his arm. 2. Are you reading the letter? 3. The old parents stay at home Christmas.

(b) Say to a child, to your parents, and to a stranger: 1. Speak louder. 2. Hold the glass. 3. Don't get angry.

ÜBERSETZUNG

1. They write an invitation to (an w. accus.) several old school-chums. 2. How shall we greet the New Year? 3. At ten o'clock (there) is not much doing on the street. 4. But shortly before and after midnight we saw great crowds of jolly people. 5. Not all the old people will stay at home tonight. 6. Give me your hand, Lotte, else you (will) fall. 7. They made a speech and touched glasses with us. 8. Many people open the windows and shout (call) "Happy New Year."

she gives him her book

LESSON TWENTY

PERSONAL PRONOUNS

112 **Personal Pronouns.** The personal pronouns are declined as follows:

SINGULAR

N.	ich, I	du, you	er, he	sie, she	es, it
G.	meiner, of me	deiner	feiner	ihrer	feiner
D.	mir, to me, me	dir	ihm	ihr	ihm
A.	mich, me	dich	ihn	sie	es

PLURAL

N.	wir, we	ihr, you	sie, they
G.	unser	euer	ihrer
D.	uns	euch	ihnen Ihnen (formal)
A.	uns	euch	sie

113 **Sie.** Exactly like sie, *they*, is declined Sie, *you:* Sie, Ihrer, Ihnen, Sie.

114 **Genitives.** The genitive of a personal pronoun does not, in German, commonly depend upon a noun. Thus ' a friend of mine ' = ein Freund von mir, or, rather more formally, einer meiner Freunde.

The sentences Bist du meiner schon müde? *Are you already tired of me?* and Ich erinnere mich seiner nicht, *I do not remember him*, show how they may be used.

115 **It is I.** For *It is I*, etc., German uses the following:

ich bin es, it is I	wir sind es, it is we
du bist es	ihr seid es
er ist es	sie sind es

The question form is Bist du es? The German " Who's Who " is called Wer ist's?

von takes dative

116 **man.** man is an indeclinable pronoun of the third person singular. It means *one, we, you, they, people, somebody.* Man sagt, *They say.* Man glaubt mir nicht, *People don't believe me.* Man kann nie wissen, *You can never tell.*

Dative and accusative are supplied from einer: Warum glaubst du einem nicht? *Why don't you believe one?*

Its possessive is sein: Im Hause nimmt man seinen Hut ab, *In the house one takes off one's hat.*

117 **Word Order of Objects.**

1. Of a direct and an indirect object the regular order is dative — accusative: Ich gebe dem Schüler ein Buch.

2. But if the accusative is a personal pronoun it precedes the dative: Er gab es dem Schüler.

3. The accusative es, contracted to 's, may, however, follow the datives mir, dir, ihm, ihr, euch: Er hat mir's schon gesagt.

4. Pronoun objects precede adverbs. Contrast Ich hatte gestern kein Geld with Ich hatte es gestern nicht.

5. In the inverted order, unemphatic pronoun objects may be put between verb and subject, contrary to § 61, Caution 2. Gestern hat ihn niemand gesehen.

118 **Damit, darauf, etc.**

1. Wo ist die Feder? Hast du damit geschrieben?
2. Wo ist die Zeitung? Hast du darin gelesen?

When a *thing* is referred to, these compounds with da= are used instead of the preposition + dative or accusative of the personal pronoun. Hence, above, damit, not mit ihr; darin, not in ihr. Compare 'therewith,' 'therein,' 'thereby.'

Before a vowel dar= is used: daran, darauf, darin, or, contracted, dran, drauf, drin.

NOTE. Ohne, *without*, does not form these compounds.

IM KINO

Bernd Förster ist noch einige Tage nach Neujahr in der Stadt geblieben, denn er hat ja noch Ferien. Am Neujahrsmorgen, etwa um 11 Uhr, klingelt das Telephon bei Martha Neumann. „Ach, Sie sind es, Herr Förster!" — „Ja, ich bin es; wie geht es Ihnen 5 denn heute, Fräulein Martha, nach solch einer fidelen Nacht?" — „Mir geht's famos, und Ihnen?" — „Danke schön, mir auch. Nach einem kalten Bad und einer Tasse schwarzem Kaffee zum Frühstück bin ich so frisch wie ein Fisch im Wasser. Aber was ich sagen wollte: Möchten Sie heute abend mit mir ins Kino gehen? 10 Es gibt einen höchst interessanten, spannenden Film, ein Freund von mir hat davon erzählt. Darf ich Sie um halb acht abholen?" — „Schön! Eigentlich wollte ich zu meinen Eltern, aber ich kann sie ja heute nachmittag besuchen."

Der Film spielte zuerst in London und handelte von zwei Schwe= 15 stern. Die ältere war verheiratet, die jüngere, sehr schöne, noch nicht. Beide waren sehr arm, der Mann der älteren konnte keine Arbeit finden. Die Frauen schneiderten und ernährten sich und ihn damit. Da erscheint plötzlich der übliche Millionär, leider aber diesmal nicht der typische, amerikanische Filmheld, jung, schön und 20 schneidig, sondern ernst, steif und sehr, sehr häßlich. Seine Häßlichkeit hat ihn menschenscheu (*misanthropic*) gemacht, er geht nie unter Menschen. Noch nie hat er eine Frau geliebt, viel weniger eine Frau ihn.

Dieser Millionär hat von der schönen Schwester gehört und hält um 25 ihre Hand an, durch seinen Sekretär'. Lange kämpft das arme Mädchen. Schwester und Schwager sagen zu ihr: „Du hilfst nicht nur dir selbst, du hilfst uns allen." Endlich gibt sie ihm ihr Jawort. Als Hochzeitsgabe bekommt sie eine halbe Million, wieder durch den Sekretär, aber kein liebes Wort. Es folgt eine glänzende Hochzeit. Viele Leute stehen an der Kirchtür, das reiche Paar zu sehen. Da hören Braut und Bräutigam ein Mädchen aus der Menge sagen: „Nicht für alles Geld in der Welt möchte ich einen Mann wie diesen."

An demselben Abend verschwindet die Braut.

(Fortsetzung folgt.)

VOKABELN

das Bad, –es, –er bath
der Bräutigam, –s, –e bridegroom
der Filmheld, –en, –en film hero, matinée idol
die Häßlichkeit ugliness
die Hochzeit, –en wedding
das Jawort, –s consent (to marry)
das Kino, –s, –s movie, cinema
die Kirchtür, –en church door
der Millionär', –s, –e millionaire
die Tasse, –n cup
die Welt, –en world
abholen wk. to call for, go and get
ernäh'ren wk. to support
erschei'nen, ie, ist erschienen to appear
handeln wk. to deal (with)
kämpfen wk. to struggle

klingeln wk. to ring
schneidern wk. to sew, do dressmaking
verschwin'den, a, ist verschwunden to disappear
eigentlich really, anyway
ernst serious
etwa about, approximately
famos' fine, capital
glänzend brilliant
häßlich ugly
schneidig smart, dashing
schwarz black
selbst -self (myself, himself, herself, themselves, etc.)
sondern but
typisch typical
unter among

REDEWENDUNGEN

danke schön! many thanks!   er hält um ihre Hand an he asks for her hand
der Film spielte the scene of the film was laid

FRAGEN

1. Warum konnte Bernd Förster noch einige Tage in der Stadt bleiben? (Er war . . .) 2. Wann klingelte das Telephon bei

Fräulein Neumann? 3. Was wollte Bernd Förster ihr zeigen?
4. Um wieviel Uhr wird er sie abholen? 5. Von wem handelt
der Film? 6. Was für ein Mann erscheint oft in amerikanischen
Filmen? 7. Beschreiben (*describe*) Sie diesen Millionär!
8. Warum liebte das Mädchen ihn nicht? 9. Warum gibt sie
ihm ihr Jawort? 10. Bleibt sie bei ihm?

ÜBUNGEN

(*a*) In the following sentences substitute personal pronouns, or their equivalents, for all noun objects and for
nouns depending upon prepositions. Watch the word
order. *Example:* 3. Er gibt sie ihr.

1. Er gibt heute der Braut eine Hochzeitsgabe. 2. Der Film
handelt von zwei Schwestern. 3. Er gibt der Braut eine halbe
Million. 4. Der Film handelt von einer Hochzeit. 5. Er
trinkt den schwarzen Kaffee aus der Tasse. 6. Nach dem Bad
bin ich frisch.

(*b*) Translate: Through me; through it; for her; for
them (i.e., *houses*); with you; with it; I thank him;
he answered me; you asked her; she helps them.

ÜBERSETZUNG

1. Was Martha tired of him? 2. Bernd had not seen
the film, and he wanted-to (wollte) see it with her. 3. A
millionaire appears in it. 4. One wants a typical dashing
matinée idol. 5. He has several millions and lures her with
them. 6. She can sew and supports herself (sich) with it.
7. He asks (bitten um) her for her consent and she gives it
to him. 8. I am fine today; how are you, dear child?

LESSON TWENTY-ONE

ORDINALS

119 **Ordinal Numbers.** The lower ordinals are formed by adding =t to the cardinals; those from 20 on add =ft. Irregular forms are underscored. Ordinals are declined like adjectives. An important difference from English is that the article is required in the predicate: ich war der zweite, *I was second.* But Zweites Kapitel, *Second Chapter.*

der erste, the first
der zweite, the second
der dritte, the third
der vierte, the fourth
der siebente, the seventh
der achte, the eighth
der neunte, the ninth

der zehnte, the tenth
der elfte, the eleventh
der zwanzigste, the twentieth
der hundertste, the hundredth
der hundert vierundzwanzigste, the hundred and twenty-fourth
der tausendste, the thousandth
der letzte, the last

Figures denoting ordinals are followed by a period: der 3. Mai, *the third of May;* Wilhelm II., *William II.*

120 **Fractionals** are formed by adding =tel (= Teil) to the ordinal, the final t of the ordinal stem disappearing. As substantives these fractionals are neuter: das Viertel, das Achtel. Especially Viertel (ie = i) is often compounded with the following noun. Viertelstunde and Vierteljahr are more common than fünfzehn Minuten and drei Monate.

121 **half.** The German equivalents of *half* are:

1. halb used as an adjective: ein halbes Brot; der halbe Sommer; *half an apple* = ein halber Apfel.

2. The substantive die Hälfte: die beiden Hälften, *the two halves; half of an apple* = die Hälfte eines Apfels; *my better half* = meine bessere Hälfte.

122 =halb. The word halb also forms compounds with the stems of the lower numerals: dritthalb Liter, *two and a half liters* (i.e., two and the third liter half); *one and a half* = anderthalb, *one and the other half*.

123 Dates. The *first of January* = der erste Januar. German does not use an *of*-construction in dates.

IM KINO (FORTSETZUNG)

In den nächsten zwei Tagen ist der Millionär sehr beschäftigt. Am dritten Tag bestellt er sein Flugzeug (*airplane*) und fliegt über den Kanal. In der Mitte desselben öffnet er die Tür und springt ins Wasser. „Wie schrecklich!" flüstert Martha. Niemand sieht es,
5 auch nicht der Flugzeugführer (*pilot*). Beim Landen findet dieser seinen Herrn nicht. Bald steht es in allen Zeitungen: der arme reiche Mann hat Selbstmord begangen.

Die nächste Szene spielt in Deutschland, im Sprechzimmer eines berühmten Arztes. Dieser hatte im Weltkrieg manchem armen,
10 verwundeten Soldaten ein neues Gesicht geschaffen (*created*). Auf höchst geheimnisvolle Weise waren immer die nötigen großen Summen Geldes aus einem fremden Lande gekommen. Nun kommt ein Mann zu diesem Arzt und will ein schönes Gesicht für sein häßliches. „Das tu' ich nicht," sagt er, „ich kann Ihnen nicht
15 helfen!" Am Ende tut er es aber doch, denn von diesem Mann hat er immer die großen Summen bekommen. „Unglaublich!" flüstert Bernd.

Die Operation' glückt. Nach einem Vierteljahr kommt ein statt=licher, elegant gekleideter Herr nach Paris. Die zweite Hälfte
20 seines Lebens soll (*is to*) glücklicher werden als die erste. In den Cafés und Thea'tern, auf Bällen und bei Pferderennen (*horse races*), überall sieht man ihn.

Seine „Witwe" ist inzwischen auch nach Paris gekommen. Sie lebt aber nicht von den Reichtümern des Toten, sie will

arbeiten. In Paris bekommt sie eine Stelle bei einer Schneiderin 25
der eleganten Welt. Durch ihre Schönheit hat sie viele Bewunderer,
aber nur einer gefällt ihr. Mit großer Mühe macht dieser ihr
endlich klar, wer er ist. Ende gut, alles gut: Die Leute gehen
zufrieden nach Hause.

Aber war er nicht ins Wasser gesprungen? Jawohl! Aber er 30
hatte seinen Fallschirm (*parachute*), und seine Jacht,[1] „Georg
V.", wartete unten auf ihn!

VOKABELN

der Bewun'derer, –s, — admirer
das Gesicht', –s, –er face
der Kanal', –s Channel
das Land, –es, ⁼er land, country
die Mühe, –n difficulty
die Schneiderin, –nen dressmaker
die Schönheit, –en beauty
der Selbstmord, –s, –e suicide
der Soldat', –en –en soldier
das Sprechzimmer, –s, — consultation room
die Summe, –n sum
die Szene, –n scene
die Witwe, –n widow
die Zeitung, –en newspaper

bege'hen *p.p.* begangen to commit
fliegen, o, ist geflogen to fly
flüstern *wk.* to whisper
glücken *wk.* ist geglückt to be successful
helfen *w. dat.* (i), a, o to help
kommen, a, ist gekommen to come
landen *wk.* ist gelandet to land
nötig necessary
schrecklich terrible
stattlich handsome, distinguished
unglaublich incredible
unten below
verwun'det wounded

REDEWENDUNGEN

es steht in der Zeitung, it is in the newspaper

auf geheimnisvolle Weise in a mysterious way

Ende gut, alles gut (proverb) All is well that ends well

FRAGEN

1. Am wievielten Tag nach der Hochzeit fliegt der Millionär über
den Kanal? 2. Was tut er in der Mitte des Kanals? 3. Wer

[1] die Jacht, –en, *yacht;* the ch is pronounced as in Nacht.

fieht das? **4.** Wie hat er sich gerettet? **5.** Bei wem spielt die nächste Szene? **6.** Was für Operationen macht der deutsche Arzt? **7.** Was für einen Mann macht die Operation aus dem häßlichen Millionär? **8.** Warum lebt er in Paris? **9.** Lebt seine Frau von seinem Geld? **10.** Gefällt Ihnen dieser Film?

ÜBUNGEN

(*a*) Lesen Sie laut: der 25. Dezember; am 8. Mai; das 3. Buch; 3. Buch; Karl V.; Katharina II.

(*b*) Schreiben Sie in Wörtern: ⅔; ⅚; ½ Pfund; ¼ Jahr.

(*c*) Antworten Sie auf deutsch: **1.** Wann ist Ihr Geburtstag? **2.** Wieviel ist ¾ + ¾?

→ √ ÜBERSETZUNG   *heißt*

1. On the fifth day it is in all the newspapers. **2.** He had given her half of his money. **3.** His yacht is-called " George V." **4.** In landing one needs a parachute. **5.** In half a year he had a new face. **6.** The first half of his life had not been happy. **7.** The widow obtains a position in Paris. **8.** A happy end makes most people contented.

Vocab ←

LESSON TWENTY-TWO ✓

RELATIVE PRONOUNS. TRANSPOSED
WORD ORDER

124 **Relative Pronouns.** The relatives der and welcher are declined as follows:

	Singular			Plural
	Masc.	*Fem.*	*Neut.*	*M. F. N.*
N.	der, who	die	das	die
G.	dessen, whose	deren	dessen	deren
D.	dem, to whom, whom	der	dem	denen
A.	den, whom	die	das	die

The declension of der differs from that of the article der in the five blocked forms only. In the spoken language der (not welcher) is customary. welcher is declined like the interrogative welcher (§ 15), but has no genitives, so that there dessen or deren must be used.

125 **Agreement.** The number and gender of the relatives are determined by the antecedent, the case by the construction in the relative clause.

The father whose son . . . , Der Vater, dessen Sohn . . .
The mother whose son . . . , Die Mutter, deren Sohn . . .
The man to whom you gave the letter . . . , Der Mann, dem Sie den Brief gegeben haben, . . .

126 **Transposed Order.** In the last sentence above, haben stands at the end of its clause. This is always the case in relative clauses because relative clauses are

Woran denkst du?

subordinate clauses and *in subordinate clauses the part of the verb that has the personal ending stands at the end of the clause.* Other words keep their regular position. This is called the Transposed Order. Lesson 28 treats it more fully.

The Normal, Inverted, and Transposed Orders may, accordingly, be contrasted as follows:

Normal: Wir essen heute nicht zu Hause, We do not eat at home today.

Inverted: Heute essen wir nicht zu Hause.

Transposed: Heute ist der Tag, an dem wir nicht zu Hause essen.

127 Use of the Relative Pronoun.

1. The relative cannot be omitted in German. *The book you sent me has greatly interested me* = Das Buch, das Sie mir geschickt haben, hat mich sehr interessiert.

2. When the antecedent is a personal pronoun of the first or second person it is regularly repeated after the relative.

Du, der du selber krank bist . . . , You who are ill yourself . . .

If it is not thus repeated the verb stands in the third person:

Ich, der schon soviel verloren hat, . . . I who have already lost so much . . .

3. Only der can be used after a personal pronoun.

4. All relative clauses are, in German, set off by commas.

128 womit, worauf, etc. Contrast

(1) Mein Schwesterchen, mit dem ich spielte, . . . with (2) Der Ball, womit ich spielte, . . .

When the reference is to a thing, German often, but not necessarily, substitutes a wo-compound (womit, 'wherewith')

for the preposition + the relative. In (2) either mit dem
or womit can be used. In (1) only mit dem is possible.

129 Demonstrative der. As a demonstrative der may be
used adjectively or substantively. It is then often
spaced, to show the emphasis.

(*a*) *Adjectively:* der Mann, *that man.*

(*b*) *Substantively:* Der ist es, *That is the man.* Die ist nie
zu Hause, **She** *is never at home.*

The word order of (*b*) shows that this is not the relative.

IM MÖBELGESCHÄFT

Bald nach Neujahr gab Lotte ihre Stelle auf, denn sie hatte keine
Zeit mehr dazu. Sie muß (*must*) doch eine Aussteuer haben, die
schön ist und nicht sehr viel kostet. Die ganze Familie spricht von
nichts als von der Wohnung, die das junge Paar gemietet hat,
von den Möbeln, die sie kaufen wollen, von dem Brautkleid, das   5
Lotte bestellt hat und von dem Frack, den der Schneider für Paul
macht.

Die Verlobten besuchten die Möbelgeschäfte und fragten nach den
Preisen. „Sieh mal, Paul, dies Wohnzimmer im Biedermeierstil,
das finde ich wunderschön!" — „Aber, Lottchen, Biedermeier! 10
Das ist doch altmodisch! Wir sind moder'ne Menschen, deren
Wohnung ein Ausdruck ihres Wesens sein soll. Darum bin ich
für moderne Möbel, die auch viel bequemer sind. Wie bequem
sitzt man z.B. auf diesem Sessel! Auf dem möchte ich immer
abends nach der Arbeit sitzen und rauchen und mit dir plaudern; 15
im Kamin brennt ein lustiges Feuer, mein Liebchen, was [1] willst
(*want*) du noch mehr?" — „Also modern!" lachte Lotte, „du hast
wohl recht. Aber dann rauche ich auch." Sie kauften zwei Sessel

[1] Mein Liebchen, was willst du noch mehr is a quotation from one of Heine's
poems.

und ein Sofa, das dazu paßte, auch einen Teppich, einen Tisch
20 aus hellem Holz und einen schönen Schreibtisch.

Die Schlafzimmermöbel sollten (*were to*) sie als Hochzeitsgeschenk
bekommen. Sie brauchten aber eine Eßzimmereinrichtung und
wollten gern moderne Stahlmöbel. Beide waren ganz entzückt
von einem Eßzimmer, dessen Tisch aus Stahl und Glas war und
25 dessen Stühle blaue Lederpolster hatten. „Und in den Glasschrank
stellen wir dein blau und weißes Meißner [1] Porzellan'," jubelte
Paul. — „Was," rief Lotte, „du, der du ein solcher Bewunderer
des Modernen bist, willst Meißner Porzellan in deinem Haus?
Das ist doch altmodisch!" — „Ach, das vergessen wir!"

30 Das Haus, worin das junge Paar eine Wohnung gemietet hatte,
war ganz neu. In der Küche war alles eingebaut, alle Schränke,
auch der elektrische Kühlschrank. Unter einem Fenster an der
Wand waren zwei Stühle und ein Tisch angebracht, die man herun=
terklappen (*let down*) konnte. Nur einen elektrischen Kochofen
35 brauchten sie zu kaufen.

VOKABELN

der Ausdruck, -s, ⁔e expression
die Aussteuer, -n trousseau
der Biedermeierstil,[2] -s Biedermeier style
das Eßzimmer, -s, — dining room
die Eßzimmereinrichtung, -en dining
 room suite
das Hoch'zeitsgeschenk', -s, -e wedding present
das Holz, -es, ⁔er wood
der Kamin', -s, -e fireplace
der Kochofen, -s, ⁔ cook-stove
das Lederpolster, -s, — leather upholstery

das Liebchen, -s, — darling, sweet-
 heart
das Möbel, -s, — piece of furniture; *plur.* furniture
die Schlafzimmermöbel, *plur.* bed-
 room furniture
der Schneider, -s, — tailor
der Schreibtisch, -es, -e writing
 desk
der Sessel, -s, — armchair
das Sofa, -s, -s sofa
der Stahl, -s steel
der Teppich, -s, -e rug, carpet
das Wesen, -s personality

[1] Meiszen (in Saxony) porcelain, in America called Dresden china.
[2] A style of house furnishing and costuming between 1820 and 1840, now
treasured by collectors of antiques.

die Wohnung, –en dwelling, apartment

brennen to burn

eingebaut built in

gab . . . auf' gave up

jubeln *wk.* to exult, jubilate

plaudern *wk.* to chat

abends of an evening

also modern' very well, let it be modern then

altmodisch old-fashioned

bequem' comfortable

darum therefore

eigen own

entzückt' delighted

hell light, bright

nichts nothing

z. B. = zum Beispiel for example, e.g.

REDEWENDUNGEN

recht haben to be right   dazu paßte matched them

FRAGEN

1. Wovon sprach die ganze Familie? 2. Was für eine Aussteuer will (*wish*) Lotte haben? 3. Was ist ein Möbelgeschäft? 4. Welchen Stil findet Paul am schönsten? 5. Was ist ein Sessel? 6. Was für ein Sofa finden sie? 7. Warum kaufen sie keine Schlafzimmermöbel? 8. Paßt Lottes Porzellan zu den modernen Möbeln? 9. Welche Küchenmöbel sind eingebaut? 10. Was war unter dem Fenster?

ÜBUNGEN

(*a*) Translate: The chair, which . . . ; the secretary who . . . ; the fiancée whose . . . ; the store in which . . . ; the armchair for which . . . ; the man whom . . .

(*b*) Supply the relative or demonstrative pronoun: 1. Die Wohnung, — wir wohnen, ist klein. 2. Der Stil, — ich liebe, ist modern. 3. Hier sind die Leute, — Haus wir mieten. 4. Ich habe einen Schneider, — ist sehr gut.

ÜBERSETZUNG

1. The wedding dress she has ordered is [out] of (aus) white silk. 2. Is this the armchair in which you would like (to) sit? 3. We buy no furniture whose price is too high. 4. The fire you have made is already burning merrily. 5. This gentleman will show you the dining room furniture. 6. Have you a dwelling which is an expression of your own personality? 7. A style that is old-fashioned does not fit into (in) our time. 8. Are you for steel furniture? — No, I am not for it.

LESSON TWENTY-THREE

INTERROGATIVE AND POSSESSIVE PRONOUNS

130 Wer, was. The interrogative pronouns wer, *who,* was, *what,* are declined as follows:

SINGULAR

N.	wēr, who?	wăs, what?
G.	wĕſſen, of whom, whose?	wĕſſen, of what?
D.	wēm, to whom? whom?	(no dative)
A.	wēn, whom?	wăs, what?

Wer geht da?
Weſſen Bild iſt das?
Wem trauſt du nicht?
Wen ſuchſt du?

Like the English *who,* wer refers to persons; of things, no matter what the gender, was must be used.

There is no plural form, and wer is limited to the singular, except that it may stand in the predicate at the head of a plural form of the verb *to be:* Wer ſind dieſe Herren? But *Who were there* = Wer war da?

131 Was is not used adjectively. *What man* is, accordingly, welcher Mann; *what child?* = welches Kind?

132 Whose? The interrogative *whose* is weſſen; the relative *whose* is deſſen, deren: Weſſen Buch iſt dies? — Der Knabe, deſſen Vater . . . , *The boy whose father* . . .

133 Was für? Was für, *what sort of,* is an invariable expression, in which für has no prepositional force and does not influence the case of the following noun:

> Was für ein Tiſch iſt das?
> Mit was für einer Feder haſt du geſchrieben?

134 Womit, worauf, etc.

(*a*) Womit hört man? Man hört mit den Ohren.
(*b*) Wodurch? *Through what?* Wofür? *For what?*

As shown by (*a*), wo-compounds take the place of the lacking dative of was. As shown by (*b*), they are usually similarly employed in the accusative, where, however, durch was? and für was? may also be used.

Before a vowel wo= becomes wor=: worauf? woran?

135 Wer, was, as Relatives.

1. Wer and was are used as compound relatives, wer meaning *he who, whoever, who;* was, *that which, whatever, what.* There is no antecedent, the compound relative carrying its own antecedent. As in all relative clauses, the verb comes last: Was nicht gut iſt, iſt ſchlecht, *What is not good is bad.* Contrast Wer ſagt das?, *Who says that?* with Wer das ſagt . . . , *He who says that* . . .

2. Was is used as a simple relative in Das ist alles, was ich brauche, *That is all that I need*, where das might have been expected. Was is used after alles, das, nichts, manches, and neuter superlatives used substantively, das Schönste, was.

136 **Possessive Pronouns.** Possessive pronouns may also be used with the definite article. Their declension is then that of the weak adjective: der meine, das meine, die seinen.

There are, besides, derivatives in ≈ig, which can be used only after the definite article: der meinige, das seinige, etc.

Neither der meine nor der meinige, etc., can be used with a noun; der meinige is more common than der meine.

There are, accordingly, four ways of expressing possessives in the predicate:

1. Das Buch ist mein.   2. Es ist meins (meines).
3. Es ist das meinige.   4. Es ist das meine.

The first, which is commonly used when the subject is a noun, may be rendered *The book belongs to me*. The verb ge≈ hören, Das Buch gehört mir, may, of course, also be used.

DIE HOCHZEIT

Der Tag der Hochzeit kam näher. Pauls Eltern werden die Hochzeit ausrichten, denn Lotte ist eine Waise. „Wen werden wir denn einladen?" fragte Herr Neumann seine Frau. „Natürlich Lottes Verwandte und die unsrigen, das macht schon über zwanzig.
5 Mit Pauls und Lottes besten Freunden werden es wohl dreißig sein. Wer zur Trauung in die Kirche kommen will, braucht keine Einladung. Wessen Handschrift ist wohl die beste in der Familie?"
— „Ich glaube, die meinige," sagte Hans. „Du darfst also die Einladungen adressieren," sagte die Mutter.

Am dritten Sonntag vor der Hochzeit las der Pfarrer in der 10
Kirche zum erstenmal das Aufgebot (*the banns*) des jungen
Paares. „Vater," fragte Hans, „was ist eigentlich (*anyway*)
ein Aufgebot?" — „Nun, siehst du, es kann sein, daß einer der
beiden schon verheiratet ist. Darum liest der Pfarrer an drei
Sonntagen vor der Hochzeit von der Kanzel die Namen derer, die 15
heiraten wollen."

Inzwischen kamen viele Hochzeitsgeschenke, schöne und häßliche,
praktische und unpraktische, Lampen, Bilder, Kuchenteller, silberne
Messer, Gabeln und Löffel, kurz, alles, was man in einem neuen
Haushalt braucht oder nicht braucht. Am Tage vor der Hochzeit 20
kamen die Verwandten von außerhalb, denn am Abend sollte
bei Neumanns Polterabend sein. „Schade," sagte Lottes Groß=
mutter zu Frau Neumann, „es gibt so viele alte Hochzeitsbräuche
(*wedding customs*), die man aber jetzt nur noch bei den Bauern
findet. Ich als (*as a*) Kind habe noch am Vorabend von Hoch= 25
zeiten Schießen und Peitschenknallen (*cracking of whips*), nicht
nur Zerbrechen von Geschirr gehört. Der Lärm sollte die bösen
Geister verscheuchen (*drive away*)."

Die Gäste waren alle gekommen, man plauderte und lachte und
neckte das Brautpaar. Frau Neumann und ihre Töchter hatten 30
einen guten He'ringssalat' (*herring salad*) gemacht, dazu trank
man Bier. Später gab es (*they had*) Kaffee und Kuchen.
Draußen krachten unaufhörlich Töpfe, Schüsseln, Teller und
Gläser gegen das Haus. Das war Hans mit den Kindern der
Nachbarn, denen dies großes Vergnügen machte. Endlich war 35
alles in tausend Stücke zerbrochen, die Kinder bekamen Kuchen
und gingen fröhlich nach Hause.

(Fortsetzung folgt.)

VOKABELN

die Gabel, –n fork
der Geist, –es, –er spirit
das Geschirr', –s dishes

die Handschrift, –en handwriting
der Haushalt, –s, –e household
die Kanzel, –n pulpit

die Lampe, –n lamp
der Lärm, –s noise, din
der Löffel, –s, — spoon
das Messer, –s, — knife
der Nachbar, –s, –n neighbor
der Polterabend celebration on the eve of a wedding, 'Polterabend'
die Schüssel, –n bowl, dish
der Topf, –es, ⸚e pot
die Trauung, –en marriage ceremony, wedding
der Verwand'te *adj. infl.* relative
der Vorabend, –s, –e eve
die Waise, –n orphan
adressie'ren *wk.* to address
du darfst you may

ein'laden (ä), u, a to invite
glauben *wk.* to believe
heiraten *wk.* to marry
es kann sein it may be
krachen *wk.* to crash
las *past of* lesen
necken *wk.* to tease
schießen, o, o to shoot
einer der beiden one of the two
böse evil
dazu' with it
gegen *w. accus.* against
silbern silver
unaufhör'lich incessant(ly)
un'praktisch impractical
wer alles ' who all '

REDEWENDUNGEN

eine Hochzeit ausrichten to make all arrangements for a wedding

von außerhalb from out of town

FRAGEN

1. Was ist eine Waise? 2. Warum soll (*is to*) Hans die Einladungen adressieren? 3. Wer alles wird zur Hochzeit kommen? 4. Wessen Namen liest der Pfarrer von der Kanzel? 5. Was schenkt man einem Brautpaar zur Hochzeit? 6. Hat man in Amerika einen Polterabend? 7. Wann ist der Polterabend? 8. Was kracht draußen gegen das Haus?

ÜBUNGEN

(*a*) Supply the proper case of wer, was, or welch: 1. In — Kirche ist die Hochzeit? 2. — schenkt man silberne Löffel? 3. Für — sind die Geschenke? 4. — (out of what) trinkt man Kaffee? 5. — Hochzeit ist es?

(*b*) Translate: Whose cousin? With whom? Through

whom? With what? On what? What knife? On what plate?

ÜBERSETZUNG

1. That is all *alles* they bought. 2. My sister and hers are coming to the wedding. 3. He who marries must buy furniture (arr. *furniture buy*). 4. Nothing *nicht war* that the relatives gave us was unnecessary. 5. On what *which* evening will the children of the neighbors make (a) din? 6. Herring salad is the best salad *which* the Germans make. 7. For what *which* people had they made the salad? 8. They break their dishes and mine.

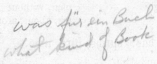

was für ein Buch
what kind of Book

LESSON TWENTY-FOUR

PREPOSITIONS. GERN

137 **Prepositions with the Dative.** The more common prepositions governing the dative are:

aus, out of
außer, besides, beyond; except
bei, at, with, at the house of, near
mit, with

nach, after; to; according to
seit, since
von, of, from
zu, to; at, in

Common contractions: beim = bei dem; vom = von dem; zum = zu dem; zur = zu der.

Nach, when meaning *according to, to judge by,* may stand after its noun: meiner Meinung nach, *according to my opinion;* seinem Alter nach, *judging by his age.* — For *to* after verbs of going use nach before places, zu before persons, an before objects.

Bei is used as follows: Ich habe den Brief nicht bei (not mit) mir, *I do not have the letter with me.* Er wohnt bei uns, *He lives with us.* Ich war eben bei deinem Vetter, *I was just now at the house of your cousin.* Beim Bäcker.

Seit. Seit drei Tagen means *for the last three days.* Contrast this idiom with vor drei Tagen, *three days ago.*

138 **Prepositions with the Accusative.** The following prepositions always govern the accusative:

bis, until, up to, to	gegen, toward, against
durch, through	ohne, without
für, for	um, about, around

Contractions with das: durchs, fürs, ums.

NOTE. Bis is usually followed by another preposition: bis in den Tod, *until death;* von Anfang bis zu Ende, *from beginning to end.* It is used alone (*a*) before names of places: von Leipzig bis Berlin; (*b*) before numbers: die geraden Zahlen von 8 bis 20; (*c*) before expressions of time: bis jetzt; bis morgen.

139 **Prepositions with the Dative and Accusative.** There are nine prepositions which may take either the dative or accusative, the accusative when motion towards a place is expressed, the dative where this is not the case. *I am in a room* and *I am walking up and down in a room* are dative notions, but *I walk into a room* is an accusative idea. Use the dative when you can ask *In what place?* the accusative when you can ask *To what place?* These prepositions are:

an, at; to (toward objects)	neben, beside, alongside
auf, on, upon	über, over, above; about [1]
hinter, behind	unter, under, among
in, in, into	vor, before
zwischen, between	

[1] When meaning *about, concerning,* über always takes the accusative.

Contractions with dem: am, im; with das: ans, aufs, ins.

Dative	*Accusative*
Wir sind in der Schule.	Wir gehen in die Schule.
Das Kind sitzt auf dem Stuhl.	Er setzt das Kind auf den Stuhl.

140 **Gern, lieber, am liebsten.** The comparative degree of *I like* is *I like better* or *I prefer*, and the superlative is *I like best*.

The German equivalent of *I like* is the appropriate verb + gern. Thus *I like tea* = Ich trinke gern Tee, and *I like meat* = Ich esse gern Fleisch.

The German equivalent of *I prefer* is the appropriate verb + lieber. Thus *I prefer eggs* = Ich esse lieber Eier.

The German equivalent of *I like best* is the appropriate verb + am liebsten. Thus *I like vegetables best* = Ich esse am liebsten Gemüse.

Other examples are: Was man wünscht, glaubt man gern, *The wish is father to the thought.* — Ich tanze lieber nicht, *I prefer not to dance.* — Am liebsten bleibe ich zu Hause, *I like staying at home best.*

DIE HOCHZEIT (FORTSETZUNG)

Am Morgen der Hochzeit geht das Brautpaar mit zwei Trauzeugen aufs Standesamt (*registry office*) zur Ziviltrauung. Ohne die geht es in Deutschland nicht. Die kirchliche (*church*) Trauung soll (*is to*) gegen Abend sein.

Die Kirche ist mit Blumen und brennenden Wachskerzen ge- 5
schmückt. Schon seit einer Stunde stehen viele Leute, besonders
Kinder, zu beiden Seiten der Kirchtür. In der Kirche sitzen die
Freunde und Bekannten der beiden Familien. „Jetzt kommen
sie!" ruft jemand draußen. Aus den ersten Wagen steigen die
Hochzeitsgäste, Martha als Brautjungfer und Bernd Förster als 10

Brautführer, alle festlich gekleidet. Endlich kommt das Braut=
paar, allein in einem eleganten Mercedeswagen. „Ach, Paul, am
liebsten möchte ich umkehren (*turn back*); sieh mal die Menge,
durch die wir in die Kirche müssen!" — „Ich möchte auch lieber
15 umkehren," sagt Paul, „aber dazu ist es jetzt zu spät. Warum hast
du es nicht vor drei Tagen gesagt?"

Ein ‚Ah‘ der Bewunderung geht durch die wartende Menge, und
man hört Rufe wie: „Was für ein schönes Paar! Sieh mal den
langen Schleier und das herrliche weiße Atlaskleid! — Was für
20 einen Kranz trägt denn die Braut? — Das ist doch ein Myrten=
kranz (*myrtle wreath*). — Und was für ein niedlicher (‘ *cute* ’),
kleiner Junge trägt die Schleppe (*train*)!" Das ist Peter, der sehr
glücklich ist, denn er darf heute bei allem dabei sein.

Lotte und Paul schreiten langsam durch die Kirche bis an den Al=
25 tar. Vor diesem stehen zwei Stühle, worauf das Brautpaar
sitzen soll, während die Orgel (*organ*) spielt und die Gemeinde
einen Choral singt. Dann tritt der Pfarrer auf die Kanzel und
hält eine kurze Traurede (*marriage sermon*). Nach dieser traut
er das Paar und steckt ihre Verlobungsringe, die sie bis zu diesem
30 Tage an der linken Hand getragen haben, als Trauringe an die
rechte. Nun sind sie ein Ehepaar.

Nach der Trauung fährt die Gesellschaft nach einem Hotel, wo es
(*there*) ein köstliches Hochzeitsmahl gibt (*is*). Zwischen den
Gängen werden [1] halb ernste und halb lustige Tischreden gehalten.
35 Am Ende einer jeden trinkt man ein Glas Sekt (*German champagne*) auf das Wohl des jungen Ehepaars. „Peter, du bist ja so
blaß!" sagt plötzlich seine Mutter, die neben ihm sitzt, „du ißt zu
viel, ist dir übel?" Schnell führt sie das weinende Kind aus dem
Saal, aber schon nach einer Viertelstunde kommen beide wieder,
40 und alles ist gut.

Während man ißt, gibt es Tafelmusik, nach dem Essen Tanzmusik.
Die Braut muß mit allen Herren tanzen, der Bräutigam mit

---

[1] werden ... gehalten, *are made.*

allen Damen. Dann erst verschwindet das junge Ehepaar, die Gäste aber tanzen bis spät in die Nacht.

Vielleicht gibt es bald eine zweite Hochzeit in der Familie. Wer weiß? 45

VOKABELN

der Altar', –s, ⸚e altar
das Atlaskleid, –s, –er satin dress
die Bewun'derung admiration
der Brautführer, –s, — best man
die Brautjungfer, –n bridesmaid
der Choral', –s, ⸚e choral, hymn
das Ehepaar, –s, –e married couple
der Finger, –s, — finger
der Gang, –es, ⸚e course
die Gemein'de, –n congregation, community
das Hochzeitsmahl, –s wedding feast
der Kopf, –es, ⸚e head
der Kranz, –es, ⸚e wreath
der Saal, –s, Säle hall
der Schleier, –s, — veil
die Ta'felmusik' dinner music
die Tischrede, –n after-dinner speech
der Trauring, –s, –e wedding ring

der Trauzeuge, –n, –n marriage witness
der Verlo'bungsring, –s, –e engagement ring
die Zivil'trauung, –en civil marriage ceremony
kommen ... wie'der return
schreiten, i, ist geschritten to walk
tragen (ä), u, a to wear
trauen wk. unite in marriage
treten (i), a, ist getreten to step
allein' alone
blaß pale
dabei' sein to be present
festlich festive(ly)
jemand, –s some one
link left
recht right (opposite of left)
während conj. while
weiß white

REDEWENDUNG

Ist dir übel? Do you feel ill?

FRAGEN

1. Wozu geht das Brautpaar aufs Standesamt? 2. Wann ist die kirchliche Trauung? 3. Wo stehen schon viele Leute? 4. Worin fährt das Brautpaar? 5. Was hat die Braut auf dem Kopf? 6. Wer geht hinter der Braut? 7. Wohin schreitet das

Brautpaar? 8. Wo tragen die Deutſchen den Verlobungsring?
Den Trauring?

ÜBUNGEN

(*a*) Translate: On the wedding morning; in front of the
church; in front of it; besides my guests; without a veil;
around me; out of what? on what? to whom; for whom;
among the people. (*b*) Translate and give comparative
and superlative: I like to dance. (*c*) Supply the correct
endings: Die Menge ſteht vor d– Kirche. — Er fliegt über d–
Kanal nach Deutſchland. — Ich ſtecke den Ring an dein– Finger.
— Das Licht iſt über d– Tiſch. — Der Pfarrer ſteht auf d–
Kanzel.

ÜBERSETZUNG

1. Wax candles are burning on both sides of the altar.
2. Many people have come to the church wedding.
3. Peter likes to carry the train of his new aunt. 4. Both
wear their (= the) wedding ring on the third finger of their
(= the) right hand. 5. The guests get into the cars and
ride (fahren) to the hotel. 6. After the hymn the pastor
preaches a short wedding sermon. 7. All laugh at (über
w. accus.) Uncle Gottlieb's funny after-dinner speech.
8. He likes to sit between his father and mother.

RELATIONSHIP TO ENGLISH

Related Words. German and English are sister languages. Fifteen hundred years ago the Anglo-Saxons (i.e., the Angles and Saxons) lived on the continent, the Angles presumably in the modern Sleswick, where there is still a district called Angeln. Hence the resemblance between German and English. The Norman conquest (1066) introduced many French words into English, but in basic vocabulary and in structure (strong and weak verbs, for example), English has remained a Germanic language. After the Anglo-Saxon invasion of England, both English and German underwent many changes, German chiefly in its consonants, English in its vowels. To a limited extent a study of the resulting correspondences between consonants is helpful to the beginner.

1. English *th* is German b: that, das; thing, Ding; three, drei; bathe, baden; earth, Erde; death, Tod.

2. English *d* is German t: do, tun; door, Tür; dead, tot; deed, Tat; bread, Brot.

3. English *t* at the beginning of a word is German z: two, zwei; ten, zehn; to, zu; tongue, Zunge; twig, Zweig.

4. English *t* in the middle or at the end of a word is ff, ß, s: eat, essen; better, besser; bite, beißen; nut, Nuß; that, das; it, es.

5. English *p* in the middle or at the end of a word is German ff (f): open, offen; hope, hoffen; sleep, schlafen; deep, tief; up, auf.

6. A *v* in the middle of an English word regularly is Ger-

man b: give, geben; live, leben; seven, fieben; silver, Silber; over, über.

DERIVATION

Derivatives. 1. The ending =e is, in the main, a feminine ending. The relatively few masculines and neuters you will soon spot (Knabe, Neffe, Franzofe, Preuße, Gemüfe). If you know nothing to the contrary you may conclude that a word in =e is feminine and weak: Schule, Küche, Speife, Zigarre, Blume, Farbe, etc. Some of the more common adjectives form abstracts in =e: Größe, Höhe, Kälte, Kürze, Länge, Treue, Wärme, etc.

2. Many verbs form verbal nouns in =ung. One may almost conclude the existence of a verb from the noun: wohnen, Wohnung; öffnen, Öffnung; retten, Rettung; landen, Landung; erzählen, Erzählung; fortfetzen, Fortfetzung; bewundern, Bewunderung. Such nouns are all feminine and belong to the weak declension.

3. Nouns in =heit are formed from many adjectives: frei, Freiheit; gleich, Gleichheit; dumm, Dummheit; befcheiden, Befcheidenheit. The ending =keit is a variation, used chiefly after =ig and =lich: richtig, Richtigkeit; wichtig, Wichtigkeit; luftig, Luftigkeit; freundlich, Freundlichkeit. The words are all feminine and weak.

4. The agent is, as in English, expressed by =er: fifchen, der Fifcher; machen, der Uhrmacher; zeigen, der Zeiger; bewundern, der Bewunderer; führen, der Brautführer.

IMPORTANT

PART TWO

✳ *LESSON TWENTY-FIVE* ✓

STRONG VERBS. CLASSES 1-2.

141 **Classification.** As an aid to memory, strong verbs are grouped in seven classes. At the head of each class is found an English verb that shows the same, or similar, vowel changes.

142 **Class 1.** The vowel-gradation is ei — i — i or ei — ie — ie. All strong verbs with ei in the infinitive belong here with the single exception of heißen (Class 7).

bite, bit, bitten

ei, i, i

beißen, biß, hat gebissen, *to bite*
greifen, griff, hat gegriffen, *to seize, grasp*
leiden, | litt, hat gelitten, | *to suffer*

schneiden, | schnitt, hat geschnitten, | *to cut*
streiten, stritt, hat gestritten, *to fight, quarrel*

NOTE. The consonant in greifen, etc., is doubled because the i is short.

ei, ie, ie

bleiben, blieb, ist geblieben, *to remain*
leihen, lieh, hat geliehen, *to lend*
scheinen, schien, hat geschienen, *to shine; seem, appear*
schreiben, schrieb, hat geschrieben, *to write*
schweigen, schwieg, hat geschwiegen, *to be or keep silent*

119

Check lesson 34

143 Class 2. The vowel-gradation is ie — ō — ō or ie — ŏ — ŏ. All stems in =ß have ŏ — ŏ. All strong verbs with ie in the present belong here, with the single exception of liegen, *to lie* (Class 5).

freeze, froze, frozen

ie, ō, ō

bieten, bot, hat geboten, *to offer*
fliegen, flog, ist geflogen, *to fly*
fliehen, floh, ist geflohen, *to flee*
ziehen, transitive, | zog, hat gezogen, | *to draw, pull*

intransitive, | zog, ist gezogen, | *to proceed, move, go*

ie, ŏ, ŏ

fließen, floß, ist geflossen, *to flow*
gießen, goß, hat gegossen, *to pour*
schießen, schoß, hat geschossen, *to shoot*
schließen, schloß, hat geschlossen, *to close, shut, conclude*
riechen, roch, hat gerochen, *to smell*

Notice the change from h to g in ziehen.

KINKELS BEFREIUNG[1] I

Das Jahr 1848 gilt in der deutschen Geschichte als das Revolutionsjahr. Deutschland war damals nicht, wie jetzt, ein Reich, sondern es gab viele Staaten, unter vielen Fürsten, die ihre Länder regierten, wie sie wollten. Das Volk hatte keine Stimme in der
5 Regierung. Schon lange aber waren demokratische Ideen in den Köpfen der besten Deutschen reif geworden. Diese verlangten von ihren Fürsten eine Verfassung, durch die das Volk auch Rechte bekam. Die Fürsten, besonders der König von Preußen, Friedrich Wilhelm IV., schienen keine Lust zu haben, ihre Macht aufzugeben,
10 und so griff das Volk zu den Waffen. Es kam zu Straßenkämpfen in mehreren deutschen Städten, auch stritten Revolutionsheere in den Jahren 1848 und 1849 in einigen Staaten gegen die Truppen

---

[1] Aus „Lebenserinnerungen" von Carl Schurz. Nacherzählt (*Retold*).

der Fürsten. Die Revolution hatte nicht das gewünschte Ende für das deutsche Volk, und viel Blut ist damals umsonst geflossen.

In seiner Selbstbiographie, „Lebenserinnerungen", hat Carl 15
Schurz, der bekannteste Deutsch=Amerikaner des neunzehnten
Jahrhunderts, über diese Kämpfe geschrieben. Als junger Mann
von neunzehn Jahren war er selbst dabei. Nach dem unglücklichen
Ende des Kampfes in Baden war er nach der Schweiz geflohen.
Er hatte schon gehört, daß der bekannte Professor und Dichter 20
Gottfried Kinkel gefangen war. Kinkel war seit 1846 Professor
der Kunstgeschichte an der Universität Bonn. Er war Schurz'
Lehrer und Freund gewesen und hatte den jungen Mann für Kunst,
Freiheit und Demokratie begeistert. Als gemeiner Soldat hatte er
in Baden gekämpft und war, verwundet, den Preußen in die 25
Hände [1] gefallen.

VOKABELN

die Befrei'ung liberation
das Blut, –es blood
die Demokratie', democracy
der Dichter, –s, — poet
die Freiheit, –en liberty, freedom
der Fürst, –en, –en prince
die Idee', –n idea
das Jahrhun'dert, –s, –e century
der Kampf, –es, –̈e struggle, fighting
die Kunst, –̈e art
die Lust, –̈e desire
die Macht, –̈e power
der Preuße, –n, –n Prussian
(das) Preußen, –s Prussia
das Recht, –es, –e right
die Regie'rung, –en government
das Reich, –s, –e realm, Reich
die Revolution', –en revolution
das Revolutions'heer, –s, –e revolutionary army

die Selbst'biographie', –n autobiography
die Stimme, –n voice
die Truppe, –n troop
die Verfas'sung, –en constitution
das Volk, –es, –̈er people, nation
aufgeben to give up
begei'stern wk. to inspire, make enthusiastic
fangen (ä), i, a to capture
regie'ren wk. to rule
verlan'gen wk. to demand
bekannt' (well) known; acquainted
damals at that time
demokra'tisch democratic
gemein' common
umsonst' in vain
un'glücklich unhappy, disastrous; distressed

---

[1] den Preußen in die Hände, *into the hands of the Prussians.*

REDEWENDUNGEN

zu den Waffen greifen resort to arms   gelten als to be regarded as, pass as

FRAGEN

1. In welchem Jahrhundert hat Carl Schurz gelebt? 2. Wie regierten die deutschen Fürsten ihre Länder? 3. Welcher deutsche Fürst besonders hörte nicht auf das Volk? 4. Warum griff das Volk zu den Waffen? 5. Was für ein Ende hatte die Revolution von 1848? 6. In welchem Werk hat Carl Schurz über die Kämpfe von 1848–1849 geschrieben? 7. Wohin floh Schurz nach den Kämpfen in Baden? 8. Wo liegt Baden (in Süd=, Nord=, West=, Ostdeutschland)? 9. Wer war Gottfried Kinkel? 10. Wie kam er in die Hände der Preußen?

ÜBUNGEN

(a) Give the second person singular, present, of: beißen, leiden, schneiden, streiten, bieten, gießen, schließen. (b) Translate and give synopses of: 1. The people (not Leute) resort to arms. 2. You (du) are cutting the bread. 3. The troops move to Baden. 4. You (ihr) fight for your rights.

ÜBERSETZUNG

1. This is the autobiography Schurz wrote later in America. 2. The teacher had lent me Schurz' book. 3. The best Germans suffered very (much) under the rule of their princes. 4. Kinkel and Schurz did not keep silent, they made speeches. 5. The soldiers shot at (auf) the people and much blood flowed. 6. Did Schurz remain in Germany or did he flee (pres. perfect)? 7. Will they close the university of Bonn? 8. The history of the 19th century offers much (that is) interesting.

LESSON TWENTY-SIX

STRONG VERBS. CLASSES 3–5

144 Class 3. The vowel-gradation is i — ă — ŭ. All strong verbs with i in the present belong to this class, except bitten and fiţen, for which see § 146.

sing, sang, sung

finden, fand, hat gefunden, *to find*
fingen, fang, hat gefungen, *to sing*
fpringen, fprang, ift gefprungen, *to jump*, *spring*
trinfen, tranf, hat getrunfen, *to drink*

Verbs whose stem ends in =mm or =nn have o in the past participle: fchwimmen, *to swim*, fchwamm, ift gefchwommen.

145 Class 4. The vowel-gradation is ĕ — ă — ŏ. Nearly all verbs of this class have an I, m, or r after the stem vowel and may thus be distinguished from Class 5, where this is never the case. Three verbs, brechen, fprechen, and treffen, have an r *before* the stem vowel.

Verbs of this class, as of Class 5, have i or ie in the 2d and 3d persons singular of the present indicative, and the singular of the imperative.

speak, spoke (biblical ' spake '), spoken

helfen (hilft), half, hat geholfen, *to help*
fterben (ftirbt), ftarb, ift geftorben, *to die*
werfen (wirft), warf, hat geworfen, *to throw*
nehmen (nimmt), nahm, hat genommen, *to take*
ftehlen (ftiehlt), ftahl, hat geftohlen, *to steal*
brechen (bricht), bräch, hat gebröchen, *to break*
fprechen (fpricht), fpräch, hat gefpröchen, *to speak*
treffen (trifft), träf, hat getroffen, *to hit;* meet, find (at home)

fommen, fäm, ift gefommen, is irregular in the vowel of its present. This verb also takes the past participle of a

verb of motion where English uses the present participle:
Ein Vogel kam geflogen, *A bird came flying.*

NOTE. The change from ff to f in trāf, the past of treffen, is due to the length of the a. A long vowel cannot be followed by a double consonant. So also kām.

146 **Class 5.** The vowel-gradation is ĕ — ā — ĕ.

eat, ate, eaten

geben (gibt), gab, hat gegeben, *to give*
lesen (liest), las, hat gelesen, *to read*
sehen (sieht), sah, hat gesehen, *to see*
treten (tritt), trat, ist getreten, *to tread, step, enter*
essen (du ißt, er ißt), aß, hat gegessen, *to eat*
fressen (frißt), fraß, hat gefressen, *to eat* (of animals)

Three verbs have i or ie in the present. They are:

bitten, bat, hat gebeten, *to ask, beg*
sitzen, saß, hat gesessen, *to sit*
liegen, lag, hat gelegen, *to lie*

bitten differs from fragen in meaning and construction:

Ich frage nach etwas, *I ask about something.*
Ich bitte um etwas, *I ask for something, request something.*
Compare bitte, *please*, which stands, of course, for ich bitte.

KINKELS BEFREIUNG II

Kinkel bekam die Todesstrafe, die aber zu lebenslänglicher Festungs=
strafe[1] gemildert wurde. Seinen Freunden und Bewunderern,
sowie einem großen Teil des Volkes schien diese Strafe grausam
genug. Immerhin, auf einer Festung behielt ein Mann seinen
5 Namen, seine bürgerliche Kleidung, seine Bücher, seine Würde.

[1] *Confinement in a fortress*, a form of punishment often imposed, in older Germany, upon political prisoners, who had done nothing dishonorable.

Dann aber kam das Schreckliche: Kinkel sollte die Strafe nicht auf einer Festung, sondern im Zuchthaus verbüßen (*serve*). Er, der Gelehrte und Dichter, sollte unter gemeinen Verbrechern, in Sträflingsjacke mit geschorenem Kopf, Zwangsarbeit tun. Weit von seinen Lieben, im Zuchthaus zu Spandau bei Berlin, saß er 10 nun und starb eines langsamen Todes. Half niemand in dieser Not?

Carl Schurz nahm es auf sich, den Freund zu retten. Er kam wieder nach Deutschland, besuchte seine Eltern und Frau Kinkel in Bonn und sprach mit ihr über seinen Plan. Kinkels 15 Freunde hatten schon eine große Summe Geld zu dem Werk seiner Befreiung gesammelt. Schurz bat seinen Vetter, Heribert Jüssen, dem er sehr ähnlich sah, um seinen Paß, und der Vetter lieh ihm diesen. Unter seinem eignen Namen konnte Schurz nicht reisen, denn die preußische Regierung suchte ihn ja als einen 20 der Aufrührer.

Am 11. August 1850 kam er in Berlin an. Auf dem Bahnhof nahm ein Polizeibeamter den Paß, las ihn, sah dem Mann ins Gesicht und ließ ihn in die Stadt ein. Schurz hatte in Berlin einige Universitätsfreunde, bei denen er ein herzliches Willkommen 25 fand. Er trat mit mehreren Leuten in Verbindung, denen Frau Kinkel und andre Demokraten trauten, und studierte diese lange. Schließlich zog er einen von ihnen ins Vertrauen, einen Arzt, Dr. Falkenthal, dem er sein Geheimnis mitteilte.

VOKABELN

der **Aufrührer**, –s, — insurgent, agitator

der **Demokrat'**, –en, –en democrat

die **Festung**, –en fortress

der **Gelehr'te** *adj. infl.* man of learning

die **Kleidung** clothing, dress

die **Not**, ⸚e distress, need

der **Paß**, –es, ⸚e passport

der **Polizei'beam'te** *adj. infl.* policeman

die **Strafe**, –n punishment, fine, sentence

die **Sträflingsjacke**, –n convict's jacket

der **Teil**, –s, –e part

der **Tod**, –es death

der **Verbre'cher**, –s, — criminal

das Willkom'men, –s welcome
die Würde, –n dignity
das Zuchthaus, –es, ⸚er penitentiary
die Zwangsarbeit, –en penal labor
behal'ten (ä), ie, a to keep
kam . . . an' arrived
ließ . . . ein' admitted
mildern *wk.* to make milder, commute
mitteilen *wk.* to communicate

sammeln *wk.* to collect
studie'ren *wk.* to study
trauen *wk., w. dat.* to trust
bürgerlich civilian
gescho'ren shorn
grausam cruel
immerhin' (but) after all
lebenslänglich for life
preußisch Prussian
schließlich finally
sowie' as well as

REDEWENDUNGEN

einem ähnlich sehen to resemble one
trat in Verbindung got in touch

ins Vertrauen ziehen to take into one's confidence

FRAGEN

1. Welche Strafe schien Kinkels vielen Freunden grausam genug? 2. Wie machte der König die Strafe noch grausamer? 3. In welches Zuchthaus warf man den Dichter? 4. Wer nimmt es auf sich, Kinkel zu retten? 5. Wie hatten Kinkels Freunde schon geholfen? 6. Mit wessen Paß reiste Schurz? 7. Mit was für Leuten ist er in Berlin in Verbindung getreten? 8. Darf (*dare*) er viele Leute ins Vertrauen ziehen?

ÜBUNGEN

(*a*) Give the imperatives of nehmen, treten, essen, brechen, lesen. (*b*) Give the second person singular, present, of sterben, nehmen, lesen, essen, fressen, sitzen. (*c*) Translate and give synopses of: 1. Does he break his word? 2. I get in touch with them. 3. What are you (du) reading? 4. We ask for freedom.

ÜBERSETZUNG

1. Some of the criminals have committed-theft (= have stolen). 2. Had the terrible (thing) come? 3. Schurz met a policeman at the station. 4. He resembled his cousin. 5. Did nobody help him? 6. He trusts the physician and speaks with him about Kinkel's liberation. 7. He will die a slow and cruel death. 8. The government did not find all the insurgents.

LESSON TWENTY-SEVEN

STRONG VERBS. CLASSES 6-7

147 Class 6. The gradation is ă — ū — ă. The second and third persons singular of the present have ä.

slay, slew, slain

fahren (fährt), fuhr, ist gefahren, *to drive, ride; go*
graben (gräbt), grub, hat gegraben, *to dig*
schlagen (schlägt), schlug, hat geschlagen, *to strike, beat*
tragen (trägt), trug, hat getragen, *to carry, bear, wear*
wachsen (wächst), wuchs, ist gewachsen, *to grow*
waschen (wäscht), wusch, hat gewaschen, *to wash*

NOTE. The chs of wachsen is pronounced as *x* in *wax*.

148 Class 7. The past has ie or i. The vowel of the present varies, *but it is always the same as that of the past participle.* All verbs with a umlaut to ä in the second and third persons singular. Laufen and stoßen umlaut to äu and ö: rufen does not modify.

fall, fell, fallen

fallen (fällt), fiel, ist gefallen, *to fall*

fangen (fängt), fing, hat gefangen, *to catch*

halten (hält), hielt, hat gehalten, *to hold; stop*

hängen, hing, hat gehangen, *to hang*

lassen (läßt), ließ, hat gelassen, *to let, leave*

raten (rät), riet, hat geraten, *to advise* (with dative of person); *guess*

schlafen (schläft), schlief, hat geschlafen, *to sleep*

laufen (läuft), lief, ist gelaufen, *to run*

heißen (du heißt or heißest, er heißt), hieß, hat geheißen, *to be called; bid, command*

stoßen (stößt), stieß, hat gestoßen, *to thrust, knock*, (an with accus., or gegen, *against*)

rufen, rief, hat gerufen, *to call*

A verb with a in the infinitive may belong to either Class 6 or 7. The verbs of both these classes are common and important.

KINKELS BEFREIUNG III

Durch Dr. Falkenthal wurde Schurz mit dem Gastwirt Krüger in Spandau bekannt, einem ehrlichen und klugen Mann, der in der Gemeinde hoch geachtet war. Krüger bot Schurz sein Haus als Wohnung und Hauptquartier an, doch dieser hielt es für besser,
5 nicht in Spandau zu wohnen, denn in einer kleinen Stadt raten die Leute bald, was ein Fremder macht. In dem großen Berlin konnte er unbekannt bleiben.

Nun fuhr er oft nach Spandau, aber nicht mit der Eisenbahn, denn auf dem Berliner Bahnhof mußte (*had to*) jeder Reisende seinen
10 Paß zeigen. Der Paß war zwar in bester Ordnung, aber einem wachsamen Polizeibeamten mußte ein zu häufiges Erscheinen desselben Passes bald verdächtig werden. Darum ging Schurz immer zu Fuß durch das Brandenburger Tor aus der Stadt und nahm dann einen Wagen nach Spandau, jedesmal einen anderen.

15 Krüger riet Schurz, eine Befreiung Kinkels mit Gewalt nicht zu versuchen. Sie zogen noch zwei junge Männer ins Vertrauen,

Poritz und Leddihn', die einige Freunde unter den Zuchthaus=
beamten hatten. Die beiden sollten Schurz einen derselben (*of
these*) bringen, den man vielleicht bestechen konnte. Dieser Teil
des Geschäfts war der schlimmste für Schurz, aber er sagte sich, 20
Bestechung ist kein Verbrechen mehr, wenn man einen Freiheits=
kämpfer aus den Banden der Tyrannen retten muß.

So kamen Poritz und Leddihn eines Tages mit einem Gefangen=
wärter und ließen ihn mit Schurz allein, der sich als einen Freund
der Familie Kinkel vorstellte. 25

VOKABELN

das Band, –es, –e bond, fetter
die Beste'chung, –en bribery
der Freiheitskämpfer, –s, — fighter
for liberty, liberator
der Gastwirt, –s, –e inn-keeper
der Gefangenwärter, –s, — (prison)
keeper
die Gewalt', –en force, violence
das Haupt'quartier', –s, –e headquarters
die Ordnung, –en order
der Reisende *adj. infl.* traveler
das Tor, –es, –e gate, gateway
der Tyrann', –en, –en tyrant
das Verbre'chen, –s, — crime

der Zucht'hausbeam'te *adj. infl.*
penitentiary official
achten *wk.* to regard, esteem
beste'chen (i), a, o to bribe
bot ... an' offered
versu'chen *wk.* to attempt
vorstellen *wk.* to introduce
doch *co-ord. conj.* but
ehrlich honest
häufig frequent
unbekannt unknown
verdäch'tig suspicious
wachsam watchful
wenn if, whenever
zwar to be sure

REDEWENDUNGEN

zu Fuß gehen to walk   halten für to consider

FRAGEN

1. Wer war Krüger? 2. Warum wohnte Schurz nicht in
Spandau? 3. Gab es damals schon eine Eisenbahn zwischen
Berlin und Spandau? 4. Wie kam Schurz immer nach Span=

dau? **5.** Wie heißt das berühmteste Berliner Tor? **6.** Warum zogen Schurz und Krüger noch zwei Männer ins Vertrauen? **7.** Welcher Teil des Geschäfts war der schlimmste für Schurz? **8.** Wen mußte er bestechen?

ÜBUNGEN

(*a*) Give the second person singular, present and past, of wachsen, waschen, halten, lassen, raten, heißen. (*b*) Translate and give synopses of: **1.** The sum is growing. **2.** Are you sleeping, Carl? **3.** What (wie) are they called? **4.** We beat the insurgents.

ÜBERSETZUNG

1. Doctor,[1] please advise me. **2.** The policeman has caught the criminal. **3.** This fighter-for-liberty bore the cruel punishment with dignity. **4.** Will he ride to Spandau on the train? **5.** At the station he held his passport in his hand.[2] **6.** Let (lassen Sie) me guess who the stranger is. **7.** The two called a keeper. **8.** The liberation of his friend was Schurz' business.

REVIEW LESSON

I. Supply the lacking endings: **1.** Gnädig⸺ Frau, möchten Sie ein frisch⸺ Brot und einig⸺ braun⸺ Kuchen? **2.** Vorig⸺ Jahr am Heilig⸺ Abend stand die ganz⸺ Familie um den herrlich⸺ Weihnachtsbaum und sang die schön⸺, alt⸺ Lieder. **3.** Nur die Alt⸺ und Krank⸺ blieben an dies⸺ kalt⸺ Abend in ihr⸺ warm⸺ Häusern. **4.** Er war ein klug⸺ klein⸺ Junge mit blond⸺ Haar und blau⸺ Augen.

[1] See §57, Note. [2] See §25.

II. (*a*) Translate and give the comparison of: 1. clear, strong, high. 2. They live happily. 3. my good neighbor. 4. I like roast goose.

(*b*) Decline in the singular and plural: kein schönes Geschenk; unser liebster Freund.

III. Read in German: Am 20. April; des 3. Buches; mit Wilhelm II.; ¼10; ⅝; 7¹⁄₁₀₀.

IV. (*a*) Supply the relative pronouns: 1. Das Haus, in — Sie wohnten, war groß genug. 2. Wir sitzen an dem Tisch, — der Kellner freigehalten hat. 3. Er war der Mann, — Geld der Arzt bekommen hatte. 4. Dies ist der Schulkamerad, mit — Hans aufs Land wanderte.

(*b*) Supply the interrogative pronouns: 1. — findet der Millionär in Paris? 2. Von — ist der Brief? 3. — Hochzeit feiern sie? 4. — können wir helfen? 5. (*Out of what*) sind die Eßzimmermöbel gemacht?

V. (*a*) Translate: Besides her; for them; around me; against us; I was behind them; into them; in you (all three words for *you*); in it; to her; through me; under it.

(*b*) Render the possessive pronouns in at least two ways: My fiancée and his; her hands and mine; whose home? ours.

VI. (*a*) Translate and give the synopses of: 1. He flies across the Channel. 2. Glass balls hang on the tree. 3. I do not swim across the lake. 4. You (ihr) sing too loudly. 5. We sit in the garden. 6. He makes a speech. 7. She cuts the bread.

(*b*) Supply the lacking pronoun subjects and translate: 1. — liest falsch. 2. — fiel ins Wasser. 3. — war gesprungen. 4. Nimmst — Gemüse? 5. — tritt in die Stube. 6. Hattet — Wasser in die Gläser gegossen? 7. — trug ein Ballkleid. 8. — liefst zu schnell. 9. — bleibt hier. 10. — bliebt hier.

LESSON TWENTY-EIGHT

CONJUNCTIONS. COMPOUND AND
COMPLEX SENTENCES

149 Principal and Subordinate Clauses. A principal clause or sentence is an independent statement, question, or command. A subordinate clause is dependent upon a principal clause, as in " After we had eaten dinner we went for a walk," where " After we had eaten dinner " merely gives the time of the walk, just as the phrase " after dinner " would do.

Subordinate clauses are most commonly introduced by relative pronouns or by subordinating conjunctions.

150 Co-ordinating Conjunctions. Co-ordinating conjunctions join clauses or phrases of equal rank. They do not affect the word order. They are:

unb, and	aber, but
ober, or	ſonbern, but
benn, for	allein', but

1. Allein is the English *only* in the sense of *but: That is all very well, only* . . . , Das iſt alles ſehr ſchön, allein . . .

2. As to aber and ſonbern, both meaning *but:*

(*a*) After a positive statement only aber can be used.

(*b*) After a negative, ſonbern introduces a statement that steps [1] into the place of the preceding negative one: Heute iſt nicht Donnerstag, ſonbern Freitag. — Ich kaufe meine Kleider nicht fertig, ſonbern ich mache ſie ſelbſt. *But on the contrary* or *but . . . instead* can here be substituted for *but.*

[1] The phrasing is, in part, that of Professor J. A. Hess.

(*c*) After a negative, aber merely supplements the preceding negative clause: Vater kann nicht fort (*get away*), aber Karl wird bald hier sein. *However* can be substituted for such a *but*.

151 **Subordinating Conjunctions.** Subordinating conjunctions express a dependence. The more common ones are:

als, when	ob, whether
bevor, ehe, before	obgleich', obwohl', although
bis, until	seit, seitdem', since (of time)
da, as, since; when	sobald', as soon as
damit', in order that	während, indem, while
(with indic. or subjunctive)	weil, because
daß, that	wenn, if, when, whenever
nachdem', after	wie, as (not causal)

152 wann, als, wenn, *when*, are distinguished as follows:

wann is used in questions, direct or indirect (§196, 3).
als refers to a single action in the past. This includes the use of the present for the past in vivid narration.
wenn is used everywhere else: with a present or future tense, and, with any tense, in the sense of *whenever, if*.

Wann ist Goethe gestorben?
Als Goethe starb, war er 82 Jahre alt.
Wenn ein großer Dichter stirbt, trauert die ganze Welt, *When a great poet dies, the entire world mourns.*
Als ich die Tür öffne, steht mein Freund da.

153 weil, denn.

1. Weil is *because*, not *while*.

2. Weil, *because*, is a subordinating conjunction, denn, *for*, a co-ordinating conjunction. Weil = *for the reason that*, denn = *and the reason is this.* " Why weren't you in school yesterday? " „Weil ich . . . "

prefix "be" usually makes verb transitive

154 vor, bevor (ehe). nach, nachdem. Vor and nach are prepositions. Bevor (ehe) and nachdem are conjunctions and introduce subordinate clauses. English makes no such distinction in the use of *before* and *after*.

Vor seinem Tode but Bevor er starb.
Nach dem Essen but Nachdem wir gegessen hatten.

But seit, *since*, is both preposition and conjunction.

155 The Complex Sentence. In a complex sentence, the subordinate clause may precede or follow the principal clause. Compare:

1. Wir blieben zu Hause, weil das Wetter schlecht war.
2. Weil das Wetter schlecht war, blieben wir zu Hause.
3. Wegen des schlechten Wetters blieben wir zu Hause.

There is inversion in (2) for the same reason that there is in (3): an adverbial phrase or clause precedes the main verb.

Other examples are:

(a) Ich schreibe Ihnen, sobald ich Zeit habe.
    Sobald ich Zeit habe, schreibe ich Ihnen.
(b) Er antwortete nicht, obgleich ich ihn zweimal fragte.
    Obgleich ich ihn zweimal fragte, antwortete er nicht.

NOTE. In a conditional sentence, i.e., a sentence with wenn, *if*, a so, literally *then*, regularly introduces the conclusion when the condition stands first. This so is also not uncommon in clauses with weil and da.

Wenn er Zeit hat, so kommt er gewiß.
Da das Wetter schlecht ist, so bleiben wir zu Hause.

KINKELS BEFREIUNG IV

Schurz beschrieb ihm den Jammer der Frau und der Kinder Kinkels und die Angst der Familie und aller Freunde, daß ein so edler Mann im Gefängnis körperlich und geistig zu Grunde gehen würde. „Kann man vielleicht dem armen Gefangenen von Zeit zu
5 Zeit heimlich etwas kräftige Nahrung, ein Stück Fleisch, einen

Schluck Wein bringen, damit er am Leben bleibt, bis der König ihn begnadigt?" fragte Schurz. „Das ist gefährlich, aber nicht unmöglich," antwortete der Mann. Da steckte Schurz ihm eine Zehntalernote in die Hand. „Tun Sie, was Sie können! Ich muß jetzt Spandau verlassen, da ich in Geschäften reise, werde 10 aber in einigen Tagen wiederkommen und von Ihnen hören, wie es dem Gefangenen geht. Nehmen Sie den herzlichsten Dank der Familie und aller Freunde!"

Nach drei Tagen fuhr Schurz wieder nach Spandau, traf den Wärter und hörte, daß dieser wirklich Kinkel ein kleines Brot und 15 eine Wurst zugesteckt hatte. „Wenn Sie ihm wieder etwas schicken wollen, bin ich gern bereit, es ihm zu geben," setzte er hinzu. Schurz gab dem Mann eine zweite Zehntalernote, diesmal auch ein Stückchen Papier für Kinkel mit den Worten [1]: „Deine Freunde sind Dir [2] treu. Halte Dich aufrecht!" 20

Als der Wärter nach einigen Tagen Schurz diesen Zettel mit einer Antwort in Kinkels Handschrift gab, glaubte Schurz, daß der Mann auch bei der Befreiung helfen würde. Sobald er aber mit ihm davon sprach, wurde es ihm klar, daß dieser erste Versuch mißglückt war. Der Mann wollte da'mit nichts zu tun haben. „Nun," 25 meinte Schurz, „da ein so mutiger Mann wie Sie die Sache nicht für möglich hält, muß ich sie aufgeben." Die Frage war nun: Wird der Mann schweigen?

Nachdem Schurz mehrere Tage stillgelegen hatte, führten Poritz und Leddihn einen zweiten Wärter zu ihm. Alles ging nach 30 Wunsch, bis Schurz fragte, ob er die Hand zur Befreiung bieten würde. Nein, das konnte und wollte er nicht. Ebenso ging es mit einem dritten und vierten Wärter.

---

[1] When meaning *connected words*, Wort has the plural Worte.
[2] In letters du and ihr are capitalized. See the letter on p. 165.

VOKABELN

die Angst, ⸚e fear, terror
der Dank, –s thanks
der Gefan'gene adj. infl. prisoner
das Gefäng'nis, –ses, –se prison
der Jammer, –s misery
die Nahrung food, nourishment
das Papier', –s paper
der Schluck, –s, –e swallow, drop
der Versuch', –s, –e attempt
der Wärter, –s, — keeper
der Wunsch, –es, ⸚e wish, desire
die Wurst, ⸚e sausage
die Zehntalernote, –n ten taler
  (taler = 3 marks) bill
der Zettel, –s, — note, piece of
  paper
begna'digen wk. to pardon
beschrei'ben, ie, ie to describe
Sie können you can
mißglü'cken wk., aux. sein to fail

schicken wk. to send
setzte er hinzu' he added
stecken wk. to put, slip
stilliegen, a, e to 'lie low,' be in-
  active
verlas'sen (ä), ie, a to leave
zugesteckt p.p. slipped
bereit' ready (for something that
  lies ahead)
ebenso just so
edel noble
gefähr'lich dangerous
geistig spiritual(ly), mental(ly)
heimlich secret(ly)
körperlich physical(ly)
kräftig nutritious
möglich possible
mutig brave, courageous
un'möglich impossible
wirklich really, actually

REDEWENDUNGEN

nach Wunsch as desired
zu Grunde gehen to go to ruin, perish

halte dich aufrecht keep up your courage
am Leben bleiben to remain alive

FRAGEN

1. Was beschrieb Schurz dem Gefangenwärter? 2. Was würde Kinkels Leben im Gefängnis etwas leichter machen? 3. War der Mann bereit, Kinkel heimlich etwas zu bringen? 4. Warum, sagt Schurz, muß er Spandau verlassen? 5. Was sollte der Wärter Kinkel das zweitemal geben? 6. Glückte dieser Versuch zur Befreiung des Freundes? 7. Wollte Schurz die Befreiung wirklich aufgeben? 8. Mit wie vielen Wärtern machte Schurz Versuche?

ÜBUNGEN

(*a*) Supply wann, wenn, or als: 1. — wird der König Kinkel begnadigen? 2. Er wird dem Wärter Geld geben, — er ihn sieht. 3. Kinkel war glücklich, — er den Zettel las. (*b*) Supply vor or bevor (ehe): — 1848 gab es nur wenige Eisenbahnen. (*c*) Supply nach or nachdem: Der Mann kaufte Wurst, — er das Geld bekommen hatte. (*d*) Supply aber (allein) or sondern: 1. Schurz reiste nicht nach Hause, — blieb in Berlin. 2. Der Wärter will nichts zur Befreiung Kinkels tun, — er ist bereit, ihm Nahrung zu bringen. (*e*) Supply weil or denn: Kinkel ist glücklich, — seine Freunde sind ihm treu.

ÜBERSETZUNG

1. While Kinkel is in prison, his family is very unhappy. 2. His friends were afraid (Angst haben) that he would go to ruin physically and mentally. 3. Will he stay alive until the king pardons him? 4. Schurz met the keeper when he again came to Spandau. 5. He did not believe the man before the latter had given Kinkel the note. 6. Kinkel was no criminal but a learned and noble man. 7. The keepers were ready whenever he asked them. 8. He roomed (wohnen) in Berlin because it was a large city.

LESSON TWENTY-NINE

IRREGULAR VERBS

156 **Irregular Weak Verbs.** Six weak verbs change their present vowel e to a in the past and past participle.

Inf.	Past Ind.	Past Part.
brennen	brannte	gebrannt, to burn
kennen	kannte	gekannt, to know
nennen	nannte	genannt, to name
rennen	rannte	ift gerannt, to run
senden	sandte	gesandt, to send
wenden	wandte	gewandt, to turn

also regular

NOTE. Spoken German uses ſchicken, *wk.*, in the place of ſenden. With ſchicken do not confuse ſchenken, *to present, give.* Associate the latter with das Geſchenk', *the present, gift.* — Nennen has two direct objects: Er nannte ihn ſeinen Herrn.

157 **Bringen, denken,** as in English, change both vowel and consonant.

Inf.	Past Ind.	Past Part.
bringen	brachte	gebracht, to bring
denken	dachte	gedacht, to think

158 **Gehen, ſtehen, tun** are irregular, as in English:

gehen (geht), ging, iſt gegangen, *to go.*
ſtehen (ſteht), ſtand, hat geſtanden, *to stand.*
tun (tut), tat, hat getan, *to do.* Present: ich tue, du tuſt, er tut, wir tun, ihr tut, ſie tun.

Do not mistake ſtand *for a present;* ſtand = *stood.*

159 **Wiſſen.** The principal parts of wiſſen, *to know,* are wiſſen, wußte, hat gewußt. The singular of the present indicative is irregular:

Können konte hat gekannt
kann
Kennen kannt " gekannt
Wissen
weiss wusste hat gewusst

<table>
<tr><td>ich weiß</td><td>wir wiſſen</td></tr>
<tr><td>du weißt</td><td>ihr wißt</td></tr>
<tr><td>er weiß</td><td>ſie wiſſen</td></tr>
</table>

The remaining inflection is regular: past indic., ich wußte, du wußteſt; imperative, wiſſe.

160 **Wiſſen, kennen.** Wiſſen = to know as a fact, have knowledge of; kennen = to have acquaintance with:

> Kennen Sie ihn? *Do you know him?*
> Wiſſen Sie, wo er iſt? *Do you know where he is?*

KINKELS BEFREIUNG V   Auf Deutſch

Inzwiſchen mußte Schurz wirklich Berlin verlaſſen, weil die Zahl derer, die ihn kannten, zu ſehr gewachſen war und jeder wiſſen wollte, warum er in der Hauptſtadt war. Er verſchwand alſo bis Ende September und wohnte nach ſeiner Rückkehr nicht in Berlin, ſondern bei Dr. Falkenthal in Moabit', das damals noch nicht zu 5 Berlin gehörte, ſondern eine Vorſtadt war. Dort hielt man ihn für einen jungen Mediziner, der dem Arzt bei ſeinen Studien half.

Die vier Gefangenwärter hatten über die Sache geſchwiegen, denn ſie wußten, wie gefährlich es für Unterbeamte des Zuchthauſes war, das zu tun, was ſie getan hatten. Da nun nicht viele Unterbeamte 10 übrig waren, bezweifelte Schurz ſchon den Erfolg ſeines Unterneh= mens. Da fand er plötzlich, was er ſo lange vergeblich geſucht hatte: ſeine Freunde brachten ihm den Gefangenwärter Brune.

Wie ſeine Kollegen war Brune Unteroffizier geweſen, hatte Frau und Kinder und ein ſehr kleines Gehalt. Aber in ſeinem Weſen war 15 nichts von der Subaltern'natur'. Als Schurz von Kinkel ſprach und dem Wunſche, ihm kräftige Nahrung zu ſchicken, machte Brune nicht das kläglich verlegene Geſicht eines Menſchen, der zwiſchen ſeiner Pflicht und einer Zehntalernote ſchwankt. „Gewiß will ich dem Manne helfen," ſagte er, „es iſt eine Schande, daß ein 20 ſo gelehrter und edler Herr unter gemeinen Verbrechern ſitzt. Ich muß für Frau und Kinder ſorgen, ſonſt würde ich ſelbſt ihm heraushelfen."

VOKABELN

der Erfolg', –s, –e success
das Gehalt', –s, ⸚er salary
die Hauptstadt, ⸚e capital (city)
der Kolle'ge, –n, –n colleague
der Medizi'ner, –s, — medical student
die Pflicht, –en duty
die Rückkehr return
die Schande shame, disgrace
die Subaltern'natur', –en a person with a sense of inferiority
der Un'terbeam'te adj. infl. subordinate official
das Unterneh'men, –s undertaking
die Vorstadt, ⸚e suburb

die Zahl, –en number
bezwei'feln wk. to doubt
denken an w. accus. to think of
gehö'ren wk.; — zu to belong to (be part of)
heraus'helfen (i), a, o to help out of a place
schwanken wk. to waver
sorgen wk. to care for
gewiß' sure(ly), certain(ly)
kläglich pitifully
übrig sein to be left
vergeb'lich in vain
verle'gen embarrassed

FRAGEN

1. Warum mußte Schurz wirklich Berlin verlassen? 2. Warum wohnte er später in Moabit? 3. Wem hatten die Gefangenwärter von der Sache gesagt? 4. Was für Beamte waren die vier? 5. Was für ein Beamter war Brune? 6. War Brunes Wesen wie das der andern? 7. Was waren diese Wärter früher gewesen? 8. Konnte ein Gefangenwärter von seinem Gehalt reich werden?

ÜBUNGEN

(a) Translate: We knew him; did he think of me? run, children! do it, Carl! we had brought it; she does not do it; the wax candles were burning. (b) Translate and give synopses of: 1. He walks to Spandau. 2. You (ihr) call (nennen) him a noble man. 3. I bring you a little piece of paper. 4. Do you (du) stand alone? 5. I think of him.

ÜBERSETZUNG

1. Too many people knew him after he had been in Berlin a few weeks. 2. But they did not know what he was doing. 3. The two men will surely bring him somebody before it is too late. 4. Do you think Brune is the right man? That I do not know. 5. The lower-officials were afraid for (um) their positions. 6. The salaries they brought home were not large enough. 7. It is a disgrace that a learned man is doing penal labor. 8. Everything had gone well until that question came.

LESSON THIRTY

INFINITIVE. PREPOSITIONS WITH THE GENITIVE

161 **Use of the Infinitive.** 1. Besides the infinitive such as *to read*, English also has a verbal in *–ing* (different from the present participle), and this will frequently render the German infinitive: das Lesen und das Schreiben, *reading and writing*. Such an infinitive noun is neuter and is capitalized.

2. The infinitive with zu is used as in English: Er bat mich zu kommen. If this infinitive has a modifier, the modifier precedes the infinitive, and the whole is set off by a comma. This holds also for rubrics 3 and 4 below. Sie baten mich, sehr früh zu kommen. — Er war bereit, seinen Freund zu retten.

3. The infinitive with um зu (at times with зu alone) denotes purpose, *in order to:* Wir arbeiten, um зu leben.

4. The infinitive with зu may depend on the prepositions ohne, *without*, and statt or anstatt, *instead of:* ohne зu grüßen, *without greeting;* statt (anstatt) зu warten, *instead of waiting.*

5. Lernen and lehren take an infinitive without зu: Ich lerne radfahren, *I am learning to ride a bicycle.* Er lehrt mich schwimmen, *He teaches me to swim.*

6. In the predicate after sein, *to be*, the infinitive with зu has a passive meaning: Was ist зu sehen? *What is to be seen?* Er ist nicht зu retten, *He is not to be (= cannot be) saved.* Es ist зu hoffen, daß..., *It is to be hoped that ...*

162 **Prepositions with the Genitive.** A number of prepositions govern the genitive in German. Notice how the *of* in the English equivalents in itself indicates a genitive relation. The more common are:

außerhalb, outside of	statt, instead of
innerhalb, inside of, within	trotz, in spite of, notwithstanding
diesseits, on this side of	um ... willen, for the sake of
jenseits, on the other side of, beyond	während, during
	wegen, on account of

EXAMPLES

trotz des Regens	diesseits der Grenze
jenseits des Berges	innerhalb eines Jahres
während des Krieges	statt eines Briefes

NOTE 1. Wegen may stand before or after the noun: des Vaters wegen, *on account of father.* With um ... willen, the noun stands between um and willen. Compare the English *for your father's sake* = um deines Vaters willen.

NOTE 2. When combined with wegen and um ... willen, the pronouns show special stem forms in -et: meinetwegen (Note 3), um seinetwillen, *for his sake.*

NOTE 3. Meinetwegen, etc., may mean either (1) *on my account* or (2) *so far as I am concerned, for aught I care.*

KINKELS BEFREIUNG VI

Als Schurz dies hörte, glaubte er, mit diesem Mann ans Ziel zu kommen, ohne die gewöhnlichen Umwege zu machen. Er sagte Brune also ohne weiteres, daß er seine Hilfe brauchte, um Kinkel aus dem Gefängnis zu befreien.

„Wenn der Lebensunterhalt Ihrer Familie Ihr größtes Bedenken 5 ist," setzte er hinzu, „so werde ich imstande sein, dafür zu sorgen. Würden Sie dann bereit sein zu helfen?" — „Es wird eine schwierige und gefährliche Sache sein," erwiderte Brune, „aber ich will mir's überlegen, ob und wie es zu machen ist. Geben Sie mir drei Tage Bedenkzeit!" 10

Das Warten war qualvoll. Schurz erzählt, wie lang ihm die drei Tage wurden und wie er versuchte, die Zeit durch Lesen zu ver= kürzen.

Am Abend des dritten Tages fuhr er wieder nach Spandau. Als er Brunes erste Worte hörte, wollte er ihm um den Hals fallen. 15 „Ich habe mir's überlegt," sagte Brune, „ich glaube, es geht. Während einer Nacht, wenn ich die Wache in den oberen Räumen des Zuchthauses habe und ein gewisser andrer Beamter unten ist, werde ich die nötigen Schlüssel aus einem gewissen Schrank holen und Kinkels Zelle öffnen. Sie treffen ihn dann innerhalb 20 des Tores. Aber es wird noch einige Zeit dauern, bis alles in rechter Ordnung ist. In der Nacht vom 5. zum 6. November sind die Nachtwachen, wie sie sein sollen (*have to*)."

„Gut," antwortete Schurz, „auch ich brauche einige Zeit für nötige Vorbereitungen." Er dachte an das Geld, das man zur Befreiung 25 Kinkels gesammelt hatte. Nicht nur diesseits, sondern sogar jenseits der deutschen Grenzen gab es Bewunderer, die größere (*rather large*) Summen gegeben hatten. Den größten Teil davon bot Schurz nun Brune zur Versorgung seiner Familie an.

VOKABELN

der Beam'te *adj. infl.* official
das Beden'ken, –s — misgiving, scruple
die Bedenk'zeit, –en time for reflection
die Grenze, –n frontier, border
die Hilfe help
der Le'bensun'terhalt, –s livelihood
der Raum, –es, ⸚e quarter, hall
der Schlüssel, –s, — key
der Umweg, –s, –e roundabout way
die Versor'gung, maintenance
die Vorbereitung, –en preparation
die Wache, –n watch

die Zelle, –n cell
das Ziel, –s, –e goal
befrei'en *wk.* to free
dauern *wk.* to last, take
erwi'dern *wk.* to reply
sich (*dat.*) etwas überle'gen *wk.* to consider something
verkür'zen *wk.* to shorten
gewöhn'lich usual
gleich immediately
gut very well
ober upper
qualvoll excruciating
schwierig difficult

REDEWENDUNGEN

ohne weiteres without more ado
es geht it can be done

imstande sein be able to
ans Ziel (*goal*) kommen achieve one's end

FRAGEN

1. Was sagte Schurz diesem Wärter ohne weiteres? 2. Was war Brunes größtes Bedenken? 3. Wieviel Bedenkzeit will Brune haben? 4. Wie versuchte Schurz, das Warten zu verkürzen? 5. Was waren Brunes erste Worte, als Schurz wieder= kam? 6. Warum konnten sie nicht gleich zu Werke gehen? 7. Hatten nur Deutsche zur Befreiung Kinkels Geld gegeben? 8. Wovon soll Brunes Familie leben, wenn man Brune [1] seine Stelle nimmt?

---

[1] Brune is dative. German expresses the *from*-notion by means of the dative.

ÜBUNG

Translate: Instead of sending it; in order to free him; it is better to wait; it is better to wait three days; within the prison; for the sake of the family; for his sake; instead of his clothing; in spite of his duty; the eating, drinking, and smoking; during that day; without thinking.

ÜBERSETZUNG *write*

1. Brune will be ready to help him. 2. Schurz is able to care for Brune's family. 3. He must (muß) open a cabinet in order to get the necessary key. 4. I did not know how it was to be done. 5. During the three days Schurz stayed in Moabit. 6. You will be free within the next four weeks. 7. It can-be-done in spite of the watchful officials. 8. We meet you outside the gate without making noise.

LESSON THIRTY-ONE

SUBJUNCTIVE AND CONDITIONAL

Note. To give a connected view, the entire paradigms are given. For the present Lesson only the blocked forms and blocked sections are needed. The underlined tenses are covered in Lesson 32, the others in Lesson 38.

163 Haben, sein, werden.

SUBJUNCTIVE

PRESENT

ich habe	ich sei	ich werde
du habest	du seiest	du werdest
er habe	er sei	er werde
wir haben	wir seien	wir werden
ihr habet	ihr seiet	ihr werdet
sie haben	sie seien	sie werden

PAST *tense has present meaning*

ich hätte, I should have	ich wäre, I should be	ich würde, I should become
du hättest	du wärest	du würdest
er hätte	er wäre	er würde
wir hätten	wir wären	wir würden
ihr hättet	ihr wäret	ihr würdet
sie hätten	sie wären	sie würden

PRESENT PERFECT

ich habe gehabt	ich sei gewesen	ich sei geworden
du habest gehabt	du seiest gewesen	du seiest geworden

PAST PERFECT

ich hätte gehabt	ich wäre gewesen	ich wäre geworden

FUTURE

ich werde haben	ich werde sein	ich werde werden

FUTURE PERFECT

ich werde gehabt haben	ich werde gewesen sein	ich werde geworden sein

CONDITIONAL

PRESENT

ich würde haben, I should have	ich würde sein, I should be	ich würde werden, I should become

PAST

| ich würde gehabt haben, I should have had | ich würde gewesen sein, I should have been | ich würde geworden sein, I should have become |

The compound tenses differ from those of the indicative merely in that the subjunctive forms of haben and sein take the place of the indicative forms. Verbs that take sein as auxiliary in the indicative also have it in the subjunctive and conditional.

164 **Umlaut.** Strong verbs always modify the vowel in the past subjunctive: ich kam, I came: ich käme, I should come; ich gab: ich gäbe; ich trug: ich trüge. Verbs like helfen, sterben, werfen (Class 4), form a past subjunctive with ü: hülfe, stürbe, würfe.

Weak verbs do not take umlaut.

165 Of the weak verb loben and the strong verb kommen (*aux.* sein) the forms are accordingly:

SUBJUNCTIVE

Present: ich lobe, du lobest, er lobe, wir loben, ihr lobet, sie loben
ich komme, du kommest, er komme, wir kommen, ihr kommet, sie kommen

---

Past: ich lobte, du lobtest (identical with past indicative)
ich käme, du kämest, er käme, wir kämen, ihr kämet, sie kämen

---

Present Perfect: ich habe gelobt, du habest gelobt, etc.
ich sei gekommen, du seiest gekommen, etc.
Past Perfect: ich hätte gelobt, du hättest gelobt, etc.
ich wäre gekommen, du wärest gekommen, etc.
Future: ich werde loben, du werdest loben, er werde loben, etc.
ich werde kommen, du werdest kommen, er werde kommen, etc.
Future Perfect: ich werde gelobt haben, du werdest gelobt haben, etc.
ich werde gekommen sein, du werdest gekommen sein, etc.

CONDITIONAL

Present: ich würde loben, du würdest loben, etc.
ich würde kommen, du würdest kommen, etc.

Past: ich würde gelobt haben, du würdest gelobt haben, etc.
ich würde gekommen sein, du würdest gekommen sein, etc.

166 Conditional Sentences. Such a sentence as " If he has money enough he will go to college " is called a conditional sentence. The subordinate clause with *if* is called the ' condition ' while the main clause is called the ' conclusion.' Contrast:

1. If he has money enough he will go to college.
2. If he had money enough he would go to college.

Sentence 1 is a simple condition and is translated into German as it stands.

Sentence 2 means that we know he has not money enough, that such a supposition is contrary to the fact: it is called a contrary-to-fact condition. In such a contrary-to-fact condition German uses the past subjunctive in both clauses, but in the conclusion the present conditional is frequently used for the past subjunctive and *must* be used in the case of weak verbs.

1. Wenn er Geld hat, (so) wird er auf die Universität gehen.
2. Wenn er Geld hätte, (so) ginge er auf die Universität.
or Wenn er Geld hätte, (so) würde er auf die Universität gehen.

As in English, the position of the clauses may be reversed:

1. Er wird auf die Universität gehen, wenn er Geld hat.
2. Er ginge auf die Universität, wenn er Geld hätte.
or Er würde auf die Universität gehen, wenn er Geld hätte.

A condition may also be expressed by inversion: Hat er Geld, so wird er auf die Universität gehen. Such a clause must stand first, and so, *then*, is used to introduce the conclusion, as it frequently does when the condition comes first.

KINKELS BEFREIUNG VII

„Vielleicht wäre es aber am besten," meinte Schurz, „wenn Sie und die Ihrigen nach der Tat nach Amerika gingen." Doch davon wollte Brune nichts wissen. Entweder hoffte er, als Helfer bei dem Unternehmen unentdeckt' zu bleiben, oder er wollte lieber seine Strafe auf sich nehmen und seine Familie im Vaterland behalten. 5

„Wenn Sie das Geld brauchen," hatte Frau Kinkel zu Schurz ge= sagt, „so müssen Sie es bei einer Dame in Berlin, einer Verwand= ten des berühmten Komponisten Felix Mendelssohn=Bartholdy, persönlich abholen." Dies tat Schurz. Die Dame gab ihm eine große Brieftasche und sagte: „Ich wußte, daß Sie um diese 10 Zeit kommen würden. Wenn Ihre Pläne nicht gut wären, so würde Frau Kinkel Sie nicht zu mir schicken. Gott schütze und segne Sie!"

Das Geld machte dem jungen Mann große Sorge. „Wenn ich es verliere, oder wenn jemand es mir stiehlt," dachte er, „so kann man 15 nicht zum zweitenmal soviel sammeln." Um ein Unglück zu ver= hüten, trug er das Geld immer in seiner Brusttasche, die er sorgfältig zunähte.

Das Schwierigste, was Schurz noch vor der Befreiung zu tun hatte, war, Transportmittel nach einem sicheren Zufluchtsort zu 20 finden. Die Grenzen der Schweiz, Belgiens und Frankreichs waren zu weit entfernt. Also blieb nichts übrig, als an die See und von dort nach England zu fliehen. Weder Bremen noch Hamburg kam in Frage. Wenn die Regierung, wie zu erwarten war, diese beiden Haupthäfen bewachte, so würde man die Flücht= 25 linge dort fangen.

VOKABELN

(das) **Belgien,** –s Belgium
die **Brieftasche,** –n wallet
die **Brusttasche,** –n breast-pocket
der **Flüchtling,** –s, –e fugitive
(das) **Frankreich,** –s France
der **Haupthafen,** –s, " main harbor

der Helfer, –s, — helper, accomplice

der Komponist', –en, –en composer

die Tat, –en deed

das Transport'mittel, –s, — means of transportation

das Unglück, –s accident, misfortune, mishap

das Vaterland, –s native country, ' fatherland '

der Zufluchtsort, –s, –e place of refuge

bewa'chen wk. to watch, guard

erwar'ten wk. to expect

hoffen wk. to hope

schützen wk. to protect

segnen wk. to bless

verhü'ten wk. to obviate, prevent

verlie'ren, o, o to lose

zunähen wk. to sew shut

entfernt' distant, away

entwe'der (or ent'weder) . . . oder either . . . or

persön'lich personal(ly)

sicher safe, certain

sorgfältig careful(ly)

soviel so much

unentdeckt undiscovered

weder . . . noch neither . . . nor

REDEWENDUNGEN

kam in Frage was to be considered   wollte nichts wissen von would not hear of (listen to)

FRAGEN

1. Warum will Brune nicht nach Amerika gehen? 2. Wo ist das Geld, das Schurz jetzt braucht? 3. Worin bekommt er das Geld? 4. Wo trug Schurz diese große Summe? 5. Warum tat er das? 6. Was mußte Schurz finden, ehe Kinkel aus dem Gefängnis kam? 7. Warum konnten sie nicht nach Belgien, Frankreich oder der Schweiz fliehen? 8. Welches sind noch jetzt die deutschen Haupthäfen?

ÜBUNGEN

(a) Translate: If he is; if he were; if you have; if you had; if I carry; if I carried; if we help; if we helped; if she learns; if she learned. (b) Translate: He will go to ruin if he remains in prison. — He would go to ruin if he remained in prison. (c) In the two sentences of (b) put the conditional clause first.

ÜBERSETZUNG

1. If he sews up his inside coat pocket he will not lose his money. 2. They would flee to France if it were not so far away. 3. The lady will give you the wallet if you call for it personally. 4. Would Brune go to America if the government were looking-for him? 5. He will open the cell if the keys are in the cabinet. 6. He would not take them if the other official were present.

LESSON THIRTY-TWO

CONTRARY TO FACT CONDITIONS IN THE PAST TIME. ALS OB. OPTATIVE AND ADHORTATIVE.

167 Contrary-to-fact Conditions in the Past Time. *He would have gone to college if he had had the money* is a contrary-to-fact condition in the past time because it expresses what would have been in the past if circumstances had been different. In such a condition, German uses the past perfect subjunctive in both clauses.

A. Er wäre auf die Universität gegangen, wenn er Geld gehabt hätte.

or *B.* Wenn er Geld gehabt hätte, so wäre er auf die Universität gegangen.

or *C.* Hätte er Geld gehabt, so wäre er auf die Universität gegangen.

168 Conditional. In the conclusion, the past conditional may be substituted for the past perfect subjunctive.

A. Er würde auf die Universität gegangen sein, wenn er das Geld gehabt hätte.
B. Wenn er das Geld gehabt hätte, so würde er auf die Universität gegangen sein.
C. Hätte er das Geld gehabt, so würde er auf die Universität gegangen sein.

SURVEY OF TENSES AND MOODS

	CONDITION		CONCLUSION	
	TENSE	MOOD	TENSE	MOOD
SIMPLE COND.	Present [1]............	Indic.	Pres. or Fut.....	Indic.
CONTR.-TO-FACT				
In Pres. Time	Past...................	Subj.	Past...................	Subj.
			or Present..............	Cond.
In Past Time	Past Perf...........	Subj.	Past Perf..........:	Subj.
			or Past...................	Cond.

169 **als ob, als wenn.** The conjunctions als ob and als wenn, *as if,* usually introduce a contrary-to-fact condition and are therefore regularly followed by either the past or past perfect subjunctive. As in conditional clauses, ob and wenn may be omitted, the clause then taking the inverted instead of the transposed word-order:

Als ob (wenn) ich nicht den ganzen Tag gearbeitet hätte!
Als hätte ich nicht den ganzen Tag gearbeitet! *As if I hadn't worked the whole day.*

170 **Optative Subjunctive.** 1. The present subjunctive is used to express a wish, the realization of which is regarded as possible: Lang lebe der König! *Long live the king!* Dein Reich komme, *Thy kingdom come.*

2. The past and past perfect are used in the same way to express a wish that cannot (past subjunctive) or could not (past perfect subjunctive) be fulfilled. Wäre er nur hier! *Would he were here.* The construction represents a contrary-to-fact condition, in the present or past time, whose conclusion is to be supplied: *If he were here, all would be well.* A clause with wenn may accordingly take the place of

[1] Theoretically, any tense except plupft. and fut. pft.

this optative: Wenn er nur hier wäre and Wenn er nur hier ge=
wesen wäre! Similarly, Das hätte ich nicht getan, where a
conditional clause can be supplied.

171 Adhortative Subjunctive.   The present subjunctive
is also used in an adhortative sense (English *let*):
Jeder Mann tue seine Pflicht! *Let every man do his duty!*

This use is especially common in the first person plural
(English *let us*): Gehen wir, *Let us go*.   Here the subject
always follows the verb, which begins the clause.   For *let us*
German also uses the imperative forms of lassen, and the
spoken language prefers these.   The du, ihr and Sie forms
are: Laß uns gehen; laßt uns gehen; lassen Sie uns gehen.
The same idea is very commonly expressed by using wollen:
Jetzt aber wollen wir essen, *Let's eat now.*

KINKELS BEFREIUNG VIII

An der Küste von Mecklenburg lag die kleinere Hafenstadt Rostock.
Schurz hätte vielleicht nicht an Rostock gedacht, wenn er dort nicht
einen treuen, demokratisch gesinnten Freund gehabt hätte.   Wäre
man nur erst über die preußische Grenze!   Die Eisenbahn war
natürlich nicht zu benutzen, aber wenn man mit schnellen Pferden   5
Spandau um Mitternacht verließe, würde man noch vor Tagesan=
bruch in Mecklenburg und in weniger als dreißig Stunden in
Rostock sein.

Nun reiste Schurz die Strecke entlang bis nach Rostock.   Er wußte
von vielen Gesinnungsgenossen, mit denen er Wagen= und Pferde=   10
wechsel verabreden konnte.   In wenigen Tagen war dies getan,
denn jeder war gern bereit zu helfen.   Um die Flüchtlinge von
Spandau bis zum ersten Pferdewechsel zu bringen, wandte Krüger
sich an einen Gutsbesitzer namens Hensel, der besonders schnelle
Pferde hatte und bereit war, selbst zu fahren.   15

„Gott sei mit Ihnen, und hoffen wir das Beste!" sagte Dr.

Falkenthal, als Schurz am 4. November von ihm Abschied nahm. In Spandau traf Schurz am Abend Brune, mit dem er noch einmal den ganzen Plan besprach, um sicher zu sein, daß alles in
20 Ordnung war.

„Nun noch eine Sache, von der ich nicht gern spreche," sagte Brune. „Ich weiß, Sie werden redlich für meine Familie tun, was Sie können, und wenn morgen nacht alles gut geht, so bin ich des Geldes so sicher, als ob ich es jetzt schon in der Tasche hätte. Aber es kann
25 auch nicht gut gehen. Was würde aus (of) meiner Familie, wenn Ihnen etwas passierte, ehe Sie mir das Geld gegeben haben? Wenn Sie die Sache recht überlegen, so müssen Sie selbst sagen, daß das Geld in meinen Händen sein muß, bevor ich meinen Kopf wage."

30 Schurz bat ihn um eine kurze Bedenkzeit. Wenn er nur mehr von diesem Mann gewußt hätte!

VOKABELN

der Abschied, –s leave
der Gesin'nungsgenos'se, –n, –n sympathizer, ally, person of the same mind
der Gutsbesitzer, –s, — owner of an estate
die Küste, –n coast
die Strecke, –n stretch, route
der Tagesanbruch, –s break of day
der Wagen- und Pferdewechsel, –s, — relay of carriages and horses

benut'zen wk. to make use of, use
bespre'chen (i), a, o to discuss
passie'ren wk., aux. sein to happen
verab'reden wk. to agree upon
wagen wk. to risk, dare, venture
wandte sich turned
gesinnt' minded, disposed
namens by the name of
recht right(ly)
redlich honest(ly), sincere(ly)

REDEWENDUNGEN

die Strecke entlang' along the route

noch eine Sache another matter

FRAGEN

1. Wo liegt Rostock? 2. Wie wollte (intended) Schurz mit Kinkel nach Rostock kommen? 3. Was mußte er nun verabreden?

4. Wie machte er das? 5. Wer sollte die beiden bis zum ersten Pferdewechsel bringen? 6. Was verlangte Brune von Schurz am Abend des vierten November? 7. Warum verlangte er das Geld? 8. Welche Antwort gab ihm Schurz?

ÜBUNGEN

(*a*) Translate: If he had driven; if they had helped; as if I had; as if she were; as if I had known. (*b*) Render the following in two ways: 1. You would have thought. 2. He would have come. (*c*) 1. Translate: If they have fast horses they will soon be in Rostock. 2. Change the German sentence to a contrary-to-fact condition in the present time. 3. Change it to a contrary-to-fact condition in the past time.

ÜBERSETZUNG

1. They (man) would have caught the two if they had gone (use fahren) by railway. 2. Let every friend be ready to help. 3. God bless your courageous deed, young man. 4. If we only had true friends. 5. Let us discuss the whole plan once more. 6. Had he only known either the man or his friends better. 7. They would have fled to France if the frontier had been nearer. 8. You talk (reden) as if you had read the story.

LESSON THIRTY-THREE

INSEPARABLE COMPOUNDS

172 Inseparable Prefixes. The inseparable prefixes are: be=, ent=, er=, ge=, ver=, and zer=. English has similar prefixes in *be-* and *for-*, vergeſſen corresponding exactly to *forget*. As in English, the accent is on the root syllable. The conjugation is that of the verb proper, except that the participle does not have ge=.

Synopsis of verſprechen, *to promise*. The principal parts are: verſprechen (i), verſprach, verſprochen.

INDICATIVE

Pres.	ich verſpreche	*Past*	ich verſprach
	du verſprichſt		du verſprachſt
Pres. Pft.	ich habe verſprochen	*Past Pft.*	ich hatte verſprochen
Fut.	ich werde verſprechen	*Fut. Pft.*	ich werde verſprochen haben

Imperative: verſprich, verſprecht, verſprechen Sie
Infinitive: verſprechen
Participles: verſprechend, verſprochen.

For the subjunctive and conditional see App., p. 221.

173 Verbs in –ieren: ſtudie′ren, ſtudier′te, hat ſtudiert′. These verbs, mostly foreign, are like inseparable compounds (*a*) in not accenting the first syllable; (*b*) in having no ge= in the past participle. They are all weak.

174 Meaning. The inseparable prefixes have certain fundamental meanings, illustrated below.

be= forms transitive verbs, from verbs, adjectives, and nouns:

beantworten, reply to	beſprechen, discuss
befreien, liberate	bewundern, admire

Note the difference in construction between simple and compound verb:

Ich antworte auf den Brief but Ich beantworte den Brief.
Ich folgte dem Rat but Ich befolgte den Rat.

ent- denotes separation: entdecken (decken, *cover*), *discover;* entlaufen, *run away;* entehren, *dishonor;* entführen, *carry off, kidnap;* entwachsen, *outgrow.*

er- denotes attainment, accomplishment: erkämpfen, *gain by fighting;* erkaufen, *acquire by purchase;* erleben, *experience;* erreichen, *attain.*

ge- has no function that can be readily defined.

ver- means (*a*) *away*, (*b*) *amiss, mis-:* (*a*) verbieten, *forbid;* verbrennen, *burn up;* verkaufen, *sell;* verspielen, *lose (in play, gaming);* versprechen, *promise.* (*b*) verführen, *lead astray;* verraten, *betray.*

zer- means *asunder, in pieces:* zerbrechen, *break in pieces;* zerreißen, *tear to pieces;* zerschneiden, *cut to pieces.*

175 **Omission of the Auxiliary.** The auxiliaries haben and sein may be omitted at the end of a subordinate clause: Er wußte nicht, was geschehen (war), *He did not know what had happened.* This omission is not usual in the spoken language.

KINKELS BEFREIUNG IX

Schurz verbrachte nun in seinem Zimmer in Krügers Gasthaus eine Stunde, die er nie vergaß.

Brune hatte zwar versprochen, Kinkel zu befreien, aber hatte er seine Ehrlichkeit schon bewiesen? Würde er nicht, nachdem er das Geld erhalten hatte, den Behörden die ganze Sache entdecken und ihn und Kinkel verraten? 5

Auf der andern Seite — Schurz verstand, daß Brune das Geld im voraus verlangen mußte, denn was würde mit seiner Frau und seinen Kindern geschehen, wenn er sie nicht mehr ernähren konnte? So [1] sehr sich Schurz auch den Kopf zerbrach, immer wieder erschien 10 Brunes ehrliches Gesicht und offnes, stolzes Wesen vor ihm. Auch

[1] So sehr ... auch, *Much as.* So sehr introduces a subordinate clause.

beschäftigte ihn der Gedanke, daß man ohne zu wagen nicht gewinnen kann. Wenn er Brunes Verlangen nicht bewilligte, so würde das Leben des Freundes und seiner Familie zerstört sein.

15 Er beschloß also, Brune das Geld zu geben, obwohl das Versprechen noch nicht erfüllt war. Als er ihn noch an demselben Abend traf, sagte er: „Das Geld ist mir anvertraut. Meine Ehre hängt daran. Ich vertraue Ihnen Geld, Ehre, Freiheit. Morgen abend um fünf Uhr werde ich das Geld in Ihre Wohnung bringen."

20 Brune schwieg einen Augenblick. Endlich sagte er: „Ich hätt's auch wirklich getan, wenn Sie das nicht versprochen hätten. Morgen um Mitternacht ist Ihr Freund ein freier Mann."

In einer Zigarrenkiste brachte Schurz das Geld zu Brune, der es nicht einmal zählen wollte.

25 „Auf Wiedersehen also heute nacht!" —
„Auf Wiedersehen und gut [1] Glück!

VOKABELN

der Augenblick, –s, –e moment
die Behör′de, –n authorities
die Ehre, –n honor
die Ehrlichkeit honesty
die Zigar′renkiste, –n cigar box
anvertrauen *wk.* to entrust
beschäftigen *wk.* to occupy
beschließen, o, o to resolve, decide, make up one's mind
beweisen, ie, ie to prove
bewilligen *wk.* to grant
entdecken *wk.* to discover, reveal
erfüllen *wk.* to fulfill

erhalten (ä), ie, a to receive
geschehen (ie), a, ist geschehen to happen
gewinnen, a, o to win, gain
verbringen *irreg.* to spend, pass
verraten (ä), ie, a to betray
verstehen *irreg.* to understand
vertrauen *wk.* to trust, entrust
zählen *wk.* to count
zerstören *wk.* to destroy
nicht einmal not even
offen open, frank
stolz proud

REDEWENDUNGEN

sich (dat.) den Kopf zerbrechen to rack one's brain

im vor′aus in advance

[1] In the phrase gut Glück the word gut remains uninflected.

FRAGEN

1. Warum war es gefährlich, Brune das Geld im voraus zu geben? 2. Was würde passieren, wenn Brune ihn verriete? 3. Was muß man oft tun, um etwas zu gewinnen? 4. Was beschließt Schurz am Ende? 5. Wie bekommt Brune das Geld? 6. Wessen Ehre hängt an dem Geld? 7. Was hätte Brune getan, wenn Schurz ihm das Geld nicht im voraus gegeben hätte? 8. Warum zählte Brune das Geld nicht?

ÜBUNGEN

(*a*) Translate and give synopses of: 1. Brune promises it. 2. I prove my honesty. 3. They rule the country. (*b*) Translate and put the verbs in the present, past, and past perfect subjunctive: 1. You (du) spend the day. 2. He decides it. 3. It happens.

ÜBERSETZUNG

1. Has he forgotten the man's honest face? 2. It had interested me to know whether he was really my friend. 3. Schurz had appeared in Brune's dwelling with a cigar box. 4. If Brune had betrayed him Schurz would have lost his honor. 5. Why did he demand the money in advance? 6. Many thoughts occupied him while he spent an hour in Krüger's tavern. 7. How could Schurz trust him before he had fulfilled his promise? 8. Do we know how much money Brune received (pres. perf.)?

LESSON THIRTY-FOUR

SEPARABLE COMPOUNDS

176 **Separable Compounds.** What is, in English, an adverb is in German considered the separable prefix of a verb: ausgehen, *to go out.*

177 **Separable Prefixes.** The number of separable prefixes is large. The more common ones are: ab, an, auf, aus, durch, ein (*in*), fort, mit, nach, über, um, unter, vor, wieder, zu, zurück, zusammen; and her and hin, treated in §182. Most of such compounds are self-explanatory: abnehmen, *to take off;* mitbringen, *to take along.* Some are not: anfangen, *to begin;* aufhören, *to cease.* Many nouns and adjectives are thus joined to verbs to form separable compounds: teil=nehmen, *to take part;* liebhaben, *to love.*

178 **Accent. Such a separable prefix is always accented, no matter where it stands:** ich gehe aus; du hast den Hut nicht abgenommen; er hat uns alle lieb.

179 **Position of Prefix.** 1. The prefix is separated only in the two simple tenses of the indicative (and subjunctive), and in the imperative. It then stands at the end of its clause or sentence: Ich fange heute morgen an, *I am beginning this morning.*

2. Ich habe heute morgen angefangen, *I began this morning.* In the infinitive and participles the prefix is not separated. In the past participle it precedes the full past participle with its ge=.

3. Ich glaube, daß wir heute morgen anfangen. In the transposed order, i.e., in a dependent clause, the verb comes last, and here prefix and verb join hands again and are written as one word.

4. Frĩ, es ist Zeit aufzustehen. The zu that is often used with the infinitive has the same position as the ge= of the participle.

180 Synopsis. In the following synopsis of aus'sprechen, *to pronounce*, take care to accent aus. To show the order, an object is given in part of the forms.

	INDICATIVE	IMPERATIVE
Pres.	ich spreche das Wort aus	sprich d. W. aus
	du sprichst das Wort aus	sprecht d. W. aus
Past	ich sprach das Wort aus	sprechen Sie d. W. aus
Pres. Perf.	ich habe d. W. ausgesprochen	INFINITIVE
Past Perf.	ich hatte d. W. ausgesprochen	aussprechen
Future	ich werde d. W. aussprechen	PARTICIPLES
Fut. Perf.	ich werde d. W. ausgesprochen haben	aussprechend
		ausgesprochen

For the subjunctive and conditional see App., p. 221.

181 Doubtful Prefixes. English has both *to undergo'* and *go un'der; to overlook'* and *look o'ver.* Just so, German has five prefixes, durch, über, um, unter, and wieder that form both separable and inseparable compounds. The accent, of course, differs. When used in their literal sense such verbs are generally separable; when used in a figurative or derived sense, inseparable: ü'bersetzen, *to ferry across;* überset'zen, *to translate;* durch'brechen, *to break through;* durchbre'chen, *to pierce;* umge'ben, *to surround.*

182 her and hin. Both her and hin imply motion, her (' hither '), motion towards the speaker, hin (' hence '), motion away from the speaker.

> Kommen Sie mal her! *Come here, please.*
> Gehen Sie mal hin! *Just go there.*

The English adverbs that once indicated direction (hither,

Ich hatte keine Zeit [das Buch anzufangen

thither; hence, thence; whither, whence) have become obsolete, so that *here* now means both *here* and *hither*, *there* both *there* and *thither*. In German, on the contrary,

hier = here, in this place; her = hither, to this place; dort = there, in that place; hin = thither, to that place.

You inquire: Wo gehst du hin? *Where are you going?* Wo kommst du her? *Where do you come from?*

With verbs, her and hin form separable compounds. So the examples above are regarded as forms of her'kommen and hin'gehen.

Compounds with other adverbs are very common: heraus', hinaus'; herein', hinein'; herun'ter, hinun'ter:

> Kommen Sie herein', *Come in.*
> Gehen Sie hinein', *Go inside.*

Such adverbs are all accented on the second syllable.

KINKELS BEFREIUNG X

Das Zuchthaus, dessen kahle Mauern von einem Tor und einer Menge kleiner Fenster durchbrochen waren, lag in der Mitte der Stadt. Straßen umgaben es auf allen vier Seiten. Kinkels Zelle im oberen Stockwerk war durch ein starkes, eisernes Gitter in
5 zwei Teile eingeteilt; in dem einen stand sein Bett, in dem andern arbeitete er. Abends schloß der Wärter die Tür im Gitter zu. Der Eingang der Zelle vom Korridor aus war mit zwei schweren Türen verwahrt, die mehrere Schlösser hatten. Auf der Straße, auf welche Kinkels Zelle hinaussah, stand Tag und Nacht eine Schild=
10 wache, eine andere bewachte während des Tages das Tor des Gebäudes an der Hauptstraße, während der Nacht einen inneren Hof.

Die Schlüssel zu Kinkels Zelle, sowie zu der Tür im Gitter, bewahrte man nachts in einem Schrank auf, der in der Stube der

Inspekto'ren stand. Von dem Schlüssel zu dieser Stube hatte 15
Brune einen Wachsabdruck (*wax impression*) gemacht, nach dem
die Spandauer Freunde einen Nachschlüssel angefertigt (*prepared*)
hatten. Der Schlüssel zu dem Schrank lag nachts immer oben auf
dem Schrank selbst. Der Inspektor legte ihn gewöhnlich selber
hin. 20

Auch zu einem Pförtchen in dem großen Tor des Zuchthauses hatte
Brune einen Nachschlüssel, den er Schurz übergab' (*handed over*).

Um Kinkel nicht unnötig lange aufzuregen (*excite*), hatte Brune
ihm erst am Abend des 5. November mitgeteilt, was im Werke war.
Er sollte wie sonst zu Bett gehen, kurz vor Mitternacht aber auf= 25
stehen, seine Kleider anziehen und bereit sein, seine Zelle zu ver=
lassen.

Schurz' Aufgabe war es, kurz nach Mitternacht, nachdem der
städtische Nachtwächter vorbeigegangen war, das Pförtchen auf=
zuschließen, in den Torweg des Zuchthauses einzutreten, dort 30
Brune und Kinkel zu erwarten, Kinkel einen Mantel umzuwerfen
und mit ihm nach Krügers Gasthaus zu eilen. Dort sollte Kinkel
sich umziehen, und beide sollten in Hensels Wagen die Flucht
antreten (*start on*).

VOKABELN

die Aufgabe, –n task
der Eingang, –s, ‑e entrance
die Flucht flight
das Gebäu'de, –s, — building
das Gitter, –s, — grating
der Hof, –es, ‑e court, courtyard
die Mauer, –n (masonry) wall
der Nachschlüssel, –s, — duplicate key
der Nachtwächter, –s, — night-watchman
das Pförtchen, –s, — little gate *or* doorway, wicket

die Schildwache, –n sentry
das Schloß, –es, ‑er lock
das Stockwerk, –s, –e story
der Torweg, –s, –e gateway
anziehen, o, o to put on
arbeiten *wk.* to work
aufbewahren *wk.* to keep
aufschließen, o, o to unlock, open up
aufstehen *irreg.* ift aufgestanden to rise
eilen *wk.*, *aux.* sein to hurry, hasten
einteilen *wk.* to divide

eintreten (i), a, e, ist eingetreten to enter

hinaus'sehen auf (ie), a, e to look out upon

hinlegen *wk.* to lay down

mitbringen *irreg.* to bring along

umwerfen (i), a, o to throw around

sich umziehen, o, o to change clothes

verwahren *wk.* to guard, secure

vorbei'gehen *irreg.* ist vorbeigegangen to go past

zuschließen, o, o to lock

eisern iron

inner inner

kahl bare; bald

nachts during the night

schwer heavy; difficult

städtisch municipal

REDEWENDUNGEN

vom Korridor aus from the corridor

was im Werke war what was going on

FRAGEN

1. Wo lag das Zuchthaus? 2. War Kinkels Zelle oben oder unten? 3. Wann war die Tür im Gitter zwischen den beiden Teilen der Zelle offen? 4. Wo standen Schildwachen? 5. Wie konnte Brune in die Stube, wo der Schrank stand? 6. Wo bewahrte der Inspektor den Schlüssel zu dem Schrank auf? 7. Warum hatte Brune Kinkel nicht früher gesagt, daß man ihn befreien würde? 8. Wo sollte Schurz die beiden erwarten? 9. Wohin sollten sie zu Fuß eilen? 10. Warum sollte Kinkel sich umziehen?

ÜBUNGEN

(*a*) Translate and give synopses of: 1. When does the night-watchman pass? 2. I hand over the key to you. 3. The two came down (herunter or hinunter?). (*b*) Translate and put the verbs in the present, past, and past perfect subjunctive: 1. He unlocks the cell. 2. You (du) enter.

ÜBERSETZUNG

1. When Kinkel goes to bed the keeper locks the door.
2. He has brought a coat along. 3. The window looked out on a street, but the prisoner could not look out. 4. It would have excited Kinkel to know what was going on. 5. Please, make (anfertigen) a duplicate key, Mr. Poritz. 6. Think it over well before you begin. 7. It will not be difficult to get up and put on your clothes, will it? 8. When did they start-on (antreten) their flight?

LESSON THIRTY-FIVE

MODAL AUXILIARIES I

Note. A survey of the entire conjugation of the auxiliaries heads the Lesson. Important forms are blocked. Lesson 35 deals with the indicative forms only and provides a drill on these. The subjunctive forms and special idioms are taken up in Lesson 36.

183 The modal auxiliaries are:

dürfen, dare, be allowed, be permitted, may (permission),

können, can, be able to, may (possibility)

mögen, may (possibility), like to

müssen, must, have to, be compelled to

sollen, shall, is to, is said to

wollen, will, want, desire, intend, be willing, be about to, profess to

Unlike the English auxiliaries, these verbs have a complete conjugation. Owing to meaning, only wollen has an imperative.

PRINCIPAL PARTS

dürfen, durfte, er hat gedurft   müssen, mußte, er hat gemußt
können, konnte, er hat gekonnt   sollen, sollte, er hat gesollt
mögen, mochte, er hat gemocht   wollen, wollte, er hat gewollt

ich darf	ich kann	ich mag	ich muß	ich soll	ich will
I may	I can	I like to	I must	I am to	I will

INDICATIVE

PRESENT

ich darf	kann	mag	muß	soll	will
du darfst	kannst	magst	mußt	sollst	willst
er darf	kann	mag	muß	soll	will
wir dürfen	können	mögen	müssen	sollen	wollen
ihr dürft	könnt	mögt	müßt	sollt	wollt
sie dürfen	können	mögen	müssen	sollen	wollen

PAST

ich durfte,	konnte,	mochte,	mußte,	sollte,	wollte
I was allowed to	I was able to	I liked to	I had to	I was to	I wanted to

PRESENT PERFECT

ich habe gedurft (gekonnt, gemocht, gemußt, gesollt, gewollt)

PAST PERFECT

ich hatte gedurft (gekonnt, gemocht, gemußt, gesollt, gewollt)

FUTURE

ich werde dürfen (können, mögen, müssen, sollen, wollen)

FUTURE PERFECT

ich werde gedurft haben (gekonnt haben, gemocht haben, etc.)

SUBJUNCTIVE

PRESENT [1]

ich dürfe	könne	möge	müsse	solle	wolle
du dürfeſt	könneſt	mögeſt	müſſeſt	solleſt	wolleſt
er dürfe	könne	möge	müſſe	solle	wolle
wir dürfen	können	mögen	müſſen	sollen	wollen
ihr dürfet	könnet	möget	müſſet	sollet	wollet
ſie dürfen	können	mögen	müſſen	sollen	wollen

PAST

ich dürfte	könnte	möchte	müßte	sollte	wollte

PRESENT PERFECT

ich habe gedurft (gekonnt, gemocht, gemußt, geſollt, gewollt)
du habeſt gedurft, etc.

PAST PERFECT

ich hätte gedurft (gekonnt, gemocht, gemußt, geſollt, gewollt)

FUTURE

ich werde dürfen (können, mögen, müſſen, ſollen, wollen)
du werdeſt dürfen, etc.

FUTURE PERFECT

ich werde gedurft haben (gekonnt haben, gemocht haben, etc.)
du werdeſt gedurft haben, etc.

CONDITIONAL

(The Conditional is little used. Present: ich würde dürfen, können, etc.
Past: ich würde gedurft haben, gekonnt haben, etc.)

IMPERATIVE

Of wollen only: wolle, wollet, wollen Sie.

INFINITIVE

dürfen	können	mögen	müſſen	ſollen	wollen

[1] Chiefly used in Indirect Discourse (Lesson 38). In the case of mögen the
optative use is also common: Möge er noch lange leben!

PARTICIPLES
PRESENT

dürfend	können	mögend	müffend	follend	wollend

PAST

geburft	gefonnt	gemocht	gemußt	gefollt	gewollt

NOTE. It will be observed that

1. In the present indic. these verbs, except follen, have in the plural a vowel different from that of the singular.

2. The endings of the singular of the present indic. are those of the past of a strong verb: ich fang, du fangft, er fang (ich darf, du darfft, er darf).

3. The vowel of the plural of the present indic., and of the present and past subj., is identical with that of the infinitive.

4. Sollen and wollen do not have umlaut anywhere.

184 zu. An infinitive depending upon a modal auxiliary has no zu, to, in either English or German: Ich kann gehen, I can go. However, English uses many paraphrases and these have to before the infinitive. I can go = I am able to go. I must go = I have to go. Do not render such a to in German.

The defective character of the English auxiliaries makes such paraphrases unavoidable. The future tense of can in English is, for example, I shall be able to, while in German it is ich werde können.

ich mußte, it should be especially observed, is I had to, not I must.

185 Ordinary Uses of the Auxiliaries.

dürfen: Das darfft du nicht (tun), You may not do that.
Darf ich Sie bitten, ... May I ask you to ...

können: Ich kann das Buch nicht finden, I cannot find the book.

mögen: Das mag wahr sein, That may be true.
Ich mag ihn gern, I like him.

müssen: Wir werden warten müssen, *We shall have to wait.*

sollen: Du sollst nicht töten, *Thou shalt not kill.*

Ihr Bruder soll mitkommen, *Your brother is to come along.*

wollen: Ich will nicht, *I don't want to.*

Wir wollen aufs Land fahren, *We intend to go to the country.*

EIN BRIEF NACH HAUSE

Lieber Vater!

Eben bekam ich Deinen Brief und muß sagen, ich kann nicht verstehen, wie Du so schlecht von mir denken kannst. Soll ich denn nichts tun als studieren? Darf ich nicht die Woche einmal ins Kino oder zu einem Tanz gehen? Das durfte ich doch sogar zu Hause.

Du schreibst, Du wirst mir das Taschengeld verkürzen müssen. Aber das geht nicht, lieber Vater. Gestern z.B. konnte ich meine deutsche Übersetzung nicht machen, denn wir sollten ein neues Buch haben, und ich wollte das Geld dazu nicht borgen. Ich hatte nur noch genug, um für mein Zimmer bezahlen (*pay*) zu können. Und der Mensch muß doch auch essen. Mein Frühstück heute mußte ich anschreiben lassen.

Soll ich vielleicht dieses Wochenende nach Hause kommen? Dann will ich Dir gern alles erklären (*explain*). Du mußt mir aber das Geld zur Fahrt schicken, denn bei dieser Kälte mag ich nicht auf der Straße stehen und warten, bis jemand mich mitnimmt.

In Liebe

Dein Sohn

Alfred

KINKELS BEFREIUNG XI

Um Mitternacht öffnete Schurz leise das Pförtchen und trat ein. Bei dem Schein einer Laterne konnte er das innere Ende des

Torwegs sehen, wo Brune mit Kinkel erscheinen sollte. Alles blieb still. Nach einer Viertelstunde dachte Schurz: „Was mag geschehen sein? Sollte Brune doch untreu sein?" Eine halbe Stunde mochte vergangen sein, da kam Brune, aber allein.

„Ich bin unglücklich," flüsterte er. „Die Schlüssel waren nicht in dem Schrank. Holen Sie morgen das Geld wieder!"

Ohne zu antworten, trat Schurz auf die Straße, schloß das Pförtchen zu, steckte den Schlüssel in die Tasche und eilte nach Krügers Gasthaus mit Poritz und Leddihn, die draußen gewartet hatten, da sie im Notfall helfen wollten.

Hensel stand bereit mit seinem Wagen. „Es ist alles mißglückt!" rief Schurz, „aber es gibt heute nacht noch etwas zu tun, ob wir es mögen oder nicht. Bis tief nach Mecklenburg hinein stehen Freunde mit frischen Pferden, die dürfen wir nicht umsonst warten lassen. Wollen Sie die Fahrt mit mir unternehmen? In drei Stunden können wir den nächsten Wagen erreichen." Statt aller (any) Antwort stieg Hensel ein, und sie rollten davon.

Es geschah wie verabredet. „Die Sache ist mißglückt," sagte Schurz traurig zu dem Kutscher des nächsten Wagens, „mehr kann ich Ihnen jetzt nicht mitteilen. Bitte, geben Sie die Nachricht an den nächsten Freund weiter, doch darf niemand sonst davon hören."

Auf der langsamen Rückfahrt konnte Schurz über das Unglück nachdenken. Er gab sich selbst die Schuld. Warum war es ihm nicht eingefallen, auch für die Zellen= und Gittertür Nachschlüssel zu machen? Er fürchtete, Kinkel würde nun für immer in dem schrecklichen Gefängnis bleiben müssen.

Nachdem die beiden in Oranienburg übernachtet hatten und am nächsten Tage nach Spandau zurückgefahren waren, ging Schurz in Brunes Wohnung. Die Zigarrenkiste stand auf dem Tisch. „Alles war in schönster Ordnung," erzählte Brune, „aber als ich den Schrank aufschloß, konnte ich die Schlüssel zur Zelle nicht finden. Heute morgen hörte ich, daß der Inspektor sie aus Ver-

sehen in die Tasche gesteckt und mit nach Hause genommen hatte. 35
Da ist das Geld, zählen Sie es erst!"

„Was nun?" sagte Schurz, „ich gebe es nicht auf. Müssen wir
warten, bis Sie wieder die Nachtwache haben?" — „Wir können
warten," antwortete Brune, „und uns inzwischen alle Nachschlüssel
verschaffen. Aber warum soll der Mann noch einen Tag länger da 40
sitzen? Ich will versuchen, ihm diese Nacht herauszuhelfen, wenn
er Mut zu einem halsbrecherischen Stück hat." — „Was, diese
Nacht?" — „Ja, diese Nacht!"

VOKABELN

der Kutscher, –s, — driver, coachman
die Later'ne, –n lantern, lamp,
street-light
der Mut, –es courage
die Nachricht, –en news, message
der Notfall, –s, ⸚e case of need
die Rückfahrt, –en journey back
der Schein, –s light, ray
davon'rollen wk., aux. sein to roll
(drive) away
einfallen (ä), ie, ist eingefallen to
occur to
einsteigen, ie, ist eingestiegen to enter, get in

erreichen wk. to reach
fürchten wk. to fear, be afraid
nachdenken irreg. to think over
übernach'ten wk. to spend the night
unterneh'men (i), a, o to undertake
verschaffen wk. to procure
weitergeben (i), a, e to pass on
wie'derholen wk. to get again, take
back
zurück'fahren (ä), u, ist zurückge=
fahren to drive back
leise soft(ly)
mit along
traurig sad(ly)
untreu faithless

REDEWENDUNGEN

aus Versehen by mistake
ein halsbrecherisches Stück an ex-
ceedingly dangerous (break-
neck) deed

gab sich selbst die Schuld blamed
himself
tief nach M. hinein far into Mecklenburg

FRAGEN

1. Wie konnte Schurz durch das Pförtchen kommen? 2. Was
wollten Poritz und Leddihn draußen auf der Straße? 3. Warum

mißglückte dieser Versuch? **4.** Was mußten Hensel und Schurz in derselben Nacht tun? **5.** Was sollte der erste Kutscher, den sie trafen, dem nächsten mitteilen? **6.** Was fürchtet Schurz nun? **7.** Will Schurz die Befreiung des Freundes aufgeben? **8.** Wann will Brune ihm heraushelfen?

ÜBUNGEN

(*a*) Supply the correct form of the auxiliary: **1.** Du (müssen) fragen. **2.** Gestern (können) ich nicht kommen. **3.** Deutsche Kinder (müssen) in die Schule gehen, bis sie fünfzehn Jahre alt sind. **4.** Ich (dürfen) nicht sagen, von wem ich es gehört habe. **5.** Ihr (mögen) ihn alle gern. (*b*) Conjugate [1]: **1.** Ich muß schon früh nach Hause. **2.** Ich werde meinen Freund nicht retten können. **3.** Ich durfte den Gefangenen besuchen. **4.** Noch heute will ich an ihn schreiben.

ÜBERSETZUNG

1. The two men intended to help but they could not. **2.** Schurz was to unlock the gate. **3.** Perhaps Mr. Hensel will want to drive himself. **4.** Will they be able to spend the night at an inn? **5.** You may count the money now. **6.** The keeper was not allowed to speak with the prisoner.

[1] I.e., give the forms of the tense in question.

LESSON THIRTY-SIX

MODAL AUXILIARIES II

186 Idiomatic and Subjunctive Uses of the Auxiliaries.

dürfen: Dürfte ich Sie bitten, *Might I ask you ...*

können: Du kannst gehen, *You may go.*

mögen: Ich möchte in einer größeren Stadt wohnen, *I should like to live in a larger city.*

sollen: Sie sollten das nicht tun, *You ought not to do that.*

This very common meaning of sollen is restricted to the past and past perfect subjunctive. English uses both *should* and *ought to* in this sense.

　　　Er soll reich sein, *He is said to be rich.*

wollen: Er will gehört haben, *He claims to have heard.*

　　　Du willst mich lieben? *You profess to love me?*

　　　Es will regnen, *It is about to rain.*

187 Infinitive and Past Participle.　Compare:

Ich mußte	Ich mußte arbeiten.
Ich habe gemußt	Ich habe arbeiten müssen.
Ich konnte	Ich konnte helfen.
Ich habe gekonnt	Ich habe helfen können.

RULE 1. The past participle of a modal auxiliary becomes an infinitive if another infinitive depends upon it.

RULE 2. Of two infinitives, the one that depends upon the other precedes: Er lernt schwimmen. — Er wird schwimmen lernen. — Er hat fragen können.

188 hätte ... können, hätte ... sollen.　These two idioms, hätte ... können, *could have*, and hätte ... sollen, *should have, ought to have*, are very important and should be practised with a number of infinitives: Ich hätte schreiben können (sollen), etc.

Note.   In the transposed order, the auxiliary here precedes the two infinitives: Wenn ich ihn nur vorher hätte sprechen können ! So when both infinitives are real infinitives: Ich sage, daß ich heute nicht werde ausgehen können, *I am saying that I shall not be able to go out today.*

189 Other Verbs.   There are a few other verbs that, when used with another infinitive, substitute their infinitive for the past participle in the compound tenses. The more common of these are: hören, sehen, helfen, lassen, *to let, cause,* heißen, *to bid.*

> Ich habe die Vögel singen hören.
> Wir haben ihn kommen sehen, *We have seen him come.*
> Er hat mir die Bücher tragen helfen.
> Ich habe meine Brille fallen lassen, *I have dropped my spectacles.*

Here also in the transposed order the auxiliary precedes the two infinitives:

> Weil er mir die Bücher hat tragen helfen.

190 Omitted Verb.   Where the goal is given, a verb of motion is frequently omitted in German after a modal auxiliary. Ich muß nach Hause, *I must go home.* Wir wollen fort, *We want to go away.*   Compare ' We must to ship.'

191 können.   können may mean *to know* when speaking of languages, lessons, poems, rules, etc.: Können Sie Deutsch? Kannst du das Gedicht (auswendig, *by heart*)?   A verb of speaking or saying (Können Sie deutsch sprechen?) is not felt to be understood.

KINKELS BEFREIUNG XII

„Der Beamte," fuhr Brune fort, „der diese Nacht die Wache auf dem oberen Korridor haben sollte, ist krank geworden. Nichts Besseres hätte passieren können, denn nun darf ich statt seiner die Wache haben. Ich könnte Kinkel auf den Söller bringen und ihn an einem Seil aus der Dachluke auf die Straße hinunterlassen. Dazu brauche ich zwar die Zellenschlüssel wieder, aber der Inspektor hätte

sie gestern nicht mit nach Hause nehmen sollen, also wird er sie
diese Nacht gewiß an den rechten Platz legen. Wenn der Herr
Professor keinen Mut zu der Sache hat, so kann er nicht so bald
heraus, fürchte ich." 10

Für Kinkels Mut konnte Schurz bürgen. Er holte nun sofort ein
Seil, das Brune unter seinem Überrock mit ins Gefängnis nahm.

Wie aber konnte man Kinkel nach Rostock bringen? Weder Pferde
noch Wagen würden diese Nacht bereit stehen. Hensel versprach,
sie zu fahren, so weit [1] seine Pferde laufen könnten. 15

Man verabredete nun, die Straße am Zuchthaus in der Nacht von
Vorbeigehenden frei zu halten. An den Ecken wollten Poritz,
Leddihn und einige andre handfeste Männer stehen und, sollte
jemand vorbei wollen, sich betrunken stellen und die Unwill=
kommenen mit lustigen Schnurren zurückhalten. Im Notfalle 20
sollten sie auch Gewalt gebrauchen.

Es könnte auch geschehen, daß das Seil Dachziegel loslöste, die
dann mit Geräusch auf die Straße fallen würden. Hensel sollte
darum am Zuchthause vorbeifahren, um mit dem Rasseln des
Wagens auf dem schlechten Pflaster das Geräusch zu übertönen. 25

VOKABELN

die Dachluke, –n dormer window
der Dachziegel, –s, — (roof) tile
das Geräusch', –es, –e noise, sound
das Pflaster, –s, — pavement
die Schnurre, –n yarn
das Seil, –s, –e rope
der Söller, –s, — garret
der Überrock, –s, ⸚e overcoat
bürgen *wk.* to vouch
fortfahren (ä), u, a to continue
gebrauchen *wk.* to use

loslösen *wk.* to loosen
rasseln *wk.* to rattle
übertö'nen *wk.* to drown, deaden
vorbei'fahren (ä), u, ist vorbei'gefahren
  to drive past
zurück'halten (ä), ie, a to keep back
handfest sturdy, stalwart
schlecht bad
sofort' at once
unwillkommen unwelcome

[1] So joined to an adjective or adverb frequently makes a subordinating
conjunction of it: so weit, *as far as;* so schnell, *as rapidly as.* Compare sobald,
as soon as. Compare so sehr, footnote 1, p. 157.

REDEWENDUNG

ſich betrunken ſtellen to pretend to be drunk

FRAGEN

1. Wann wollte Brune einen zweiten Verſuch machen?
2. Warum dachte er, daß die Schlüſſel dieſe Nacht am rechten
Platz ſein würden? 3. Wie ſollte Kinkel diesmal das Gefängnis
verlaſſen? 4. Wie brachte Brune das Seil ins Gefängnis?
5. Wie konnten Schurz und Kinkel dieſe Nacht fliehen? 6. Wie
wollte man um Mitternacht die Straße frei halten? 7. Was
könnte ein lautes Geräuſch machen? 8. Wie wollte Henſel dies
Geräuſch übertönen?

ÜBUNG

Translate: I have been able; I have been able to run; he
had not wanted; he had not wanted to count the money;
it ought to happen; it ought to have happened; it could
happen; it could have happened; I hear the tiles fall; I
have heard the tiles fall; they let nobody pass; they have
let nobody pass.

ÜBERSETZUNG

1. He could (get) out if he had courage. 2. Schurz should
have thought of everything. 3. Have you seen the horses
run? 4. Several men. could stand on the corners to keep
the street free. 5. They could also have used force.
6. Neither Kinkel nor Schurz knew English. 7. They
must (go) across the Prussian border. 8. If Hensel had
not driven past, the officials could have heard the noise of
the falling tiles.

Drei Kameraden Pg. 68-71

LESSON THIRTY-SEVEN

IMPERSONAL VERBS. LASSEN

192 **Impersonal Verbs.** 1. Common to English and German are impersonal verbs expressing phenomena of nature: Es regnet, *it rains;* es donnert, *it is thundering;* es schneit, *it is snowing;* es hagelt, *it is hailing.* Such verbs are conjugated like other verbs (Es hat gestern geregnet) but used in the third person singular only.

2. Similarly of a physical or mental state: Mich friert, *I am cold;* Es gefällt mir hier, *I like it here;* mich dünkt, *methinks;* Ist dir übel? *Are you ill?*

3. Without parallels in English are: Es klopft, *There is a knock at the door;* es klingelt, *the bell is ringing;* es brennt, *there is a fire;* es tut mir leid, *I am sorry.*

4. Many verbs may be used both the impersonal and personal ways: Es ist mir nicht gelungen (geglückt), ihn zu befreien, *I did not succeed in freeing him,* but Der erste Plan gelang nicht (mißglückte).

193 **Es gibt. Es ist.** Es gibt, *There is, There are,* asserts existence in general or within wide limits; es ist and es sind denote presence in a circumscribed space. As no hard and fast line can be drawn between existence within wide limits and presence in a circumscribed space, there are many cases where either expression may be used:

Es gibt noch viele India'ner in den Vereinigten Staaten, *There are still many Indians in the United States.*

Es waren viele Indianer unter den Zuschauern, *There were many Indians among the spectators.*

Heute gibt's keinen Nachtisch (keine Speise), *There is no dessert to-day.*

Es tut mir leid, daß es heute keinen Nachtisch gibt.

Both es ist and es gibt may be used in other tenses and moods: Früher gab es keine Eisenbahnen, *Formerly there were no railroads.*

NOTE. Apart from meaning, es gibt and es ist show differences of construction:

(*a*) Es gibt always remains singular. Es ist varies its number to agree with the predicate.

(*b*) Es gibt is followed by the accusative case, es ist (sind) by the nominative: Es gibt grünen und schwarzen Tee.

(*c*) Es of es gibt is retained in the inverted and transposed orders, while es of es ist (sind) is omitted: Ich sehe, daß nur ein Stuhl im Zimmer ist.

194 **The Causative lassen.** Lassen means not only *to let, to permit, to leave,* but also *to have some one do something, to have something done.* It may therefore be called the causative auxiliary. It is always followed by the active infinitive.

Ich lasse den Sekretär den Brief abschreiben, *I am having the secretary copy the letter.*
Ich ließ das Lied noch einmal singen, *I had the song sung again.*
Er ließ die Türen schließen, *He had the doors shut.*

Es läßt sich tun - it lets itself do it

KINKELS BEFREIUNG XIII

Um Mitternacht standen alle wieder bereit, Schurz in einem dunklen Torweg dem Zuchthaus gegenüber, die Freunde an den Ecken. Es gefiel Schurz nicht, daß die Nacht so still war. Wenn es nur gestürmt und geregnet hätte!

5 Es waren nur wenige Laternen da, und diese gaben wenig Licht, — elektrisches Licht, sogar Gaslaternen gab es ja damals noch nicht — so daß Schurz die Dachluken kaum sehen konnte. Da erschien das verabredete Zeichen: aus einer der Dachluken fiel ein heller Schein, der sich dreimal auf und ab bewegte. Das war Brunes Laterne.
10 Schnell gab Schurz auch sein Zeichen, indem [1] er Feuer schlug. Eine Sekunde später sah er einen dunklen Körper langsam herunter=

---

[1] indem er . . . schlug, *by striking fire.*

kommen. Was er gefürchtet hatte, geschah: es regnete Dachziegel, die mit großem Lärm auf das Pflaster fielen. Aber schon kam Hensels Wagen rasselnd vorbeigefahren.[1]

Der dunkle Körper hatte den Boden erreicht, schnell war Schurz bei ihm. Ja, es war der Freund, da stand er lebendig auf seinen Beinen. 15

„Das ist eine kühne Tat!“ war sein erstes Wort.

„Gott sei Dank!“ antwortete Schurz. „Nun schnell das Seil ab und dann fort!“ Vergeblich versuchte er, den Knoten des Seils zu 20 lösen. „Es tut mir leid,“ sagte Kinkel, „ich kann dir nicht helfen, denn meine Hände sind ganz blutig.“ Schließlich gelang es Schurz, das Seil mit einem Messer zu zerschneiden. Kinkel ließ sich den Mantel umwerfen, blickte aber angstvoll nach dem umkehrenden Wagen und den dunklen Gestalten, die näher kamen. „Unser 25 Wagen und unsre Freunde!“ beruhigte ihn Schurz.

In einiger Entfernung sangen Männerstimmen: „Wir [2] sitzen so fröhlich beisammen.“ — „Was ist denn das?“ fragte Kinkel. — „Deine Kerkermeister bei einer Bowle Punsch!“ — „Famos!“ In Krügers Gasthaus feierte man heute nacht Geburtstag, unter 30 den Gästen waren mehrere Zuchthausbeamte. Man hatte einen Punsch brauen lassen, den Krüger besonders gut (*strong*) gemacht hatte.

Während Kinkel im Gasthaus einen schwarzen Anzug und einen großen Bärenpelz anzog und eine Mütze aufsetzte, trat Krüger ins 35 Zimmer mit einigen gefüllten Gläsern. „Herr Professor, im Nebenzimmer sitzen einige Ihrer Gefängnisbeamten beim Punsch. Ich habe sie eben gefragt, ob sie mir ein Glas erlauben wollten für ein paar Berliner Freunde. Sie hatten nichts dagegen. Nun trinken wir Ihr erstes Wohl aus der Bowle Ihrer Kerkermeister!“ 40

[1] See §145.
[2] A jovial student song. The second line runs: „Und haben einander so lieb.“

VOKABELN

der Anzug, –s, ⸗e suit
der Bärenpelz, –es, –e bear-fur coat
das Bein, –es, –e leg
der Boden, –s, ⸗ ground
die Bowle (pron. without the w), –n bowl
die Entfer'nung, –en distance
die Gas'later'ne, –n gas street-lamp
der Kerkermeister, –s, — jailer
der Knoten, –s, — knot
der Körper, –s, — body
die Männerstimme, –n male voice
die Mütze, –n cap
der Punsch, –es punch
das Zeichen, –s, — sign, signal
aufsetzen wk. to put on (hat)

beruhigen wk. to reassure, quiet
sich bewegen wk. to move
blicken wk. to look
erlauben wk., w. dat. of person to permit
füllen wk. to fill
lösen wk. to loosen
regnen wk. to rain
stürmen wk. to storm (of wind)
zerschneiden, i, i to cut in two
ab off; auf und ab up and down
beisam'men together
blutig bloody
gegenü'ber opposite
kühn bold
leben'dig living, alive

FRAGEN

1. Warum wünschte Schurz, daß es in dieser Nacht stürmte und regnete? 2. Welche Zeichen hatten Brune und Schurz verabredet? 3. Was machte dem geretteten Kinkel große Angst? 4. Wo kamen die Männerstimmen her? 5. Wer war unter denen, die in Krügers Gasthaus tranken und sangen? 6. Was zog Kinkel an, und was setzte er auf? 7. Warum hatte Krüger den Punsch so gut gemacht? 8. Womit trank man auf Kinkels Wohl?

ÜBUNGEN

(a) Translate and put in the tenses of the indicative (excepting the fut. pft.) and in the present, past, and past perfect subjunctive: He has a carriage come. (b) Conjugate: 1. I have succeeded. 2. I like it (gefallen).

ÜBERSETZUNG

1. Do you know whether there was electric light at that time? 2. We are glad (froh) that there were no people on the street. 3. Was there a wedding at Krüger's inn? — No, there were men there who were celebrating a birthday. 4. They had a bowl of punch brewed. 5. There is no water in the glasses. 6. He will not succeed in loosening the knot. 7. Krüger had had a black suit brought for Kinkel. 8. If it storms no one will hear the noise in the street.

LESSON THIRTY-EIGHT

INDIRECT DISCOURSE

195 Indirect Discourse. *He said they were friends.* The report of a spoken or written statement, thought, or question in an object clause after a verb of saying, thinking, or asking in the main clause is called indirect discourse.

196 Subjunctive in Indirect Discourse.

Direct statement: Ich habe den Schlüssel.
Indirect statement: Brune sagte, daß er den Schlüssel hätte (habe), or Brune sagte, er hätte (habe) den Schlüssel.

1. German uses the subjunctive in indirect discourse for the purpose of reporting a statement without stating it as a fact or vouching for the truth of it. For the use of present or past subjunctive see below.

2. As shown in the example above, the object clause may stand without the conjunction baß. If so, the normal word order follows. In general this use without baß is preferable.

3. Clauses dependent on verbs of asking are introduced by ob, or by any pronoun or adverb that can introduce a direct question (wer, was, wie, wo, wann, etc.). Being dependent clauses, these indirect questions take the transposed word order. Haben Sie den Schlüssel? becomes Schurz fragte Brune, ob er den Schlüssel hätte (habe).

197 Indicative in Indirect Discourse.

1. Schurz wußte, daß es gefährlich war. German uses the indicative in indirect discourse after verbs or phrases implying certainty, such as wissen, zeigen, sehen, beweisen (*prove*), es ist klar, etc.

2. Ich sage dir, daß es möglich ist or Ich sage dir, es ist möglich. When the verb of saying, thinking, asking is in the first person singular, present tense, the speaker thus expressing his own present conviction, the indicative is retained.

3. Schurz denkt, daß alles verloren ist. — Der Freund fragt, wer helfen will. After a governing verb in the present tense, second or third person, the indicative is also becoming more and more common in the spoken language. Verbs of asking in the present tense always take the indicative.

198 Survey of Tenses in Indirect Discourse.

DIRECT	INDIRECT
Present	Present or Past Subj.
Past	**Pres. Perf. or Past Perf. Subj.**
Present Perfect	Pres. Perf. or Past Perf. Subj.
Past Perfect	Past Perf. Subj.
Future	Fut. Subj. or Pres. Conditional
(Imperative)	Pres. or Past Subj. of sollen or mögen

EXAMPLES

Direct: Mein Freund sagte zu mir: „Du hast recht."
Indirect: Mein Freund sagte zu mir, daß ich recht hätte (habe).

Direct: Er sagte zu mir: „Du hattest recht."
Indirect: Er sagte zu mir, ich hätte (ich habe) recht gehabt.

Direct: Schurz fragte Krüger: „Hat der Mann geschwiegen?"
Indirect: Schurz fragte Krüger, ob der Mann geschwiegen hätte (habe).

Direct: Hensel sagte: „Ich werde vorbeifahren."
Indirect: Hensel sagte, er werde (würde) vorbeifahren.

Direct: Krüger bat die Beamten: „Bitte, geben Sie mir ein Glas Punsch für meine Freunde!"
Indirect: Krüger bat die Beamten, sie möchten ihm ein Glas Punsch für seine Freunde geben.

199 **Rules.** Observe, accordingly, the following rules in changing from direct to indirect discourse:

1. With the exceptions noted below, use, in general, the same tense that was or would have been used in direct discourse.

2. Or, follow, as in English, the sequence of tenses, i.e., after a governing verb in the past tense use a past tense in the subordinate clause.

3. Change the Past of the direct discourse to Pres. Perf. or Past Perf. Subj. of indirect discourse.

4. If the form of the subjunctive happens to be the same as that of the indicative, use the other possible tense.

5. The present, present perf., and future subjunctive are formal and are therefore used less and less in the spoken language.

6. The imperative becomes a form of sollen or mögen (more polite): Ich sagte, Sie sollten (möchten) hier bleiben.

I told him "Go Home"

" " " , that he should go home

KINKELS BEFREIUNG XIV

Schurz und Kinkel sprangen in Hensels Wagen, und fort ging es, so schnell die Braunen traben konnten, zuerst in der Richtung nach Hamburg, damit Verfolger glauben sollten, sie wären dorthin geflohen; bald aber bog Hensel in die Straße nach Rostock ein.

5 Kinkel erzählte, daß die Nacht vorher die schrecklichste seines Lebens gewesen wäre. Als es eins schlug und Brune noch nicht da war, glaubte er, er sei dem Wahnsinn nahe. Auch diese Nacht sei die Rettung beinahe mißglückt. Brune habe den falschen Schlüssel zu der Gittertür gebraucht, ohne zu wissen, daß er den richtigen auch 10 in der Hand hielt. Schließlich habe er eine Art geholt und mit lauten Schlägen die Stäbe der Tür auseinander gebogen. Auf einem Korridor hätten sie einen Beamten, der nicht im Geheimnis war,[1] vorbeilassen müssen. Nun aber, schloß Kinkel, habe er als einzige Wunde nach einem so harten Kampf und großen Sieg seine 15 blutigen Hände, die von dem Seil ganz zerschunden waren.

Nachdem die Pferde acht deutsche Meilen zurückgelegt hatten, wurde es klar, daß man halten mußte, um sie zu füttern und ihnen eine kurze Rast zu geben. Am Morgen, als man über die preußische Grenze war, wusch Hensel sie im ersten Gasthaus mit warmem 20 Wasser, was auf (for) kurze Zeit ein wenig half. Am Nachmittag, nach einer Fahrt von mehr als dreizehn Meilen, erreichten die Flüchtlinge Neustrelitz, wo sie an dem Stadtrichter Petermann einen begeisterten Freund und Helfer hatten. Hier nahmen sie Abschied von dem treuen Hensel. Seine beiden schönen Braunen 25 hatten sich niedergelegt, sobald sie in den Stall kamen, — einer, um nicht wieder aufzustehen.

Bei Petermann gab es ein gutes Essen und einen herrlichen Wein, wozu er einige Freunde eingeladen hatte. Schurz fürchtete, Peter=mann werde aus Freude über Kinkels Befreiung nicht schweigen 30 können. Dann ließ Petermann Wagen und Pferde kommen, fuhr mit, und am nächsten Morgen, am 8. November, erreichten sie Rostock.

---

[1] Schurz uses this phrase: nicht um (about) das Geheimnis wußte is better.

VOKABELN

die Axt, ⸚e axe
der Braune *adj. infl.* bay horse
die Raft, –en rest
die Rettung, –en rescue
die Richtung, –en direction
der Schlag, –es, ⸚e blow
der Sieg, –es, –e victory
der Stab, –es, ⸚e stave, bar
der Stadtrichter, –s, — city judge
der Verfolger, –s, — pursuer
der Wahnsinn, –s insanity
die Wunde, –n wound
biegen, o, o to bend
einbiegen, o, ist eingebogen to turn

mitfahren (ä), u, ift mitgefahren to
drive along
sich niederlegen *wk.* to lie down
traben *wk.* to trot
vorbeilassen (ä), ie, a to let pass
zerschinden, zerschindete, zerschunden
to skin
zurücklegen *wk.* to put behind one
(of distance)
auseinander apart
begeistert enthusiastic
einzig only *adj.*
hart hard

FRAGEN

1. Warum fuhr Hensel zuerst in der Richtung nach Hamburg?
2. Was sagte Kinkel von der Nacht vorher? 3. Warum konnte
Brune die Gittertür nicht aufschließen? 4. Wie kam Kinkel doch
heraus? 5. Welche Wunde hatte Kinkel in dem Kampf bekom=
men? 6. Was ist eine deutsche Meile? 7. Wie weit ist Neustre=
litz von Spandau? 8. Wer sorgte nun weiter für die Flüchtlinge?
9. Was geschah mit Hensels Pferden? 10. Am wievielten
kamen die Flüchtlinge in Rostock an?

ÜBUNGEN

(a) Put into indirect discourse: 1. Hensel sagte: „Ich muß
die Pferde füttern." 2. Schurz fragt: „Wieviel Meilen ist es von
Spandau nach Neustrelitz?" 3. Kinkel erzählte: „Niemand kam,
und ich war dem Wahnsinn nahe." 4. „Fahren Sie durch die
Straße!" sagte Schurz zu Kinkel. 5. Brune wußte: „Jetzt ist
unten alles bereit." (b) Put into direct discourse: 1. Schurz
fragte Brune, ob er schweigen könne. 2. Man sagte ihnen später,
daß Hensel eins seiner Pferde verloren habe. 3. Krüger bat die
Gäste, sie möchten ihm etwas Punsch für seine Freunde geben.

ÜBERSETZUNG

1. The pursuers thought the fugitives were on their (the) way to Hamburg. 2. I did not know that I had the right key. 3. The official went past without seeing them. 4. Kinkel said his bloody hands were a slight (leicht) wound for such a great victory. 5. Schurz wrote that they had gone across the Prussian frontier in the morning. 6. I think it is clear.

LESSON THIRTY-NINE

REFLEXIVE VERBS

200 Reflexive Verbs. A verb like *to wash oneself* is called a reflexive verb because the action of the subject is exerted upon itself.

Many German verbs can be used reflexively only (ſich ſchämen), others are reflexive and non-reflexive (waſchen and ſich waſchen).

201 German and English reflexives differ in two respects.

1. Ich waſche mich, du wäſcht (wäſchſt) dich. In the first and second persons, German uses the simple personal pronouns.

2. Er wäſcht ſich, ſie wäſcht ſich, ſie waſchen ſich, Sie waſchen ſich. For the third person, German has a special form ſich. It is used for all genders, both numbers, and dative and accusative.

Du ſchmeichelſt dir, *you flatter yourself.* With verbs that take the dative, the reflexive also stands in the dative.

202 Conjugation. Reflexive verbs use haben as auxiliary. Paradigms, ſich ſchämen, *to be ashamed* and ſich an'ziehen, *to dress oneself.*

INDICATIVE

Present ich ſchäme mich	ich ziehe mich an
du ſchämſt dich	du ziehſt dich an
er ſchämt ſich	er zieht ſich an
wir ſchämen uns	wir ziehen uns an
ihr ſchämt euch	ihr zieht euch an
ſie ſchämen ſich	ſie ziehen ſich an

Past ich ſchämte mich	ich zog mich an
Pres. Perf. ich habe mich geſchämt	ich habe mich angezogen
Past Perf. ich hatte mich geſchämt	ich hatte mich angezogen
Future ich werde mich ſchämen	ich werde mich anziehen
Fut. Perf. ich werde mich geſchämt haben	ich werde mich angezogen haben

IMPERATIVE

ſchäme dich, ſchämt euch, ſchämen Sie ſich	ziehe dich an, zieht euch an, ziehen Sie ſich an

The Subjunctive and Conditional moods are similarly formed. See Appendix, pp. 218, 219.

203 ſelber, ſelbſt, *-self, -selves,* are invariable. They follow the noun or pronoun to which they refer: Schurz ſelbſt, *Schurz himself;* wir ſelber, *we ourselves.* They are sometimes used with the reflexive pronouns, for emphasis: Du ſchadeſt dir ſelber, nicht mir, *You are hurting yourself, not me.*

Before a noun or pronoun, ſelbſt means *even* and is a synonym of ſogar': ſelbſt er, *even he;* ſelbſt Schurz, *even Schurz.*

204 einan'der. The reciprocal relation, as in 'They love *each other*' is expressed by einander, which is invariable. However, the plural reflexive pronouns (uns, euch, sich) are also very commonly used reciprocally: Wir sehen uns bald wieder, *We shall meet again soon.* Einander is always reciprocal.

NOTE. Prepositions combine to form one word with einander: miteinander, durcheinander.

KINKELS BEFREIUNG XV

In Rostock holte Petermann sofort Moritz Wiggers, Schurz' Freund, einen bedeutenden Bürger der Stadt, der sich herzlich über Kinkels Rettung freute. „Ein Freund von mir," sagte Wiggers, „der reiche Kaufmann Brockelmann, will Sie beide auf einem seiner
5 eignen Schiffe nach England bringen lassen. Auf den können wir uns fest verlassen." Brockelmann kam, und die drei begrüßten sich, als ob sie alte Freunde wären.

Bis das Schiff, die „Kleine Anna", segelfertig und der Wind günstig war, wohnten Kinkel und Schurz in Brockelmanns
10 gastlichem Hause. Selbst Kinkel fing an, sich von der schrecklichen Zeit im Gefängnis zu erholen. Schurz erinnerte sich sein Leben lang, wie liebevoll die Familie und ihre Freunde sich den Flücht-lingen widmeten, wie die Hausfrau den Gästen die köstlichsten Leckerbissen vorsetzte und wie sie selber Kinkels verwundete Hände
15 wusch und verband. Auch wurde im Hause abends gut musiziert,[1] worüber die beiden sich sehr freuten.

Am 17. November gingen die Flüchtlinge an Bord (*aboard*). Die „Kleine Anna" war ein Segelschiff von etwa 80 Tonnen, das eine Ladung Weizen nach Newcastle bringen sollte. „Wann werden
20 wir wohl (*I wonder*) zurückkehren?" fragten sich die beiden, als sie hinten auf dem Deck standen, bis der letzte Streifen deutscher Küste verschwunden war.

[1] Impersonal passive, an anticipation of §210, *there was good music . . . .*

Anfangs ging alles gut, eine leichte Brise schwellte die Segel, und die „Kleine Anna" glitt sanft durch die wenig aufgeregten Wellen. Aber schon am nächsten Morgen war Kinkel seekrank. Das Wetter 25 wurde immer schlimmer, und Kinkel wurde immer kränker. Schurz, der sich sehr wohl fühlte, versuchte umsonst, ihn aufzumuntern. Kinkel glaubte, daß er sterben müsse. War er seinen Feinden entkommen, um hier elend zu verenden?

VOKABELN

die Brise, –n breeze	gleiten, i, ist geglitten to glide
der Bürger, –s, — citizen	schwellen wk. to swell, fill
das Deck, –es, –e deck	verbinden, a, u to bandage, dress
der Feind, –es, –e enemy	verenden wk., aux. sein to die, perish
die Hausfrau, –en housewife	sich verlassen (ä), ie, a to rely (on,
die Ladung, –en load, cargo	auf w. accus.)
der Leckerbissen, –s, — tidbit	vorsetzen wk. to set before
das Schiff, –es, –e ship	sich widmen wk. to devote o.s.
das Segel, –s, — sail	zurückkehren wk., aux. sein to return
der Streifen, –s, — strip	anfangs in the beginning
die Tonne, –n ton	bedeutend important
der Weizen, –s wheat	elend miserable
der Wind, –es, –e wind	fest firmly, thoroughly
aufmuntern wk. to cheer (up)	gastlich hospitable
sich begrüßen wk. to greet each other	günstig favorable
entkommen, a, ist entkommen to escape	hinten behind, in the rear
	leicht light
sich erholen wk. to recuperate	liebevoll loving
sich erinnern wk. to remember	sanft gentle
sich freuen to rejoice, be glad (at über w. accus.)	segelfertig ready to sail
sich fühlen wk. to feel	wohl well

FRAGEN

1. Wer war Wiggers? 2. Wie wollte Brockelmann die beiden nach England bringen lassen? 3. Warum konnten sie nicht sofort fahren? 4. In wessen Hause wohnten sie, bis sie reisen konnten? 5. Was für ein Schiff war es, und wie hieß es?

6. Wie war die Fahrt zuerst? 7. Wie fühlte sich Kinkel am nächsten Morgen? 8. Wie fühlte sich Schurz? 9. Was fürchtete Kinkel? 10. Können Sie das verstehen, oder sind Sie noch nie seekrank gewesen?

ÜBUNGEN

(a) Translate: We greet each other; beside each other; he himself; even the housewife; she washes herself; she herself washes his hands; do you remember? rejoice; I feel well; he will recuperate. (b) Translate and conjugate: I relied on him. — I buy myself a cap.

ÜBERSETZUNG

1. Even Brockelmann's friends devoted themselves to the fugitives. 2. On the seventeenth of November they took leave from each other. 3. I know you (ihr) will see each other again. 4. We could have stayed (wohnen) in their hospitable home. 5. He has them taken to Newcastle as soon as the wind is favorable. 6. Kinkel soon began to feel miserable. 7. He wrote that he had always remembered those days (an w. accus.). 8. Your friends are faithful, you can rely on them.

LESSON FORTY

PASSIVE VOICE

205 **Active and Passive** may be contrasted as follows:

Father pays the bill, Der Vater bezahlt die Rechnung.
The bill is (being) paid by father, Die Rechnung wird von dem Vater bezahlt.
Father has paid the bill, Der Vater hat die Rechnung bezahlt.
The bill has been paid by father, Die Rechnung ist von dem Vater bezahlt worden.

It will be noticed that

1. The agent is expressed by von (English *by*).

2. The auxiliary is werden (in English *to be*).

3. The participle in the perfect tenses becomes worden.

206 **Conjugation.** The conjugation of a German passive follows:

INDICATIVE

Pres. ich werde gerufen, I am (being) called

Past ich wurde gerufen, I was (being) called

Pres. Pft. ich bin gerufen worden, I have been called

Past Pft. ich war gerufen worden, I had been called

Fut. ich werde gerufen werden, I shall be called

Fut. Pft. ich werde gerufen worden sein, I shall have been called

NOTE that German says gerufen werden and gerufen worden, English *be called* and *been called*. For the Subjunctive, Conditional, etc., see App., pp. 216, 217.

207 **werden.** Note three uses of werden:

1. As a separate verb: Wir werden beide alt, *We are both getting old.* It is often followed by zu: Der Wind wurde zum (*developed into*) Sturm.

2. To express the future: Ich werde dich abholen, *I shall come for you.*

3. In the passive, as above.

208 Use of the Passive. Instead of the passive, we often find in German:

1. The active with man: Man sagt, *It is said.*

2. Reflexives: Das macht sich leicht, *That is easily done.*

209 True and False Passive. German makes a sharp distinction between:

Die Rechnung wird bezahlt and Die Rechnung ist bezahlt.

The first is a *process* and the true passive, meaning that at this moment some one is paying the bill. The false passive, on the other hand, is a *result* and means that the bill is a paid bill.

Das Haus wird gebaut (process: men are at work on it).
Das Haus ist gebaut (result: it is finished).
Das Haus wird verkauft (process: I can hear the auctioneer).
Das Haus ist verkauft (result: it is sold).

210 Intransitive Verbs form an impersonal passive:

[handwritten: Es wurde Hause gut musizirt]

Man musizierte gut im Hause becomes Im Hause wurde gut musiziert.
Er hilft mir   becomes Mir wird von ihm geholfen.
Die Mutter hilft dem Schüler becomes Dem Schüler wird von der Mutter ge=
                                                                holfen.

[handwritten left margin: antworten / folgen / helfen / denken]

211 Transitive Verbs used without an object can also form an impersonal passive:

Man sang und tanzte becomes Es wurde gesungen und getanzt.
                    There was dancing and singing.
Similarly: Um Antwort wird gebeten (abbrev. U.A.w.g.).
           An answer is requested (R.s.v.p.).

[handwritten bottom: when a verb requires an indirect object (the dative) / Dative must be kept up in passive voice / Gott hilft dir. — Dir wird von Gott geholfen. —]

KINKELS BEFREIUNG XVI

Der Wind wurde zum Sturm, noch ehe die „Kleine Anna“ um
Dänemark herum in die Nordsee kam. Wie eine Nußschale wurde
sie umhergeworfen, die See wusch Tag und Nacht über das Deck,
und es war ein Wunder, daß das Schiff von den dagegen donnernden
Wogen nicht zerschmettert wurde. Kinkel blieb mehrere Tage 5
seekrank, erholte sich aber dann trotz des Sturmes und begann, wie
Schurz, sich für die Schönheit des wütenden Meeres zu interessieren.
„Mir wurde nun vergeben“, schreibt Schurz, „daß ich mich über
sein Elend lustig gemacht hatte.“

Zehn Tage dauerte das böse Wetter. Die „Kleine Anna“ war 10
ganz von ihrem Wege abgetrieben worden, und da der Himmel
immer mit Wolken bedeckt war, konnten keine Beobachtungen
gemacht werden. Selbst der Kapitän wußte tagelang nicht, wo sie
sich befanden. Als der Himmel sich endlich klärte, steuerte er auf
Newcastle zu, wurde aber wieder abgetrieben und landete schließlich 15
nach weiteren vier Tagen in Leith, dem Hafen von Edinburg in
Schottland.

Dem Leser, der sich für Schurz’ und Kinkels weitere Schicksale
interessiert, wird geraten, Schurz’ Buch selbst zu lesen. Hier sei nur
noch gesagt, daß Kinkel mit seiner Familie in England blieb, bis 20
ihm durch eine Amnestie’ des Königs von Preußen im Jahre 1866
die Tore des Vaterlands wieder geöffnet wurden. Schurz ging
1852 nach Amerika und besuchte Deutschland zum erstenmale
wieder im Jahre 1862, auf der Rückfahrt nach Amerika von
Spanien (*Spain*), wohin er von Präsident Lincoln als Gesandter 25
der Vereinigten Staaten geschickt worden war.

Und Brune? Er war als Helfer bei Kinkels Befreiung entdeckt
und zu drei Jahren Gefängnis verurteilt worden. Nachdem er
seine Strafe verbüßt hatte, zog er mit seiner Familie nach seiner
Heimat Westfalen, wo er als geachteter Bürger ein hohes Alter 30
erreichte. Die anderen Mithelfer wurden freigesprochen.

VOKABELN

das Alter, –s age, old age; **ein hohes Alter,** a ripe old age
die Beob'achtung, –en observation
das Elend, –s misery
der Gesand'te *adj. infl.* minister, envoy
der Hafen, –s, ⸗ harbor
die Heimat, –en home [1]
der Kapitän', –s, –e captain
der Leser, –s, — reader
das Meer, –es, –e ocean
der Mithelfer, –s, — accomplice
die Nordsee North Sea
die Nußschale, –n nutshell
der Präsident', –en, –en president
das Schicksal, –s, –e fate, fortune
die Schönheit, –en beauty
der Sturm, –es, ⸗e storm
die Vereinigten Staaten the United States

die Woge, –n (turbulent) wave
die Wolke, –n cloud
das Wunder, –s, — miracle
abtreiben, ie, ie to drive off
bedecken *wk.* to cover
sich befinden to be (somewhere or somehow)
freisprechen (i), a, o to acquit
sich klären *wk.* to clear up
umher'werfen (i), a, o to throw about
vergeben (i), a, e to forgive *w. dat. of person*
verur'teilen *wk.* to condemn
zerschmettern *wk.* to crush
zusteuern *wk.* to steer for, head for
noch ehe even before
tagelang for days
um . . . herum around
wütend raging

REDEWENDUNG

sich lustig machen über to make fun of

FRAGEN

1. Wie nennt man einen starken Wind? 2. Wie lange dauerte das böse Wetter? 3. Wo befand sich die „Kleine Anna", als das Wetter besser wurde? 4. Wieviel Tage dauerte die ganze Reise? 5. Bis wann blieb Kinkel in England? 6. Wohin wurde Schurz von Präsident Lincoln geschickt? 7. Was wurde nach Kinkels Befreiung mit Brune getan? 8. Wohin zog er, als er aus dem Gefängnis kam? 9. Starb er jung, oder wurde er ein alter Mann? 10. Wo kann man mehr über Schurz' und Kinkels Leben lesen?

[1] Not to be used for a house, which in this sense is **Heim.**

ÜBUNGEN

(a) Change to the passive voice: Die Wogen zerschmettern das Schiff. **2.** Der Kapitän machte Beobachtungen. **3.** Präsident Lincoln hat Schurz nach Spanien geschickt. **4.** Die Freunde werden Kinkel befreien. **5.** Man riet mir ... **6.** Wir werden dir helfen. *(b)* Translate: **1.** Um sechs wird gegessen. **2.** Im Nebenzimmer wurde gesungen und getrunken. **3.** Sonnabends wird um zwölf geschlossen. **4.** Im Hause darf nicht geraucht werden. **5.** Beim Polterabend wurde früher geschossen.

ÜBERSETZUNG

1. The sky is covered with clouds, we cannot make observations. **2.** The Little Anna will be thrown about like a nutshell. **3.** After the harbor was reached they went on (an) land with each other. **4.** Not much more can be told, you must read it yourself. **5.** You are forgiven, said Kinkel. **6.** He was allowed (erlauben, w. dat.) to return to his homeland. **7.** While Kinkel was let down with the rope Hensel drove by. **8.** Brune could not be acquitted.

FINAL REVIEW AND SURVEY

1. Pronounce: Knabe, gnädig, diesseits, Beispiel, Einstein.

2. Of noch and jetzt, which is *yet*, which *now?*

3. Geld ist heutzutage kaum Gold.

4. Ich bitte dich. — Ich frage dich zum letztenmal. — How do you say " Please " in German? How " Many thanks "?

5. Er war heute bei mir. — Besonders von dir eingeladen?

6. Er stand neben mir.

7. Er fuhr fast zu schnell.

8. Falsch: Ich habe zwei Uhren auf ihn gewartet.

9. Ist das jüngste von vier Kindern das vierte oder das Viertel?

10. Vor drei Tagen heißt auf englisch . . .

11. Ein armer Student ist einer, der . . .
Ein schlechter Student ist einer, der . . .

12. Jener Mann, jedermann. — schicken, schenken. — zu Hause, nach Hause. — vor, bevor. — nach, nachdem.

13. Was bedeutet: ausgehen, aussterben, mitsingen, hinauslaufen, herunternehmen, beantworten, betreten, entfliehen, entreißen, ergreifen, erheiraten, erkämpfen, verblühen, verbrennen, zerdrücken, zertreten?

14. Falsch: Der Mann ich fragte, wußte es nicht.
Richtig: Der Mann, den ich fragte, wußte es nicht.

15. „Ich sage dir, es ist gefährlich." Warum steht ‚ist' nicht am Ende?

16. Zu übersetzen: (a) 1. He is working. 2. That I did not say. 3. All were silent. 4. The cook was called Ella. 5. She was called into the room.

(b) 1. Brune was to find the key. 2. He could not find it. 3. He did not dare make noise. 4. You ought to read Schurz' memoirs. 5. I should like to read them. 6. I intend to read them during the vacation. 7. You could have asked once more. 8. I should have asked once more.

17. Im Eßzimmer wird gegessen. — Im Lesezimmer . . . — Im Spielzimmer . . . — Im Studierzimmer . . . — Im Rauchzimmer . . . und Karten . . .

18. Der Schornsteinfeger[1] (*chimney sweep*) kommt auf den Hof und ruft: „Morgen früh wird gefegt!"

Wenn mancher Mann wüßte, wer mancher Mann wär',
Gäb' mancher Mann manchem Mann manchmal mehr Ehr'.

[1] The owner of the apartment building has chimneys cleaned periodically.

APPENDIX

PRONUNCIATION

SILENT LETTERS. Except for h when it shows vowel length and of e in ie (= long i), there are no silent letters. Thus f and p are pronounced in Knie, *knee,* and Pneu, *pneumatic tire.*

VOWELS

QUANTITY. German long vowels are longer than English long vowels, short vowels shorter. Basic rules are:

1. A vowel is always short when followed by a double consonant, i.e., one and the same consonant doubled: Mann, *man;* Neffe, *nephew;* kommen, *to come.*

2. A vowel is long when doubled or followed by h. Such an h is silent: Paar, *pair;* Sohn, *son;* Stuhl, *chair.*

3. A syllable is said to be *open* if it ends in a vowel, *closed* if it ends in a consonant. A stem vowel in an open syllable is always long: Fe=der, *pen;* Va=ter, *father;* o=der, *or;* a=ber, *but.* (A single consonant between vowels always goes with the next syllable.)

4. If a stem vowel, in the course of inflection, occurs in both open and closed syllables, it is a long vowel. Thus the a of Tag, *day,* is long since the plural is Tage (Ta=ge), where the a stands in an open syllable. Similarly, er fragte (frag=te), *he asked,* since the infinitive is fra=gen.

5. In general, a vowel followed by one consonant is long, by two or more consonants, short, but to this rule there are many exceptions. Long: nur, *only;* ſchon, *already;* ſtets, *always.* Short: Bank, *bench;* und, *and;* es, *it.*

In this book, vowels have in doubtful cases been marked − (long) and ᴗ (short). — A correct pronunciation can be acquired only through the ear, and the English equivalents of German sounds given below are in many cases merely approximations.

PRONUNCIATION. The vowels are pronounced as follows:

ā is like the *a* in *art:* ja, *yes;* haben, *to have.*

ă is like the *a* in *artistic:* Bank, *bench;* was? *what?*

ē is like *ey* in *they:* Feder, *pen;* geben, *to give.*

ĕ is the *e* in *let:* es, *it;* Neſt, *nest.*

e in an unaccented syllable is slurred like *a* in *comma:* Tinte, *ink;* Mutter, *mother.* Do not pronounce it like *ay* in *outlay.*

ī (usually written ie) is like *e* in *me:* wie? *how?* hier, *here.*

ĭ is the *i* of *it:* Tinte, *ink;* Winter, *winter.*

ō is like the *o* in *know:* groß, *great;* rot, *red.*

ŏ resembles the *o* of *forty:* Sommer, *summer;* dort, *there.*

ū is like *oo* in *boot,* but with more protrusion of the lips: Fuß, *foot;* Bruder, *brother.*

ŭ is like *oo* in *foot,* but with the lips more protruded: jung, *young;* Mutter, *mother.*

y occurs mostly in words taken from Greek. The choicer pronunciation is ü but i is also heard: Ypſilon (name of the letter), *y;* Symbōl', *symbol.*

Umlaut. The term umlaut means a modification of the vowels α, o, u to ä, ö, ü; and of the diphthong αu to äu. The same change is found in such English plurals as *feet, geese, men, mice, teeth.* The pronunciation is as follows:

ä long is like *ei* in *their:* ſpät, *late;* Mädchen, *girl.*

ä short is the same as e (as in *let*): Hände, *hands;* Blätter, *leaves.*

ö long does not exist in English. Students who cannot acquire the sound through imitation may produce it by pronouncing long e and rounding the lips as for long o: hören, *to hear;* böſe, *evil.*

ö short also has no English counterpart. To produce it, hold the tongue in position for short e and then round the lips, but less decidedly than for long ö: öffnen, *to open;* Körper, *body;* Löffel, *spoon.*

ü long does not exist in English. Pronounce long i and round the lips as if for long u: grün, *green;* grüßen, *to greet;* müde, *tired.*

ü short also has no English equivalent. Hold the tongue in position for short i and then round the lips but less decidedly than for long ü: fünf, *five;* hübſch, *pretty.*

äu. See below under Diphthongs.

Diphthongs. There are three diphthongs in German: ei, αu, and eu or äu. " They are shorter than the corresponding English ones: not drawled, but staccato (snappy)." (Bloomfield.)

ei, for which αi also occurs in a few words, is short α + short ι, resembling the English *i* in *mine:* mein, *mine;* ſein, *his;* Mai, *May.*

Caution

Do not confuse ei and ie.
Associate ei with such names as Rhein, Heidelberg.
For ie compare English *brief, grief, lief*.
The final letters of ei and of ie, as pronounced in English,
give the German values.

ei as *i* in *mine*

ie as *e* in *even*

au is like *ou* in *house:* Haus, *house;* Auge, *eye.*

eu approaches *oi* in *oil:* heute, *to-day;* Leute, *people.*

äu, the umlaut of **au,** is the same sound as **eu:** Häuser, *houses;* Gebäu'de, *building.*

CONSONANTS

Voiced and Voiceless Consonants. A consonant is called *voiced* if, while the consonant is uttered, the vocal chords vibrate. If they do not vibrate, it is called *voiceless.* Thus, in English, *p, t, k, f, s* are voiceless consonants, and *b, d, g, v, z* are the corresponding voiced consonants.

To observe the vibration of the vocal chords, alternate *s* with *z,* stopping the ears. The buzz with *z* is caused by the vibration of the vocal chords.

Final Consonants. In German the voiced consonants b, d, g, v at the end of a word or syllable, or when standing next to a voiceless consonant, become voiceless. Thus b is pronounced as p, in ob, *whether;* ihr habt, *you have;* and d as t in und, *and;* Geld, *money;* g as f in Tag, *day;* v as f in Nerv, *nerve.*

Double Consonants. Double consonants are pronounced like single consonants. They merely indicate that the preceding vowel is short.

Pronunciation. The individual consonants are pronounced as follows:

b as *b* in *bank:* Baum, *tree;* aber, *but.* Pronounce *p* in lieb, *dear;* gibt, *gives;* Obst, *fruit.*

c occurs only in foreign words. It is pronounced

(a) as *k* before a, o, u: Café, café.

(b) as *ts* (= German z) before other vowels (e, i, ä, ö, y): Cäsar, *Cæsar;* Cicero (pron. *tseetsero*).

ch is produced by the friction of breath between the tongue and the palate. The point of friction is fixed by the position the tongue has taken for the preceding vowel. Two such points are distinguished, the back after a, o, u, au, and the front after the other vowels (e, i, ä, ö, ü, ei, eu, äu) and after a consonant. For short these are called the ach-sound and the ich-sound.

(a) The ach-sound is produced between the back of the tongue and the soft palate. " The sound may best be learned by whispering ' koo ' . . . and dwelling on the sound that follows the *k* "[1] or repeat, in very rapid succession, the *k*-sound: k-k-k-k . . ., and then instead of stopping the passage of breath with each successive *k* allow it to pass on with friction: ach, *oh;* Dach, *roof;* doch, *yet;* noch, *still;* Buch, *book;* auch, *also;* machen, *to make;* kochen, *to cook;* Kuchen, *cake.*

(b) The ich-sound " may best be learned by whispering ' key ' and dwelling on the sound that follows the *k* ": ich, *I;* mich, *me;* dich, *thee;* recht, *right;* solch, *such.*

Note. The diminutive suffix =chen always has the front ch: Frauchen, *little woman, wife;* Mädchen, *girl.*

(c) Initial ch = *k* in a few words derived from Greek: Cha=

[1] Hempl, *German Orthography and Phonology,* § 180 and Notes.

raf'ter, *character;* Chor, *chorus.* However, Chemie' and China, with the ich-sound.

NOTE. chs in such words as sechs, *six,* and wachsen, *grow,* is pronounced *ks* (English *x*).

ck is the sign for double k: backen, *to bake;* Stück, *piece.* A vowel followed by ck is always short.

d initial and medial, as *d* in *deep:* dunkel, *dark;* baden, *to bathe;* as *t* in und, *and;* Mädchen, *girl.*

dt sounds as *t:* Städte, *cities.*

f = *f* in *far:* finden, *to find.*

g 1. Pronounce g as in *go* in gut, *good;* sagen, *to say;* Flagge, *flag;* that is, at the beginning of a word or syllable and when doubled.

2. Pronounce g as *k* in Tag, *day;* Weg, *way;* fragt, *asks;* fragte, *asked;* that is, at the end of a word or syllable, or before a consonant.

3. Pronounce g as front ch in the ending ⸗ig: König, *king;* billig, *cheap.*

4. For ng see under n.

NOTE. Fully as common a pronunciation, but one with less authority, is to pronounce final g as ch, in Tag with an ach-sound, in Weg with an ich-sound. Medially (Tage, *days;* Wege, *ways*) this ch becomes voiced, a difficult sound to acquire.

h = *h* in *hold* at the beginning of a word (including parts of compounds) or a suffix: haben, *to have;* Hausherr, *master of the house;* Freiheit, *freedom.* Elsewhere it merely marks the preceding vowel as long.

j " a tightly squeezed " English *y* in *year:* ja, *yes;* jetzt, *now.*

k = English *k* as in *keep:* kalt, *cold;* denken, *to think.*

l differs from the English *l*. The edge of the tongue — flat, not drawn to a point — lies against the back of the upper teeth, the sound escaping from the sides. The corners of the mouth are drawn back. In English *l*, the point of contact of the tongue with the roof of the mouth is much higher up, and the front part of the tongue has a concave shape, instead of convex as in German: lang, *long;* ſchnell, *quick.*

m = English *m:* Mann, *man;* nehmen, *to take.*

n = English *n*, but with the tip of the tongue against the back of the upper teeth, not, as in English, against the roots of these teeth: neu, *new;* nein, *no.*

ng = *ng* in *singer*, never the *ng* of *finger:* Finger, *finger;* ſingen, *to sing.* So also when final, although *k* is also heard there: jung, *young.*

p = English *p:* Paar, *pair;* Papier', *paper.*

pf is like *pf* in *helpful:* Pfund, *pound;* Kopf, *head.*

ph occurs in foreign words only and is pronounced ſ: der Philoſoph', *the philosopher.*

q occurs only before u; qu = *kv:* Qual, *suffering.*

r is pronounced in two ways:

1. As a tongue or lingual r, like the English *r* in *rat*, but distinctly trilled. While this is not as common in Germany as the uvular r, it is good usage and is recommended to the beginner. Take care to vibrate the r distinctly.

2. The uvular r is made by the vibration of the uvula, as in gargling. The front of the tongue lies flat, while the back part is raised, the vibration resulting from the forcing of the air through the passage thus formed.

Rad, *wheel;* reden, *to speak;* richtig, *correct;* Rose, *rose;* rund, *round;* Brief, *letter;* fragen, *to ask;* Stern, *star.*

Caution

Do not let an r affect the sound of a preceding vowel, as in English. Thus in Stern, *star,* the e is pronounced as *e* in *nest,* not as *e* in *stern.*

ſ, ß 1. = *s* in *sit* when final or next a voiceless consonant: Glas, *glass;* Haus, *house;* Herbſt, *autumn.*

2. = *z* in *zeal* when initial or between vowels: Sohn, *son;* Gläſer, *glasses;* Häuſer, *houses.* Note that this is the same difference as between *house* and *houses.*

3. = ſch (as *sh* in *short*) in initial ſp and ſt: Stuhl, *chair;* ſpät, *late;* Sprache, *language;* Bleiſtift, *lead-pencil.*

ſch = *sh* in *short:* Schule, *school;* waſchen, *to wash.*

ſſ and ß = *ss* in *hiss:* Waſſer, *water;* heiß, *hot.*

NOTE. Alphabetically, ß has the same place as ſſ.

t = *t* as in *ten:* Teil, *part;* dort, *there.*
   = *ts* before i in a few foreign words: Operation', *operation;* Lektion', *lesson.*

th is pronounced as *t.* It occurs in Greek words: Thea'ter, *theater;* Thron, *throne.* German does not have the English *th*-sound.

ß = *ts:* Katze, *cat.*

v = *f* as in *fire:* viel, *much;* Vater, *father.*
   = *v* in foreign words, except where final, when it becomes *f:* nervös', *nervous;* Nerv, *nerve.*

$\mathfrak{w} = v$ in *very* but with less friction. It is produced by breath forced between lower lip and upper teeth: wie, *how;* Waffer, *water.*

$\mathfrak{x} = x$ *(ks)* in *ox:* Heye, *witch;* Axt, *ax.*

$\mathfrak{z} = ts$: zehn, *ten;* tanzen, *to dance;* kurz, *short.*

SYLLABICATION

Words are divided into syllables as follows:

1. **A single consonant between two vowels goes with the following syllable:** Va=ter; Schü=ler; Fe=der, *pen.*

2. ß, ſch, ch (representing but one sound) when standing between vowels go with the syllable following: hei=ßes Waffer, *hot water;* wa=ſchen, *to wash;* brau=chen, *to need.*

3. Otherwise, of two or more consonants between vowels, only the last goes with the following syllable; ſt, however, is not separated and goes with the next syllable: Waſ=ſer, *water;* ſel=ten, *seldom;* Fen=ſter, *window;* mei=ſtens, *mostly.*

4. ck, the sign for double k, at the end of a line becomes k=k: backen: bak=ken.

ACCENT

1. Native words accent the stem syllable. The only important exceptions to this rule are verbs in =ieren and nouns in =ei: ge'ben, *to give;* buchſtabie'ren, *to spell;* Liebelei', *philandering.*

2. Compound nouns accent the first syllable, as in English: Sonn'tag, *Sunday;* Wohn'zimmer, *living room.*

3. Words of foreign origin frequently accent the last syllable: Papier', *paper;* intereſſant', *interesting.*

CAPITALS

1. All nouns and words used as nouns begin with a capital: das Buch, *the book;* die Armen, *the poor.*

2. The pronoun Sie, *you,* and its possessive Ihr, *your,* begin with a capital.

3. Neuter adjectives following viel, manch, etwas, nichts, and expressing a substantive idea, begin with a capital: viel Gutes, *much that is good;* nichts Neues, *nothing new.*

4. The pronoun ich, *I,* is not written with a capital.

5. Adjectives denoting nationality do not begin with a capital: das deutsche Volk, *the German people.*

PUNCTUATION

COMMA. German uses the comma more freely than English.

1. The comma sets off all subordinate clauses from principal clauses. Thus all relative and all conditional clauses have commas: Dies ist der einzige Fehler, den Sie gemacht haben, *This is the only mistake that you have made.*

2. Infinitive clauses that have modifiers are set off by commas: Es ist eine schlechte Gewohnheit, immer die Hand in der Tasche zu haben, *It is a bad habit always to have your hands in your pockets.*

3. A comma is put before und (aber, oder) when it introduces a complete sentence, a sentence with a subject and a verb: Ich gehe morgen, und er kommt in einigen Tagen, *I am going to-morrow and he comes in a few days.*

4. No comma is used before und in a series, or before the abbreviation usw., *etc.:* Gott, der Mensch und die Welt, *God,*

man, and the world. Die geraden Zahlen sind zwei, vier, sechs usw., *The even numbers are two, four, six, etc.*

5. In the middle of a sentence, the German equivalents for *however*, aber and jedoch, are not set off by commas: Es ist aber zu spät, *However, it is too late.*

EXCLAMATION POINT. The exclamation point is used more freely than in English:

1. After imperatives: Karl, hole schnell ein Pfund Butter! *Charles, quickly get a pound of butter.*

2. With the salutation in letters: Lieber Karl! *Dear Charles:*

HYPHEN. The hyphen is a double stroke (=). It also indicates that the second part of a compound is to be supplied from the following noun: Sonn= und Feiertage, *Sundays and holidays.*

German does not have the hyphened compounds so common in English. The three categories of compounded words in English, (1) words written separately, (2) hyphened words, (3) words written solid, are all written solid in German. This is the main reason why German words look longer than English words: die Abendzeitung, *the evening newspaper;* der Stundenzeiger, *the hour-hand;* der Buchbinder, *the bookbinder.*

QUOTATION MARKS. Quotation marks are written thus: „Wände haben Ohren", " *Walls have ears.*"

ITALICS. Instead of italics German uses either spaced type or bold type to indicate emphasis. Neither device is common.

NOUNS

STRONG DECLENSION

CLASS 1   CLASS 2   CLASS 3

Singular

der Onkel	der Ofen	der Tag	die Hand	das Rad
des Onkels	des Ofens	des Tages	der Hand	des Rades
dem Onkel	dem Ofen	dem Tage	der Hand	dem Rade
den Onkel	den Ofen	den Tag	die Hand	das Rad

Plural

die Onkel	die Öfen	die Tage	die Hände	die Räder
der Onkel	der Öfen	der Tage	der Hände	der Räder
den Onkeln	den Öfen	den Tagen	den Händen	den Rädern
die Onkel	die Öfen	die Tage	die Hände	die Räder

WEAK DECLENSION   MIXED   IRREGULAR   FOREIGN

Singular

der Knabe	die Blume	das Auge	der Name	das Studium
des Knaben	der Blume	des Auges	des Namens	des Studiums
dem Knaben	der Blume	dem Auge	dem Namen	dem Studium
den Knaben	die Blume	das Auge	den Namen	das Studium

Plural

die Knaben	die Blumen	die Augen	die Namen	die Studien
der Knaben	der Blumen	der Augen	der Namen	der Studien
den Knaben	den Blumen	den Augen	den Namen	den Studien
die Knaben	die Blumen	die Augen	die Namen	die Studien

ADJECTIVES

THE STRONG AND WEAK ADJECTIVE

Singular

Masc.	Fem.	Neut.
N. guter Mann	gute Frau	gutes Kind
der gute Mann	die gute Frau	das gute Kind
G. guten Mannes	guter Frau	guten Kindes
des guten Mannes	der guten Frau	des guten Kindes
D. gutem Manne	guter Frau	gutem Kinde
dem guten Manne	der guten Frau	dem guten Kinde
A. guten Mann	gute Frau	gutes Kind
den guten Mann	die gute Frau	das gute Kind

Plural

Masc.	Fem.	Neut.
N. gute Männer	gute Frauen	gute Kinder
die guten Männer	die guten Frauen	die guten Kinder
G. guter Männer	guter Frauen	guter Kinder
der guten Männer	der guten Frauen	der guten Kinder
D. guten Männern	guten Frauen	guten Kindern
den guten Männern	den guten Frauen	den guten Kindern
A. gute Männer	gute Frauen	gute Kinder
die guten Männer	die guten Frauen	die guten Kinder

THE ADJECTIVE AFTER ein, kein, etc.

Singular

Masc.	Fem.	Neut.
kein guter Mann	keine gute Frau	kein gutes Kind
keines guten Mannes	keiner guten Frau	keines guten Kindes
keinem guten Manne	keiner guten Frau	keinem guten Kinde
keinen guten Mann	keine gute Frau	kein gutes Kind

Plural

keine guten Männer	keine guten Frauen	keine guten Kinder
keiner guten Männer	keiner guten Frauen	keiner guten Kinder
keinen guten Männern	keinen guten Frauen	keinen guten Kindern
keine guten Männer	keine guten Frauen	keine guten Kinder

VERBS

AUXILIARIES OF TENSE

INDICATIVE

PRESENT

ich habe, I have	ich bin, I am	ich werde, I become
du hast	du bist	du wirst
er hat	er ist	er wird
wir haben	wir sind	wir werden
ihr habt	ihr seid	ihr werdet
sie haben	sie sind	sie werden

PAST

ich hatte, I had	ich war, I was	ich wurde, I became
du hattest	du warst	du wurdest
er hatte	er war	er wurde
wir hatten	wir waren	wir wurden
ihr hattet	ihr wart	ihr wurdet
sie hatten	sie waren	sie wurden

PRESENT PERFECT

ich habe gehabt, I have had	ich bin gewesen, I have been	ich bin geworden, I have become

PAST PERFECT

ich hatte gehabt, I had had	ich war gewesen, I had been	ich war geworden, I had become

FUTURE

idʒ werde ħaben, I shall have	idʒ werde ſein, I shall be	idʒ werde werden, I shall become
du wirſt ħaben	du wirſt ſein	du wirſt werden

FUTURE PERFECT

idʒ werde geħabt ħaben, I shall have had	idʒ werde geweſen ſein, I shall have been	idʒ werde geworden ſein, I shall have become

SUBJUNCTIVE

PRESENT

idʒ ħabe	idʒ ſei	idʒ werde
du ħabeſt	du ſeieſt	du werdeſt
er ħabe	er ſei	er werde
wir ħaben	wir ſeien	wir werden
iħr ħabet	iħr ſeiet	iħr werdet
ſie ħaben	ſie ſeien	ſie werden

PAST

idʒ ħätte	idʒ wäre	idʒ würde
du ħätteſt	du wäreſt	du würdeſt
er ħätte	er wäre	er würde
wir ħätten	wir wären	wir würden
iħr ħättet	iħr wäret	iħr würdet
ſie ħätten	ſie wären	ſie würden

PRESENT PERFECT

idʒ ħabe geħabt	idʒ ſei geweſen	idʒ ſei geworden
du ħabeſt geħabt	du ſeieſt geweſen	du ſeieſt geworden
er ħabe geħabt	er ſei geweſen	er ſei geworden

PAST PERFECT

idʒ ħätte geħabt	idʒ wäre geweſen	idʒ wäre geworden

FUTURE

ich werde haben	ich werde sein	ich werde werden
du werdest haben	du werdest sein	du werdest werden
er werde haben	er werde sein	er werde werden

FUTURE PERFECT

ich werde gehabt haben	ich werde gewesen sein	ich werde geworden sein

CONDITIONAL

PRESENT

ich würde haben, I should have	ich würde sein, I should be	ich würde werden, I should become
du würdest haben	du würdest sein	du würdest werden
er würde haben	er würde sein	er würde werden
wir würden haben	wir würden sein	wir würden werden
ihr würdet haben	ihr würdet sein	ihr würdet werden
sie würden haben	sie würden sein	sie würden werden

PAST

ich würde gehabt haben, I should have had	ich würde gewesen sein, I should have been	ich würde geworden sein, I should have become

IMPERATIVE

habe	sei	werde
habt	seid	werdet
haben Sie	seien Sie	werden Sie

INFINITIVE

haben	sein	werden

PARTICIPLES

PRESENT

habend	seiend	werdend

PAST

gehabt	gewesen	geworden

WEAK VERBS

ACTIVE AND PASSIVE VOICES

Active	Passive

INDICATIVE

Present

Active	Passive
ich lobe, I praise	ich werde gelobt, I am (being) praised
du lobst	du wirst gelobt
er lobt	er wird gelobt
wir loben	wir werden gelobt
ihr lobt	ihr werdet gelobt
sie loben	sie werden gelobt

Past

Active	Passive
ich lobte, I praised	ich wurde gelobt, I was praised
du lobtest	du wurdest gelobt
er lobte	er wurde gelobt
wir lobten	wir wurden gelobt
ihr lobtet	ihr wurdet gelobt
sie lobten	sie wurden gelobt

Present Perfect

Active	Passive
ich habe gelobt, I have praised	ich bin gelobt worden, I have been praised
du hast gelobt	du bist gelobt worden

Past Perfect

Active	Passive
ich hatte gelobt, I had praised	ich war gelobt worden, I had been praised
du hattest gelobt	du warst gelobt worden

Future

Active	Passive
ich werde loben, I shall praise	ich werde gelobt werden, I shall be praised
du wirst loben	du wirst gelobt werden

Active	Passive

FUTURE PERFECT

ich werde gelobt haben, I shall have praised	ich werde gelobt worden sein, I shall have been praised
du wirst gelobt haben	du wirst gelobt worden sein

SUBJUNCTIVE

PRESENT

ich lobe	ich werde gelobt
du lobest	du werdest gelobt
er lobe	er werde gelobt
wir loben	wir werden gelobt
ihr lobet	ihr werdet gelobt
sie loben	sie werden gelobt

PAST

ich lobte	ich würde gelobt
du lobtest	du würdest gelobt
er lobte	er würde gelobt
wir lobten	wir würden gelobt
ihr lobtet	ihr würdet gelobt
sie lobten	sie würden gelobt

PRESENT PERFECT

ich habe gelobt	ich sei gelobt worden
du habest gelobt	du seiest gelobt worden
er habe gelobt	er sei gelobt worden

PAST PERFECT

ich hätte gelobt	ich wäre gelobt worden

FUTURE

ich werde loben	ich werde gelobt werden
du werdest loben	du werdest gelobt werden
er werde loben	er werde gelobt werden

Future Perfect

ich werde gelobt haben	ich werde gelobt worden sein
du werdest gelobt haben	du werdest gelobt worden sein
er werde gelobt haben	er werde gelobt worden sein

CONDITIONAL

Present

ich würde loben, I should praise	ich würde gelobt werden, I should be praised

Past

ich würde gelobt haben, I should have praised	ich würde gelobt worden sein, I should have been praised
du würdest gelobt haben	du würdest gelobt worden sein

IMPERATIVE

lobe	werde gelobt
lobt	werdet gelobt
loben Sie	werden Sie gelobt

INFINITIVE

loben	gelobt werden

PARTICIPLES

Present

lobend	gelobt werdend

Past

gelobt	gelobt worden

REFLEXIVE VERBS

INDICATIVE

PRESENT

ich schäme mich
du schämst dich
er schämt sich
(sie schämt sich)
wir schämen uns
ihr schämt euch
sie schämen sich
(Sie schämen sich)

PAST

ich schämte mich
du schämtest dich
er schämte sich
(sie schämte sich)
wir schämten uns
ihr schämtet euch
sie schämten sich
(Sie schämten sich)

PRESENT PERFECT

ich habe mich geschämt

PAST PERFECT

ich hatte mich geschämt

FUTURE

ich werde mich schämen

FUTURE PERFECT

ich werde mich geschämt haben

SUBJUNCTIVE

PRESENT

ich schäme mich
du schämest dich
er schäme sich

PAST

ich schämte mich
du schämtest dich
er schämte sich

PRESENT PERFECT

ich habe mich geschämt
du habest dich geschämt
er habe sich geschämt

PAST PERFECT

ich hätte mich geschämt
du hättest dich geschämt
er hätte sich geschämt

FUTURE

ich werde mich schämen
du werdest dich schämen
er werde sich schämen

FUTURE PERFECT

ich werde mich geschämt haben
du werdest dich geschämt haben
er werde sich geschämt haben

CONDITIONAL

PRESENT
ich würde mich schämen

PAST
ich würde mich geschämt haben

IMPERATIVE

schäme dich
schämt euch
schämen Sie sich

INFINITIVE

sich schämen

PARTICIPLES

PRESENT

sich schämend

PAST

sich geschämt

STRONG VERBS

Conjugation of bleiben, blieb, ist geblieben

INDICATIVE

PRESENT
ich bleibe, I remain

du bleibst
er bleibt
wir bleiben
ihr bleibt
sie bleiben

PAST
ich blieb, I remained

du bliebst
er blieb
wir blieben
ihr bliebt
sie blieben

PRESENT PERFECT
ich bin geblieben, I
have remained
du bist geblieben
er ist geblieben
wir sind geblieben
ihr seid geblieben
sie sind geblieben

PAST PERFECT
ich war geblieben, I
had remained

FUTURE
ich werde bleiben, I
shall remain

FUTURE PERFECT
ich werde geblieben
sein, I shall have
remained

SUBJUNCTIVE

PRESENT
ich bleibe
du bleibest
er bleibe
wir bleiben
ihr bleibet
sie bleiben

PAST
ich bliebe
du bliebest
er bliebe
wir blieben
ihr bliebet
sie blieben

PRESENT PERFECT
ich sei geblieben
du seiest geblieben
er sei geblieben
wir seien geblieben
ihr seiet geblieben
sie seien geblieben

PAST PERFECT	FUTURE	FUTURE PERFECT
ich wäre geblieben	ich werde bleiben	ich werde geblieben sein
du wärest geblieben	du werdest bleiben	du werdest geblieben sein
er wäre geblieben	er werde bleiben	er werde geblieben sein

CONDITIONAL

PRESENT	PAST
ich würde bleiben, I should remain	ich würde geblieben sein, I should have remained

IMPERATIVE	INFINITIVE	PARTICIPLES
bleibe	bleiben	PRESENT
bleibt		bleibend
bleiben Sie		PAST
		geblieben

INSEPARABLE AND SEPARABLE COMPOUNDS

INDICATIVE

PRESENT

ich verspreche
du versprichst

ich spreche aus
du sprichst aus

PAST

ich versprach

ich sprach aus

PRESENT PERFECT

ich habe versprochen

ich habe ausgesprochen

PAST PERFECT

ich hatte versprochen

ich hatte ausgesprochen

FUTURE

ich werde versprechen

ich werde aussprechen

FUTURE PERFECT

ich werde versprochen haben

ich werde ausgesprochen haben

SUBJUNCTIVE

PRESENT

ich verspreche   ich spreche aus
du versprechest   du sprechest aus

PAST

ich verspräche   ich spräche aus

PRESENT PERFECT

ich habe versprochen   ich habe ausgesprochen
du habest versprochen   du habest ausgesprochen

PAST PERFECT

ich hätte versprochen   ich hätte ausgesprochen

FUTURE

ich werde versprechen   ich werde aussprechen
du werdest versprechen   du werdest aussprechen

FUTURE PERFECT

ich werde versprochen haben   ich werde ausgesprochen haben

CONDITIONAL

PRESENT

ich würde versprechen   ich würde aussprechen

PAST

ich würde versprochen haben   ich würde ausgesprochen haben

IMPERATIVE

versprich   sprich aus
versprecht   sprecht aus
versprechen Sie   sprechen Sie aus

INFINITIVE

versprechen   aussprechen

PARTICIPLES

PRESENT

verſprechend   ausſprechend

PAST

verſprochen   ausgeſprochen

STRONG AND IRREGULAR VERBS

Compounds are included in the list only when they happen to be used more frequently than the simple verbs. The 3d person singular is given in parentheses after the meaning if the form changes its vowel or ends in et instead of t. When a verb takes ſein as auxiliary this is shown by giving, in full, the 3d person singular of the present perfect. Special forms of the past subjunctive are enclosed in parentheses. Only the more common verbs are given.

Infinitive	Past	Past Participle
backen, bake (bäckt)	buk, backte	gebacken
befehlen, command (be= fiehlt)	befahl (Su. be= föhle, befähle)	befohlen
beginnen, begin	begann (Su. be= gönne, begänne)	begonnen
beißen, bite	biß	gebiſſen
biegen, bend	bōg	gebogen
bieten, offer (bietet)	bōt	geboten
binden, bind (bindet)	band	gebunden
bitten, beg (bittet)	bāt	gebeten
blaſen, blow (bläſt)	blies	geblaſen
bleiben, remain	blieb	iſt geblieben
braten, roast (brät)	briet	gebraten
brĕchen, break (bricht)	brāch	gebrŏchen
brennen, burn	brannte (Su. brennte)	gebrannt

Infinitive	Past	Past Participle
bringen, bring	brachte	gebracht
denken, think	dachte	gedacht
dringen, press	drang	ift gedrungen
dürfen, may (darf)	durfte	gedurft
einladen, invite (lädt ein)	lud ein	eingeladen
empfangen, receive (emp= fängt)	empfing	empfangen
empfeh′len, recommend (empfiehlt)	empfahl (Su. emp= föhle, empfähle)	empfohlen
effen, eat (du iffeft or ißt, er ißt)	äß	gegeffen
fahren, drive (fährt)	fuhr	ift gefahren (intr.) hat gefahren (trans.)
fallen, fall (fällt)	fiel	ift gefallen
fangen, catch (fängt)	fing	gefangen
fechten, fight (ficht)	focht	gefochten
finden, find (findet)	fand	gefunden
fliegen, fly	flōg	ift geflogen
fliehen, flee	floh	ift geflohen
fließen, flow	flöß	ift gefloffen
freffen, eat (of animals) (frißt)	fräß	gefreffen
frieren, freeze	frōr	gefroren
geben, give (gibt)	gāb	gegeben
gehen, go	ging	ift gegangen
gelingen, succeed	gelang	ift gelungen
gelten, be worth (gilt)	galt (Su. gölte, gälte)	gegolten
genießen, enjoy	genöß	genoffen
gefchehen, happen (gefchieht)	gefchah	ift gefchehen
gewinnen, gain	gewann (Su. ge= wönne, gewänne)	gewonnen
gießen, pour	göß	gegoffen

Infinitive	Past	Past Participle
gleiten, glide (gleitet)	glitt	iſt geglitten
graben, dig (gräbt)	grūb	gegraben
greifen, seize	griff	gegriffen
halten, hold (hält)	hielt	gehalten
hängen, hang (tr. and intr.)	hing, (intr.) hängte (trans.)	gehangen (intr.) gehängt (tr.)
heben, lift	hōb (hūb)	gehoben
heißen, call, be called	hieß	geheißen
helfen, help (hilft)	half (Su. hülfe, hälfe)	geholfen
kennen, know	kannte (Su. kennte)	gekannt
klingen, sound	klang	geklungen
kommen, come	kām	iſt gekommen
können, can (kann)	konnte	gekonnt
laſſen, let (läßt)	ließ	gelaſſen
laufen, run (läuft)	lief	iſt gelaufen
leiden, suffer (leidet)	litt	gelitten
leihen, lend	lieh	geliehen
leſen, read (lieſt)	lās	geleſen
liegen, lie	lāg	gelegen
lügen, lie (tell a lie)	lōg	gelogen
mißlin'gen, fail	mißlang	iſt mißlungen
mögen, may (mag)	mochte	gemocht
müſſen, must (muß)	mußte	gemußt
nehmen, take (nimmt)	nahm	genommen
nennen, name	nannte (Su. nennte)	genannt
raten, advise (rät)	riet	geraten
reiben, rub	rieb	gerieben
reißen, tear	riß	geriſſen
reiten, ride (reitet)	ritt	iſt geritten
rennen, run	rannte (Su. rennte)	iſt gerannt

Infinitive	Past	Past Participle
riechen, smell	röch	gerochen
rufen, call	rief	gerufen
saufen, drink (of animals) (säuft)	soff	gesoffen
schaffen, do, be busy; create	schaffte schuf	geschafft geschaffen
scheiden, part (scheidet)	schied	ist geschieden
scheinen, seem	schien	geschienen
scheren, shear, shave	schör	geschoren
schieben, shove	schob	geschoben
schießen, shoot	schöß	geschossen
schlafen, sleep (schläft)	schlief	geschlafen
schlagen, strike (schlägt)	schlug	geschlagen
schließen, shut	schlöß	geschlossen
schmelzen, melt (schmilzt)	schmolz	ist geschmolzen (intr.) hat geschmolzen (trans.)
schneiden, cut (schneidet)	schnitt	geschnitten
schreiben, write	schrieb	geschrieben
schreien, cry	schrie	geschrieen
schreiten, stride (schreitet)	schritt	ist geschritten
schweigen, be silent	schwieg	geschwiegen
schwimmen, swim	schwamm (Su. schwömme, schwämme)	ist geschwommen
sehen, see (sieht)	sah	gesehen
sein, be (ist)	wār	ist gewesen
senden, send (sendet)	sandte (Su. sendete)	gesandt
singen, sing	sang	gesungen
sinken, sink	sank	ist gesunken
sitzen, sit	sāß	gesessen
sollen, shall, will (soll)	sollte (Su. sollte)	gesollt
sprechen, speak (spricht)	sprāch	gesprochen
springen, spring	sprang	ist gesprungen

Infinitive	Past	Past Participle
stechen, prick (sticht)	stach	gestochen
stehen, stand	stand (Su. stünde, stände)	gestanden
stehlen, steal (stiehlt)	stahl	gestohlen
steigen, climb, mount	stieg	ist gestiegen
sterben, die (stirbt)	starb (Su. stürbe, stärbe)	ist gestorben
stoßen, push (stößt)	stieß	gestoßen
streiten, fight (streitet)	stritt	gestritten
tragen, carry (trägt)	trūg	getragen
treffen, hit (trifft)	trāf	getroffen
treiben, drive	trieb	getrieben
treten, tread (tritt)	trāt	ist getreten
trinken, drink	trank	getrunken
tūn, do (tut)	tāt	getān
verbergen, hide (verbirgt)	verbarg (Su. verbärge, verbürge)	verborgen
vergessen, forget (vergißt)	vergāß	vergessen
verlieren, lose	verlōr	verloren
verschwinden (verschwindet)	verschwand	ist verschwunden
wachsen, grow (wächst)	wūchs	ist gewachsen
wäschen, wash (wäscht)	wūsch	gewäschen
wenden, turn (wendet)	wandte (Su. wendete)	gewandt
werden, become (wird)	wurde	ist geworden
werfen, throw (wirft)	warf (Su. würfe, wärfe)	geworfen
wiegen, weigh (tr. and intr.)	wōg	gewogen
wissen, know (weiß)	wußte	gewußt
wollen, will (will)	wollte (Su. wollte)	gewollt
verzeihen, pardon	verzieh	verziehen
ziehen, draw; move	zōg	hat gezogen (trans.) ist gezogen (intrans.)

GERMAN SCRIPT

a   *a*   *A*   n   *n*   *N*

b   *b*   *B*   o   *o*   *O*

c   *c*   *C*   p   *p*   *P*

d   *d*   *D*   q   *q*   *Q*

e   *n*   *E*   r   *r*   *R*

f   *f*   *F*   s   *ſ ß*   *S*

g   *g*   *G*   t   *t*   *T*

h   *h*   *H*   u   *u*   *U*

i   *i*   *I*   v   *v*   *V*

j   *j*   *J*   w   *w*   *W*

k   *k*   *K*   x   *x*   *X*

l   *l*   *L*   y   *y*   *Y*

m   *m*   *M*   z   *z*   *Z*

GERMAN SCRIPT
Modified Sütterlin

Es ist Sonntag. Die Kinder besuchen die Eltern. „Guten Tag!" sagen sie. „Ach, wie schön, daß ihr kommt!" sagen Vater und Mutter. Die eine Kinder, zwei Söhne und zwei Töchter, sind schon groß. Hans ist noch zu Hause, er geht noch zur Schule. Paul ist Kaufmann. Martha ist Lehrerin. Marie ist verheiratet. Das Haus ist warm, und das Essen ist fertig. Die Familie geht zu Tisch.

SUPPLEMENTARY EXERCISES

LESSON 1

I. Supply the definite articles before the following nouns:
— Tisch; — Schule; — Haus; — Lehrerin; — Essen; — Mann;
— Familie; — Tag; — Vater; — Kind.

II. In the following sentences, use the pronouns er, sie, es,
instead of the noun subjects: 1. Marie ist verheiratet. 2. Der
Kaufmann ist zu Hause. 3. Das Haus ist warm. 4. Der Tag ist
schön. 5. Die Familie kommt zu Tisch. 6. Der Tisch ist groß.
7. Das Kind geht schon zur Schule. 8. Die Schule ist gut.
9. Paul ist nicht verheiratet.

LESSON 2

I. Supply the definite article in the nominative case: —
Küche; — Teller; — Enkel; — Söhnchen; — Speise; — Gemüse; — Mädchen; — Zigarre; — Stück; — Köchin.

II. Translate: 1. the mother's cook. 2. the father's cigar.
3. the kitchen of the house. 4. the house of the family.
5. the man's grandson.

III. Complete the following sentences with the nouns which
are supplied: 1. Die Köchin bringt . . . the roast, the salad,
the vegetable, the spinach. 2. Das Mädchen holt . . . the
plate, the soup, the food, the dessert.

IV. (**Model:** Ich gebe dem Vater die Zigarre.) According to this model, complete the following sentences, introducing each with Ich gebe: 1. — — the dessert to the little son. 2. — — the piece to the mother. 3. — — the plate to the cook. 4. — — the soup to the father. 5. — — the food to the man. 6. — — the salad to the daughter.

V. Use the correct words for "*you are*" (or "*are you?*") in the following sentences: 1. Vater, — böse? 2. Herr Neumann, — Kaufmann? 3. Kinder, — hungrig? 4. Peter, — unartig. 5. — die Lehrerin des Mädchens? 6. Mutter, — eine gute Köchin. 7. Vater und Mutter, — zu Hause?

LESSON 3

I. 1. Use the correct form of dieser before the following nouns: — Baum; — Woche; — Leute; — Farbe; — Garten.
2. Use the correct form of jeder before the following nouns: — Blume; — Seite; — Stuhl; — Lehrerin; — Familie.
3. Use the correct form of welcher before the following nouns: — Sträucher; — Kuchen; — Haus; — Tisch; — Tag.

II. Translate: 1. the color of this flower. 2. the garden of that man. 3. the mother of many a girl. 4. which father's children? 5. the afternoon of that day. 6. the kitchen of every house. 7. the daughter of such parents.

III. In the following sentences, supply the correct word for "*what*": 1. — trinkt die Familie? 2. — Baum ist hinter dem Haus? 3. — Blumen blühen jetzt? 4. — Kind trinkt Milch? 5. — bringt Anna?

IV. Use the nouns in parentheses in the dative after the prepositions mit, *with;* auf, *on;* in, *in;* unter, *under:* 1. mit (dieſe Tulpen). 2. in (jeder Garten). 3. auf (welcher Baum)? 4. mit (ſolche Blumen). 5. auf (jener Stuhl). 6. in (manches Stück). 7. unter (dieſer Lindenbaum).

LESSON 4

I. Use the following nouns in answers to the question: Was iſt das? (**Model:** Das iſt ein Veilchen.): Roſe; Baum; Strauch; Stuhl; Fenſter; Hut; Zimmer; Wohnſtube.

II. Use the following nouns with the indefinite article as direct objects after any form of the present tense of haben (**Model:** Wir haben einen Großvater.): garden; grandmother; little-son; cook; grandson; house; home; friend; table; room.

III. Translate and conjugate throughout the entire tense, changing the possessive to agree with the subject: 1. I had my friend (you had your friend, etc.). 2. I was in my house (you were in your house, etc.).

IV. Supply the correct endings: 1. Habt ihr ein— Obſtbaum in eur— Garten? 2. In jen— Beet blühen jetzt unſer— Roſen. 3. Unter ein— Baum habe ich ein— Tiſch; wir trinken hier jed— Nachmittag unſer— Kaffee. 4. Aus d— Fenſter ihr— Wohnſtube haben ſie ein— Blick auf (*with acc.*) d— Berg. 5. Mein— Köchin bringt d— Milch und d— Obſt für mein— Familie. 6. Anna, wo haben Sie Ihr— Hut? (It) iſt in mein— Schlaf= ſtube auf d— Stuhl.

V. Translate the answers to the following questions: 1. Dieſes Zimmer? — Yes, this one. 2. Jeder Mann? — No, not each one. 3. Kein Kuchen? — No, none. 4. Welches Fenſter? — That one. 5. Mein Vater? — No, not yours.

6. Dein Stück? — Yes, mine. 7. Haft du einen Stuhl? — Yes, I have one. 8. Haben Sie keinen Freund? — No, I have none.

LESSON 5

I. Put in the plural: mancher Amerikaner; dieser Bäcker; unser Garten; kein Schinken; mein Schüler; unsre Mutter; ihr Vater; dein Bruder; sein Kasten; solches Plätzchen.

II. Translate: 1. with these Englishmen. 2. in your rooms. 3. on the plates. 4. with his grandsons. 5. from her daughters. 6. in which gardens?

III. Change all plurals to singulars and singulars to plurals: 1. Hattet ihr einen Ofen in eurem Zimmer? 2. Wo war der Teller mit dem Kuchen? 3. Die Gemüse dieser Gärtner waren meistens frisch. 4. Beim Fleischer und beim Bäcker. 5. Hatten eure Mütter Dienstmädchen? 6. Der Garten meines Bruders.

LESSON 6

I. Put in the plural: welcher Abend; manches Paar; dieses Geschäft; kein Geheimnis; meine Schwiegertochter; kein Schuh; welcher Tisch; auf jenem Baum; mit ihrem Freund; in meiner Hand; von unsrem Hund; für diesen Tag.

II. Put in the singular: in den Nächten; mit solchen Schuhen; in den Händen der Lehrer; für die Freunde der Brüder; auf den Tischen und Stühlen; vor drei (three) Jahren.

III. Translate: 1. I am not getting rich. 2. The apples were getting red. 3. It was turning cool. 4. The fruit is getting ripe. 5. Flowers are becoming expensive. 6. Did you have time? 7. We do have a telephone.

LESSON 7

I. Put in the plural: 1. unſer Haus; kein Kind; welcher Mann; dieſer Wald; jenes Dorf; ſein Brief; ein Kalb; ein Huhn; ihr Sonntagskleid; das Schloß.
2. das Dach auf dem Haus; das Pferd im Stall; das Ei im Neſt; ein Wirtshaus im Dorf; der Mann auf dem Rad; der Reichtum des Mannes; im Schloß und im Bauernhaus; der Wein im Keller; auf dem Feld und im Wald; ein Abend und eine Nacht.

II. Translate (The verbs in this exercise, conjugated like fragen, are all listed in previous vocabularies): 1. Where are you living now, Ernest? 2. I buy my eggs at the market. Where do you buy yours? 3. They show the little-son the animals. 4. My brother is getting chairs for his friends. 5. Children, do you like (lieben) dogs? 6. She needs a hat and shoes. 7. Does his father smoke? 8. Our teachers praise the pupils all the time. 9. The tulips are not blooming now. 10. They take a trip into the country.

LESSON 8

I. Read in German: 0; 5; 6; 16; 21; 33; 66; 101; 264; 789; 1456; 45 960; 1942; 3 000 000; three times; ten times.

II. Antworten Sie auf deutſch! 1. Wie viele Tage hat die Woche? 2. Wie viele Tage hat dieſer Monat? 3. Wie viele Minuten hat die Stunde? 4. Wie viele Sekunden hat die Minute? 5. Wie viele Schultage hat die Woche? 6. Wie viele Schüler ſind in unſrer Klaſſe? 7. Wieviel iſt 18 + 19? 8. Wieviel iſt 37 − 14? 9. Wieviel iſt 6 × 9? 10. Wieviel iſt 45 ÷ 15?

LESSON 9

I. Model

Present:	Ich habe mein Geld
Past:	du hattest dein Geld
Present perfect:	er hat sein Geld gehabt
Past perfect:	wir hatten unser Geld gehabt
Future:	ihr werdet euer Geld haben
Future perfect:	sie werden ihr Geld gehabt haben

Reproduce the following sentences according to the above model. In other words give a sliding synopsis of each statement: 1. Ich bin nicht bei meinem Freund. 2. Ich werde bald müde. 3. Ich habe heute keine Zeit (yesterday, gestern; tomorrow, morgen).

II. Translate: 1. She has the letter. 2. She does not have the letter. 3. She has not had the letter. 4. She has not had the letter in her (the) hand. 5. She has not had the letter in her hand today.

LESSON 10

I. Give the genitive singular and nominative plural, with articles, of the following nouns: Blume; Franzose; Engländer; Neffe; Bruder; Sohn; Student; Frau; Mensch; Mann; Dame; Kartoffel.

II. Translate: 1. the wives of these men. 2. the students at (auf) the universities. 3. my son's friends (boys). 4. my nephew's friends (girls). 5. the sisters of this gentleman. 6. masters and mistresses. 7. boy and girl pupils. 8. grandsons and granddaughters. 9. American men and women. 10. English men and women.

LESSON 11

I. In the following sentences make the inverted order necessary by placing the element in boldface type before the subject: 1. Der Zug hält **auf dem Bahnhof des Seebads.** 2. Die Ferien sind **leider** bald zu Ende. 3. Man liegt **viele Stunden** am Strande. 4. Martha hatte **dieses Jahr** viel zu tun.

II. Choose a predicate element yourself, place it first, then complete the sentence: 1. Wir werden Anfang Juli im Kaufhaus sehr beschäftigt sein. 2. Die Landleute tanzen und singen am Abend im Wirtshaus. 3. Sie gehen am Sonntag in die Kirche.

III. Translate: 1. Now I am six years old. 2. In the afternoon we have guests. 3. Then we play in the living room. 4. In the dining room they have (there is) birthday cake.

LESSON 12

I. Answer the question Wieviel Uhr ist es? by translating the following expressions: 12 o'clock; half past four; a quarter past five; a quarter to eight; five minutes after seven; ten minutes to eleven.
2. Referring to train time translate: 2:30; 6:20; 10:10.

II. Translate: 1. Tuesday at two o'clock. 2. Friday at half past nine. 3. yesterday evening. 4. this evening. 5. tomorrow evening. 6. yesterday morning. 7. this morning. 8. tomorrow morning.

III. Translate: 1. Frank's (Franz) birthday. 2. Mrs. Schulz' guests. 3. Lotte's uncle. 4. Berlin University. 5. Frankfurt sausage. 6. the city of Cologne. 7. the cities of France. 8. the king of Italy.

LESSON 13

I. Give the genitive singular and nominative plural of the following nouns: die See; der See; der Haufe; der Staat; der Arzt; das Museum; der Vetter; der Inspektor.

II. Translate: 1. the nerves of the eyes and ears. 2. at the ends of the streets. 3. on the lakes of every state. 4. the people of this name. 5. the pains are in his heart. 6. the visit of our nephew. 7. Are crocodiles amphibia or reptiles? 8. Peasant women make butter and cheese and feed the chickens.

LESSON 14

I. Give synopses (without future perfect) of: 1. Die Musikanten spielen einen Wiener Walzer. 2. Paul winkt dem Kellner. 3. Ich brauche ein Ballkleid. 4. Wir folgen dem Takt der Musik.

II. Give sliding synopses (without future perfect) of: 1. Ich tanze mit meinem Freund (use the feminine pronoun in the present perfect). 2. Ich summe eine Melodie.

III. Translate: 1. Paul, take your fiancée to the ball. 2. Madam (unmarried), please, dance this polka with me (mir). 3. Paul and Lotte, please, do not smoke.

LESSON 15

I. 1. Conjugate in the present tense: Ich grüße meinen Lehrer. 2. Conjugate in the past tense: Ich wartete auf meinen Schulkameraden. (In both 1. and 2. make the possessive agree with the subject.)

II. Give a sliding synopsis of: Jch rede mit meiner Nichte.

III. Translate: 1. Frank, do not be so lazy. 2. Don't get sick, boys. 3. [My] gentlemen, don't be angry. 4. [My] ladies, don't get angry. 5. Children, wait for your aunt. 6. Marie, feed the chickens.

IV. Antworten Sie auf deutsch! 1. Wie lange sind Sie schon auf der Universität? 2. Wie lange haben Sie schon Deutsch? 3. Seit wann ist Herr Roosevelt schon Präsident? 4. Jhr Hund ist tot? Wie lange hatten Sie den Hund schon?

LESSON 16

I. Supply the adjective endings: 1. Lustig—, gesund— Kinder in hübsch— Sommerkleidern spielen an heiß— und kühl— Tagen am Strande in naß— Sand. 2. Die Köchin bäckt gut— Kuchen mit frisch— Milch und reif— Obst. 3. Wir haben herrlich— Wetter und baden jed— Tag in kalt—, klar— Wasser. 4. Kaufe etwas Schön—, aber nichts Teur—!

II. Translate: 1. good tobacco. 2. blond hair. 3. red silk. 4. three new books. 5. in warm coats. 6. more rich people. 7. something important. 8. much (that is) cheap. 9. all kinds of interesting people.

III. „Guten Tag" heißt: " *How do you do* " or " *goodbye*." 1. Wie grüßt man am Morgen? 2. Wie grüßt man am Abend? 3. Was sagt man, wenn man zu Bett geht?

LESSON 17

I. Supply the adjective endings: 1. Jn d— gut— Stube steht ein groß— Baum mit viel— bunt— Glaskugeln, vergoldet—

Nüssen und hell— Lichtern. 2. Hatte d— gut— Mutter früher auch elektrisch— Lichter auf ihr— schön— Weihnachtsbaum? 3. Nein, in den alt— Zeiten schmückte man den lieb— Baum mit grün— und rot— Wachskerzen. 4. Viel— geheimnisvoll— Pakete liegen auf d— rund— Tisch, und auf jed— Platz steht ein groß— Teller mit allerlei köstlich— Süßigkeiten.

II. Translate: 1. the famous picture; a famous picture. 2. every lazy pupil; his lazy pupil. 3. these narrow (eng) streets; several narrow streets. 4. the old and the young. 5. the rich (woman) and the poor (woman). 6. a sick (man) and a dead (man). 7. many sick and dead (people).

LESSON 18

I. Give the comparison in German of: 1. interessant; schlank; dumm; kurz. 2. our young cousin; much money; er raucht viel.

II. Decline in singular and plural in German: 1. kein besseres Geschenk. 2. the fastest horse.

III. Supply the endings and translate the words in parenthesis: 1. Mein älter— Neffe ist der best— Schüler in d— ganz— Klasse. 2. Er ist viel klüg— als sein— jünger— Brüder und lernt am schnellst—. 3. D— größt— Zimmer ist am Morgen (coolest), aber am Nachmittag wird es (warmer and warmer).

LESSON 19

I. Conjugate throughout the tense used: 1. Ich spreche nicht laut. 2. Ich halte eine Rede. 3. Ich hielt eine Rede. 4. Ich schreibe meinem Schulkameraden (change possessive).

II. Translate and give synopses of: 1. Do you (du) see the gay life in the streets? 2. She helps her older sister. 3. The sun is shining (ſcheinen).

III. Supply the pronoun subjects and the infinitives of the following verbs: — ſpricht, — ſprecht, — ſprach; — bleibt, — blieb, — bliebt, — bliebſt; — hält, — haltet, — hielt, — hieltet; — ſchreiben, — ſchrieben; — ſiehſt, — ſeht, — ſaht; — lieſt, — leſt; — gibt, — gebt, — gab.

LESSON 20

I. In the following sentences change all nouns to pronouns: 1. Grüße deinen Vater! 2. Ich liebe meine Freunde. 3. Die Mutter gibt dem Kind die Suppe. 4. Paul ſagte den Eltern das Geheimnis. 5. Bernd dankt ſeinem Freund. 6. Haſt du deiner Freundin gedankt?

II. Translate: over me; for you (in three ways); from him; with her; with us (i.e. at our house); in them.

III. Answer the following questions using compounds with da for the phrases in boldface type: 1. Iſt das Brot **in dem Kaſten**? (Ja, das Brot iſt darin.) 2. Haſt du **mit dieſem Bleiſtift** geſchrieben? 3. Haben ſie **aus den Gläſern** getrunken? 4. Werden Sie mir **von Ihrer Reiſe** erzählen? 5. Was liegt dort **auf dem Tiſch**? 6. Kauft er einen Wagen **für das Geld**?

LESSON 21

I. Read aloud in German: 1. Heute iſt der 3. Juli. Am 15. Auguſt fahre ich nach Hauſe. 2. Das Datum am Anfang eines Briefes ſchreibt man wie folgt: . . . , den 26. Mai 1942. 3. Morgen ift mein 18. Geburtstag. 4. Das Reich Karls V.; von Heinrich VIII. 5. ¾, ½ Liter (m.), 3½ Meile (f.).

II. Give synopses of: 1. Er fliegt über den Kanal. 2. Die Operation glückt. 3. Sie kommen nach Paris. 4. Ich arbeite bei einer Schneiderin. 5. Wo landet ihr?

LESSON 22

I. Supply the relative or demonstrative pronoun: 1. Der Film, — wir gesehen haben, handelt von einem Millionär, — über den Kanal fliegt. 2. Das Flugzeug, mit — er fliegt, landet in Deutschland. 3. Dort geht er zu einem Arzt, — Operationen berühmt waren. 4. Mit dem neuen Gesicht, — der Arzt ihm schafft, kommt er nach Paris und sucht seine Frau. 5. — ist auch in Paris und arbeitet bei einer Schneiderin, zu — die eleganten Damen kommen.

II. Express the relative pronouns in two ways wherever possible: 1. Dies ist der Sessel, (on which) ich sitzen möchte. 2. Wir haben einen Kamin, (in which) jeden Abend ein Feuer brennt. 3. Wie heißt die Dame, (with whom) Sie geplaudert haben? 4. Dies sind die Möbel, (for which) das Brautpaar eine große Summe bezahlt hat.

III. Change each pair of simple sentences into principal and relative clause: 1. Paul schreibt an seinen Freund. Der wohnt in einer Kleinstadt. 2. Das Sofa paßt zu den Sesseln. Es ist auch modern. 3. Der Tisch steht in der Ecke. Der Kellner hat ihn freigehalten.

IV. Translate: 1. The newspaper I am reading is good. 2. Here is the letter he has written. 3. The chairs you have bought are too expensive. 4. Where is the house they had rented?

LESSON 23

I. Supply the correct form of wer, was, was für, or welch—:
1. — lieſt du? 2. Von — haſt du es gehört? 3. Für — Leute
ſind die Möbel? 4. — Jacht iſt das? 5. Aus — Glas hat er
getrunken? 6. — Stil gefällt dir am beſten? 7. (What kind
of a) Geſchenk wird er dir geben? 8. (What kind of a) Salat
haben die Töchter gemacht?

II. Translate: 1. Who came? 2. the guest who came . . .
3. the people whose guest . . . 4. whose guest? 5. the
children for whom . . . 6. for whom? 7. Whom do they
tease? 8. the engaged couple whom they tease . . . 9. for
what? 10. from what? 11. from whom? 12. from what
town? 13. from which relatives?

III. Translate the possessives in the following phrases in two
ways, using possessive adjectives and pronouns (**Model:**
Sein Haus und meins. Sein Haus und das meinige (or das
meine).): 1. my book or his. 2. her handwriting and yours.
3. your guests and mine. 4. his cake and not hers. 5. with
our children and theirs. 6. I see my spoon but not yours.

LESSON 24

I. Supply the endings: 1. In welch— Kleid geht ſie in d—
Kirche? 2. Aus ein— Wagen ſteigt das Brautpaar. 3. Sie
ſchreiten durch d— Menge, die an d— Tür ſteht, bis vor d— Altar.
4. Vor d— Trauung ſpielt die Orgel. Der Pfarrer ſteht auf d—
Kanzel, vor d— das Brautpaar ſitzt. 5. Nun tritt er vor d—
Brautpaar und ſteckt ihre Ringe an d— rechte Hand. In Deutſchland
trägt man den Trauring an d— rechten Hand. 6. Peter ſitzt
zwiſchen ſein— Vater und ſein— Mutter. 7. Die Kellner ſetzen
den Wein auf d— Tiſch. 8. Mit w— hat die Braut bei d—
Hochzeit getanzt?

II. Antworten Sie auf deutsch! 1. Gehen Sie gern ins Kino?
2. Wo wohnen Sie lieber, in der Stadt oder auf dem Lande?
3. Was machen Sie im Sommer am liebsten? 4. Womit fahren
Sie lieber, mit dem Auto oder mit der Eisenbahn?

LESSON 25

I. Give synopses of: 1. Im Kriege fließt viel Blut. 2. Das
Volk leidet Not. 3. Ich leihe dir Schurz' Buch. 4. Sie fliehen
nach der Schweiz.

II. 1. Give the second person singular past of: schließen;
gießen; schneiden; beißen; leiden.
2. Give the second person plural present and past of: leiden;
schneiden; streiten; bieten.

III. Translate: 1. We were flying. 2. They have been
suffering. 3. She did cut. 4. The sun is shining. 5. He
had been shooting. 6. You were writing. 7. It was pouring.

LESSON 26

I. Give synopses of: 1. Ich ziehe ihn ins Vertrauen. 2. Findet
ihr den Vetter? 3. Verbrecher sitzen im Gefängnis. 4. Does he
die in the penitentiary? 5. You (du) meet a policeman.

II. Supply the pronoun subject and translate: — nehmt,
— nahmt, — nahm; — hilft, — helft; — treffen, — trafen, —
traft; — fand, — fandet; — stiehlst, — stehlt; — stirbt, — sterbt,
— starbt; — bat, — batet; — sitzt, — saßt, — saß.

III. Translate: 1. Eat your egg and drink your milk, Peter.
2. Dear friends, help me. 3. " Take my passport ", says
the cousin. 4. Please, speak with my parents, Mr. Brown,
and ask for (um) my hand.

LESSON 27

I. Translate and give synopses of: 1. Schurz rides to Spandau. 2. Do you (du) advise me that? 3. You (ihr) consider it better (halten für).

II. Supply the pronoun subjects and translate: — stößt, — stoßt, — stießt; — läßt, — ließt, — laßt; — trug, — tragt, — trägt; — ruft, — rief; — lauft, — läuft, — liefst; — haltet, — hielt, — hieltet; — fiel, — fielt, — fällt.

LESSON 28

I. Combine the following pairs of simple sentences to make compound or complex sentences. Use the conjunctions in parenthesis: 1. Kinkel war Professor in Bonn gewesen. (Aber) Er war als Aufrührer den Preußen in die Hände gefallen. 2. Schurz kam wieder nach Deutschland. (Nachdem) Er war nach der Schweiz geflohen. 3. (Sobald) Schurz hatte seines Vetters Paß. Er reiste nach Berlin. 4. Er konnte nicht unter seinem eignen Namen reisen. (sondern) er mußte seines Vetters Paß gebrauchen. 5. Er zog den Arzt ins Vertrauen. (denn) Er traute ihm. 6. Er zog den Arzt ins Vertrauen. (weil) Er traute ihm.

II. Supply the correct one of the conjunctions in parenthesis: 1. Ich werde dem Wärter eine Zehntalernote geben, (wenn, wann, als) ich wiederkomme. 2. (Nach, nachdem) einigen Tagen fuhr Schurz nach Berlin. 3. (Vor, bevor, ehe) Schurz einen Wagen nahm, ging er zu Fuß durch das Brandenburger Tor. 4. Schurz ging nicht zu Fuß, (aber, sondern) nahm einen Wagen. 5. Der Mann will nicht bei Kinkels Befreiung helfen, (weil, denn) es gefährlich ist. 6. (Da, seit) der Mann nicht helfen wollte, mußte man einen zweiten suchen.

LESSON 29

I. Give synopses of: 1. Geht die Sache gut? 2. Wir wenden uns an Brune. 3. Du tust nichts Schlechtes. 4. Ich weiß den Namen des Gastwirts nicht.

II. Give sliding synopses, changing the possessive: 1. Ich denke an meine Familie. 2. Ich sende meine Grüße (greetings). 3. Ich kenne meine Freunde.

III. Wissen or kennen? Translate: 1. Did he know that his friends were true to him? 2. Schurz knew several families in Berlin. 3. The government knows Schurz, but does not know where he is.

LESSON 30

I. Translate: A. 1. the coming and going. 2. the thinking and doing. 3. the giving and taking. 4. the shooting. 5. hearing and seeing. 6. instead of waiting. 7. instead of opening the cell. 8. without thinking. 9. without thinking of his family. 10. without knowing you. B. 1. I am ready to help. 2. I am ready to help him. 3. I am ready to help him with money. C. 1. Schurz needed a passport in order to travel. 2. Schurz needed a passport in order to travel by train. 3. Schurz needed a passport in order to show it at the station. D. 1. He learned to wait. 2. Nothing was to be seen. 3. What is to be done? 4. Es ist kaum zu glauben.

II. Translate: 1. on account of the key. 2. during the month of September. 3. outside of the capital. 4. for their sake. 5. for the prisoner's sake. 6. instead of this official.

LESSON 31

I. 1. Change the following verbs to the same form of the subjunctive: Er hatte; du machtest; sie waren; ich wurde; du famſt; wir taten; ſie fand; ihr nahmt; ich lag; er zog; du bliebſt; ich aß.

2. Conjugate the present conditional of laufen.

II. Es geht, wenn Brune die Wache hat. 1. Change this real condition to a contrary-to-fact condition. 2. In your new sentence (1), change the verb in the conclusion to the other possible tense. 3. Rewrite sentence 2, putting the conditional clause first. 4. Rewrite sentence 3, using inversion instead of wenn. 5. Go through the same four steps with the following sentence: Ich komme, wenn es nicht zu ſpät iſt.

LESSON 32

In the second and third person singular present subjunctive there is no vowel change in verbs like geben (gibt), or umlaut in verbs like fahren (fährt). The infinitive stem is used without exception plus the subjunctive endings –e, –eſt, –e, –en, –et, –en. (Only ich ſei and er ſei are without ending.) Therefore: present indicative of wiſſen: ich weiß; present subjunctive: ich wiſſe; of eſſen: er ißt, er eſſe; of waſchen: er wäſcht, er waſche.

I. Change the following verbs to the same form of the subjunctive: ich bin; wir ſind; er hat; ihr habt; du weißt; du gibſt; er macht; ſie läuft; du nimmſt; er ſpricht; du lieſt; er fällt; ich war gerannt; wir hatten getan; du warſt gegangen.

II. Render the following in two ways (present conditional or past subjunctive; past conditional or past perfect subjunctive): 1. he would have. 2. you would hold. 3. I should take. 4. you would have found. 5. I should have read. 6. they would have fled.

III. Wenn er ehrlich iſt, wird er das Geld nicht nehmen. 1. Change this real condition to a contrary-to-fact condition in the present time. 2. Change sentence 1 to a contrary-to-fact condition in the past time. 3. In sentence 2, express the condition by inversion. 4. Use the other possible tense in the conclusion of sentence 1 and 2.

LESSON 33

I. List the principal parts of all the inseparable compound verbs in Kinkels Befreiung IX, pp. 157–158.

II. Translate and give synopses of: 1. He never forgets it. 2. Do you (du) betray your friend? 3. I gain nothing.

III. Give synopses in the subjunctive (present, past, past perfect) and both tenses of the conditional: 1. Er erhält das Geld. 2. Du verstehst mich nicht.

LESSON 34

I. Write the principal parts of all compound verbs in Kinkels Befreiung X, pp. 162–163.

II. Translate and give synopses of: 1. A wall surrounds the prison. 2. I lay the key down. 3. We get up early. 4. Do you (ihr) translate the story?

LESSON 35

I. Translate: 1. May I? 2. You may. 3. You may (must) not. 4. we are able. 5. We were able to understand. 6. You must. 7. He had to hurry. 8. He will have to get up.

9. She is to work.   10. She was to bring it.   11. I intend to go in.   12. Did you want to look out?   13. Do you like it? 14. I did not like to hear it.

II. Translate: 1. Ohne Schlüssel wird Brune die Zelle nicht aufschließen können. 2. Der Beamte muß es gesehen haben. 3. Sie dürfen Ihren Freund nicht verraten. — Das habe ich auch nicht gewollt. 4. Wir durften die Leute nicht warten lassen. 5. Wenn Sie das Geld haben wollen, müssen Sie es bei mir abholen. 6. Es mochte Mitternacht sein.

III. Translate: 1. I wanted to visit the prisoner, but I was not allowed.   2. Kinkel was to get up and throw a cloak around (himself).   3. They will have to open the little gate softly.   4. May he take the lantern?   5. We did not like to drive to Mecklenburg in the night.

LESSON 36

I. Give synopses of: 1. Ich darf die Wache haben. 2. Können die Pferde weit laufen? 3. Du willst die Fahrt unternehmen. 4. Er sieht die Männer an der Ecke stehen. 5. Wir lassen einen Nachschlüssel machen.

II. Give the following in the past and past perfect subjunctive and translate: 1. Ich kann ihm heraushelfen. 2. Der Inspektor soll den Schlüssel nicht mitnehmen. 3. Sollen sie Gewalt gebrauchen? 4. Wir können vorbeifahren.

III. Translate: 1. Kinkel soll ein bekannter Dichter gewesen sein. 2. Kannst du ein Gedicht von ihm? — Nein, ich kann keins und kenne auch keins. 3. Schurz hätte dem ehrlichen Brune um den Hals fallen mögen. 4. Haben Sie die Dachziegel fallen hören? 5. Hensel will es gehört haben. 6. Wir möchten nach Bremen, aber wir können nicht.

LESSON 37

I. Translate and conjugate: 1. I was sorry. 2. I have liked it (gefallen).

II. Give synopses of: 1. Es gibt keinen Nachtisch. 2. Ich lasse mir ein Paar Schuhe machen. 3. Es regnet den ganzen Tag.

III. Translate: 1. They had (*say:* there was) punch. 2. Did they have punch? 3. I know that they had punch. 4. There was punch on the table. 5. Was there punch on the table? 6. I know that there was punch on the table.

LESSON 38

I. Change to indirect discourse: 1. Schurz sagte zu Kinkel: „Das sind deine Kerkermeister." 2. Schurz erzählte: „Hensel fuhr sehr schnell." 3. Brune sagte: „Der Beamte ist krank geworden." 4. Die Freunde fragten Kinkel: „Hatten Sie Männerstimmen gehört?" 5. Brune versprach: „Ich werde Kinkel an einem Seil hinunterlassen." 6. Er sagte zu mir: „Fahren Sie um Mitternacht vorbei!"

II. Translate: 1. I think it will snow. 2. Krüger asks whether Kinkel wants a glass of punch. 3. He knew that Brune was honest. 4. Did you think Kinkel was a criminal? 5. He asked who the dark figures (Gestalten) were. 6. It was clear that they were friends.

LESSON 39

I. Conjugate: 1. Ich setze mich auf das Sofa (sich setzen, to sit down). 2. Ich habe mich gut erholt. 3. Ich zog mich aus (to undress).

II. Addressing: a) a child; b) the children; c) an acquaintance, express in three ways: 1. Rejoice. 2. Wash (yourself). 3. Rely on me. 4. Dress. 5. Undress. 6. Buy yourself a carriage.

III. Translate: 1. from each other. 2. to each other. 3. We understand each other. 4. We meet each other every day. 5. even the Prussians. 6. the Prussians themselves.

IV. Translate: 1. Kinkel cut himself on (an) the rope. 2. Schurz cut the rope himself. 3. I can remember. 4. Are you feeling well? 5. We must dress now. 6. The horses lie down.

LESSON 40

I. Translate and give synopses of: 1. Brune is not (being) acquitted. 2. The prisoners are (being) freed.

II. Change to passive voice: 1. Ein Freund bringt die beiden nach England. 2. Hensel fütterte die Pferde. 3. Die Hausfrau hat ihnen guten Wein vorgesetzt. 4. Das Seil hatte Kinkels Hände zerschunden. 5. Petermann wird die Freunde einladen.

III. True or false passive? 1. Nachdem Brune freigesprochen (war or wurde?), zog er nach Westfalen. 2. Während Kinkel am Seil heruntergelassen (ist or wird?), fährt Hensels Wagen vorbei. 3. Als das Essen gekocht (war or wurde?), setzten wir uns zu Tisch und aßen. 4. In einer Stunde wird der Brief geschrieben (sein or werden?), dann kannst du ihn zur Post tragen. 5. Der Brief muß sofort geschrieben (sein or werden?), wenn er heute fort soll.

VOCABULARIES

ABBREVIATIONS

accus.	= accusative	irreg.	= irregular
adj.	= adjective	p.	= page
adv.	= adverb	plur.	= plural
aux.	= auxiliary	poss.	= possessive
comp.	= comparative	p.p.	= past participle
conj.	= conjunction	prep.	= preposition
dat.	= dative	pro.	= pronoun
dem.	= demonstrative	pron.	= pronounce
gen.	= genitive	rel.	= relative
imper.	= imperative	sing.	= singular
indecl.	= indeclinable	sup.	= superlative
infl.	= inflection	tr.	= transitive
interj.	= interjection	w.	= with
interr.	= interrogative	wk.	= weak

VOCABULARIES

NOUNS. Gender is indicated by a ber, bie, or baß before the noun. If, as with most proper nouns, a noun does not commonly have the article, the latter is put in parentheses. Of masculine and neuter nouns, the endings of the genitive singular and the nominative plural are given; of feminine nouns, the ending of the nominative plural only. Where no plural is given, none is in common use.

VERBS. Weak verbs are marked *wk*. Of strong verbs, the principal parts are indicated in both Vocabularies. Separable compounds are printed with a hyphen: auf=ftehen. Whenever a verb, whether strong or weak, takes fein as an auxiliary, the 3d person singular present perfect is given in full. This fixes the form in mind rather better than the formula " aux. fein."

ACCENT AND QUANTITY. Accents and other marks of pronunciation have been used wherever they were deemed helpful.

GERMAN–ENGLISH VOCABULARY

A

ab, off

der Abend, -s, -e, evening

abends, in the evening

aber, but; however

ab-holen, wk., to call for

der Abschied, -s, leave

das Abteil, -s, -e, compartment

ab-treiben, ie, ie, to drive off

ach, ah, oh

achten, wk., to regard, esteem

adressie'ren, wk., to address

ähnlich, alike; einem ä. sehen, to resemble one

all, all; alles, everything

allein', alone; but

allerlei', indecl., all kinds of

als, as; than; when

also, so then, therefore; well then

alt, old

der Altar', -s, -e, altar

das Alter, -s, —, age, old age

altmodisch, old-fashioned

am = an dem

(das) Ame'rika, -s, America

der Amerika'ner, -s, —, American

die Amnestie', amnesty

amüsie'ren, wk., to amuse

an, w. dat. or accus., at, on, to

an-bieten, o, o, to offer

an-bringen, irreg., to fasten

ander, other

der Anfang, -s, -e, beginning

an-fangen (ä), i, a, to begin

anfangs, in the beginning

an-fertigen, wk., to prepare, make

angebracht, p. p. of anbringen

die Angel, -n, fishing pole and line

angeln, wk., to angle, still-fish

die Angst, -e, fear, terror; — haben, to be afraid

angstvoll, fearful

an-halten (ä), ie, a, to sue, ask in marriage

an-kommen, a, ist angekommen, to arrive

ans = an das

an-schreiben, ie, ie, to charge; a. lassen, have charged

die Ansichtskarte, -n, picture post card

an-stoßen (ö), ie, o, to touch glasses

an-treten (i), a, e, to start on

die Antwort, -en, answer

antworten, wk., to answer

an-vertrauen, wk., (p.p. anvertraut) to entrust

an-ziehen, zog an, angezogen, to put on (dress)

der Anzug, -s, -e, suit

der Apfel, -s, -, apple

der Apfelkuchen, -s, —, apple-tart

der Apparat', -s, -e, apparatus

das Aqua'rium, -s, -rien, aquarium

die Arbeit, -en, work; task

arbeiten, wk., to work

arm, poor

iii

der Arm, –es, –e, arm

die Armbanduhr, –en, wrist watch

der Arzt, –es, ⸚e, physician

das Atlaskleid, –s, –er, satin dress

ātmen, wk., to breathe

auch, also; so sehr auch, however much

auf, w. dat. or acc., on, upon; to; auf und ab, up and down

auf=bewahren, wk., (p.p. aufbewahrt), to keep

die Aufgabe, –n, task

auf=geben (i), a, e, to give up

das Aufgebot, –s, –e, banns

aufgeregt, excited; turbulent

auf=machen, wk., to open (up)

auf=muntern, wk., to cheer up

auf=passen, wk., to watch, look out

aufrecht, upright; sich — halten, to keep up one's courage

der Aufrührer, –s, —, insurgent, agitator

auf=schließen, o, o, to unlock

auf=setzen, wk., to put on (hat)

auf=stehen, irreg., ist aufgestanden, to rise

das Auge, –s, –n, eye

der Augenblick, –s, –e, moment

aus, w. dat., out, out of; over

der Ausdruck, –s, ⸚e, expression

auseinan'der, apart

der Ausflug, –s, ⸚e, excursion, trip

aus=geben (i), a, e, to spend

aus=graben (ä), u, a, to dig up

aus=richten, wk., to make all arrangements for

außerhalb w. gen., outside; von —, from out of town

äußerst, extremely, most

aus=sprechen (i), a, o, to pronounce

aus=steigen, ie, ist ausgestiegen, to alight, get out

die Aussteuer, –n, trousseau

die Auswahl, choice, selection

die Axt, ⸚e, axe

B

backen (ä), u, a, to bake

der Bäcker, –s, —, baker

baden, wk., to bathe

der Bahnhof, –s, ⸚e, railway station

bald, soon

der Ball, –s, ⸚e, ball

das Ballkleid, –s, –er, ball dress

der Ballsaal, –s, –säle, ballroom

das Band, –es, –e, bond, fetter

der Bärenpelz, –es, –e, bear-fur coat

der Bauer, –s, –n, farmer

das Bauernhaus, –es, ⸚er, farm-house

der Baum, –es, ⸚e, tree

der Beam'te (adj. infl.), official

bedecken, wk., to cover

das Beden'ken, –s, —, misgiving, scruple

die Bedenk'zeit, time for consideration

bedeuten, wk., to mean

bedeu'tend, important

die Bedeu'tung, –en, meaning

das Beet, –es, –e, (garden) bed

befestigen, wk., to fasten

sich befinden, a, u, to be (somewhere, etc.)

befreien, wk., to free

die Befrei'ung, –en, liberation

begehen, irreg., to commit

begeistern, wk., to inspire, make enthusiastic

begießen, o, o, (' bepour '), to drink to

beginnen, a, o, to begin

begnadigen, wk., to pardon

begrüßen, wk., to greet; sich —, greet each other

behalten (ä), ie, a, to keep

die Behör'de, –n, authorities

bei, w. dat., with, at; near

beibe, both; two

beim = bei dem

das Bein, —es, —e, leg

beina'he, (or bei'nahe) almost

beisam'men, together

bekam, —en, past of bekommen

bekannt', known, well-known; quainted

bekommen, a, o, to receive, get

(das) Belgien, —s, Belgium

bellen, wk., to bark

benutzen, wk., to use

das Benzin', —s, gasoline

die Beob'achtung, —en, observation

bequem', comfortable

der Berg, —es, —e, mountain

(das) Berlin', —s, Berlin

beruhigen, wk., to quiet, reassure

berühmt', famous

beschäftigen, wk., to occupy

beschäf'tigt, busy

beschei'den, modest

beschließen, o, o, to decide, resolve

beschreiben, ie, ie, to describe

der Besi'ßer, —s, —, owner

beson'ders, especially

besprechen (i), a, o, to discuss

besser, better

bestechen (i), a, o, to bribe

die Beste'chung, —en, bribery

bestellen, wk., to order

der Besuch', —s, —e, visit, company

besuchen, wk., to visit

beten, wk., to pray

betrun'ken, drunk

das Bett, —es, —en, bed

bevor', conj., before

bewachen, wk., to watch

sich bewegen, wk., to move

beweisen, ie, ie, to prove

bewilligen, wk., to grant

der Bewun'derer, —s, —, admirer

die Bewun'derung, admiration

bezahlen, wk., to pay

bezweifeln, wk., to doubt

biegen, o, o, to bend

das Bier, —es, —e, beer

das Bild, —es, —er, picture

billig, cheap

bis, until

ein bißchen, a little

bitte (= ich bitte), please

bitten, a, e; — um, to ask for, request

blank, shiny

blaß, pale

das Blatt, —es, —er, leaf; page

blau, blue

das Blei, —es, lead

bleiben, ie, ist geblieben, to stay, remain

der Bleistift, —s, —e, lead-pencil

der Blick, —es, —e, look, view

blicken, wk., to look

blond, blond

blühen, wk., to bloom

die Blume, —n, flower

das Blut, —es, blood

blutig, bloody

der Boden, —s, ", ground

das Boot, —es, —e, boat

borgen, wk., to borrow

böse, evil; angry

bot . . . an, past of anbieten

die Bowle, —n, bowl

der Braten, —s, —, roast

brauchen, wk., to need

braun, brown, tanned

die Braut, —e, fiancée

der Brautführer, —s, —, best-man

der Bräutigam, —s, —e, bridegroom

die Brautjungfer, —n, bridesmaid

das Brautkleid, —s, —er, wedding-dress

das Brautpaar, —s, —e, engaged couple

brechen (i), a, o, to break

brennen, irreg., to burn

der Brief, —es, —e, letter

die Brieftasche, –n, wallet

bringen, *irreg.*, to bring, take

die Brise, –n, breeze

das Brot, –es, –e, (loaf of) bread

das Brötchen, –s, —, roll

der Bruder, –s, ", brother

die Brusttasche, –n, inside coat-pocket

das Buch, –es, "er, book

das Bücherbrett, –s, –er, bookshelf

die Buchhandlung, –en, bookshop

bunt, gay-colored, motley

die Burg, –en, stronghold, fortress

bürgen, *wk.*, to vouch (for)

C

das Café', –s, –s, café

der Choral', –s, "e, choral, hymn

D

da, there, then; bin wieder da, am back again

dabei', present; — sein, to be in something

das Dach, –es, "er, roof

die Dachluke, –n, dormer-window

der Dachziegel, –s, —, tile

damals, at that time

die Dame, –n, lady

damit', in order that

danach, after that

(das) Dänemark, –s, Denmark

der Dank, –es, thanks

danken, *wk., w. dat.*, to thank; danke schön, many thanks

dann, then

darf, darfst, *see* dürfen

darum', therefore

das, that (*dem.*)

daß, *conj.*, that

dauern, *wk.*, to last

davon'=rollen, *wk.*, ist davongerollt, to drive away

davor', in front (of it)

dazu', for that, with that

das Deck, –es, –e, deck

die Deklination', –en, declension

der Demokrat', –en, –en, democrat

die Demokratie', –n, democracy

demokra'tisch, democratic

denken, *irreg.*, to think (of, an *w. accus.*)

denn, then; for; *in questions*, see Note, p. 12, footnote 3.

dersel'be, the same

deutsch, German; auf —, in German

der Deutsche (*adj. infl.*), German

(das) Deutschland, –s, Germany

dich *accus. of* du

der Dichter, –s, —, poet, author

der Diener, –s, —, servant

der Dienstag, –s, –e, Tuesday

das Dienstmädchen, –s, —, servant-girl

dieser, this

diesmal, this time

diesseits, *w. gen.*, on this side of

das Ding, –es, –e, thing

dir, *dat. of* du

doch, nevertheless, after all; but; is he not, etc.

der Doktor, –s, –to'ren, doctor

der Dom, –s, –e, cathedral

die Donau, Danube

donnern, *wk.*, to thunder

der Donnerstag, –s, –e, Thursday

das Dorf, –es, "er, village

die Dorfleute (*plur.*), village people

dort, there

draußen, *adv.*, outside

drei, three

dreifach, threefold, triple

der dritte, the third

drücken, *wk.*, press, pinch

du, thou, you; say
dumm, stupid
die Düne, –n, dune, down
dunkel, dark
durch, *w. accus.*, through
durcheinan'der, at the same time, in confusion
durchleuch'ten, *wk.*, to illumine
durchs = durch das
dürfen, may, dare, be allowed
der Durst, –es, thirst
das Dutzend, –s, — *or* –e, dozen

E

eben, just now, just then
ebenso, just so
die Ecke, –n, corner
edel, noble
das Ehepaar, –s, –e, married couple
die Ehre, –n, honor
ehrlich, honest
die Ehrlichkeit, honesty
das Ei, –es, –er, egg
eigen, own
eigentlich, really, anyway
eilen, *wk.*, to hurry
einan'der, each other
ein-bauen, *wk.*, to build in
ein-biegen, o, ist eingebogen, to turn in
ein-fallen (ä), ie, ist eingefallen, to occur to (*w. dat.*)
der Eingang, –s, ⸚e, entrance
einige, some
der Einkauf, –s, ⸚e, purchase; Ein-käufe machen, to shop
ein-laden (ä), u, a, to invite
die Einladung, –en, invitation
ein-lassen (ä), ie, a, to let in
einmal, once; nicht einmal, not even
eins, one
ein-steigen, ie, ist eingestiegen, to enter, get in

ein-stimmen, *wk.*, to join in
ein-teilen, *wk.*, to divide into
ein-treten (i), a, ist eingetreten, to enter
der Einwohner, –s, —, inhabitant
einzig, only (*adj.*)
das Eis, –es, ice
die Eisenbahn, –en, railway, train
eisern, iron, of iron
elegant', elegant, smart
elek'trisch, electric
elend, miserable
das Elend, –s, misery
die Eltern (*plur.*), parents
das Ende, –s, –n, end; am E., in the end; zu E. sein, to be at an end
endlich, finally
eng, narrow, tight, small
(das) England, –s, England
der Engländer, –s, —, Englishman
der Enkel, –s, —, grandson
entdecken, *wk.*, to discover, reveal
entfernt', distant
die Entfer'nung, –en, distance
entkommen, a, ist entkommen, to escape
entlang'; die Strecke entlang, along the route
entwe'der (*or* ent'weder) . . . oder, either . . . or
entzückt', delighted
die Erde, the earth
der Erfolg', –s, –e, success
erfüllen, *wk.*, to fulfil
erhalten (ä), ie, a, to receive
erheben, o, o, to raise
sich erholen, *wk.*, to recuperate
die Erho'lung, rest, recreation
sich erinnern, *wk.*, to remember (an *w. accus.; or gen.*)
erklären, *wk.*, to explain; declare
erlauben, *wk.*, to permit (*w. dat. of person*)
ernähren, *wk.*, to support; sich —, make one's living

ernſt, serious
erreichen, wk., to reach
erſcheinen, ie, iſt erſchienen, to appear;
    das Erſcheinen, appearance
der erſte, the first; erſt, not until
ertönen, wk., iſt ertönt, to resound
erwarten, wk., to await
erwidern, wk., to reply, retort
erzählen, wk., to narrate, tell
eſſen (i), a, gegeſſen, to eat
das Eſſen, –s, food, dinner
die Eßſtube, –n, dining-room (less
    pretentious than Eßzimmer)
das Eßzimmer, –s, —, dining-room
etwa, approximately
etwas, something; some; somewhat
euch, dat. or accus. of ihr
euer, your, poss. of ihr

F

fahren (ä), u, iſt (hat) gefahren, to go,
    travel, drive
die Fahrt, –en, trip, journey, drive
fallen (ä), ie, iſt gefallen, to fall
der Fallſchirm, –s, –e, parachute
falſch, false, wrong
die Fami'lie, –n, (pron. –milye),
    family
famōs', capital, excellent
fangen (ä), i, a, to catch
die Farbe, –n, color
faſt (= beinahe), almost
faul, lazy
die Feder, –n, feather, pen
fegen, wk., to sweep
fehlen, wk., to ail; be absent
feierlich, festive, solemn
feiern, wk., to celebrate
der Feind, –es, –e, enemy
das Feld, –es, –er, field
das Fenſter, –s, —, window
die Ferien (plur.), vacation

die Ferienreiſe, –n, vacation trip
fertig, ready, ready-made
feſt, firm, thorough
feſtlich, festive, holiday
die Feſtung, –en, fortress
die Feſtungsſtrafe, confinement in a
    fortress
das Feuer, –s, —, fire
fidēl', hilarious, jolly
der Film, –es, –e, film
der Filmheld, –en, –en, film hero,
    matinée idol
finden, a, u, to find; like
der Finger, –s, —, finger
der Fiſch, –es, –e, fish
der Fiſcher, –s, —, fisherman
das Fiſcherdorf, –s, ̈–er, fishing village
das Fleiſch, –es, meat
der Fleiſcher, –s, —, butcher
fleißig, industrious
der Flieder, –s, lilac
fliegen, o, iſt geflogen, to fly
fliehen, o, iſt geflohen, to flee
die Flucht, flight, escape
der Flüchtling, –s, –e, fugitive
das Flugzeug, –s, –e, airplane
flüſtern, wk., to whisper
folgen, wk., iſt gefolgt, to follow
fort, away
fort-fahren (ä), u, a, to continue
fort-ſetzen, wk., tr., to continue
die Fortſetzung, –en, continuation
der Frack, –es, ̈–e, dress-suit
die Frage, –n, question
fragen nach, wk., to ask about
(das) Frankreich, –s, France
der Franzo'ſe, –n, –n, Frenchman
die Frau, –en, woman, wife, Mrs.
das Fräulein, –s, —, young lady,
    Miss
frei, free; vacant
frei-halten (ä), ie, a, to reserve
die Freiheit, –en, liberty, freedom

der **Freiheitskämpfer.** –s, —, fighter
for liberty

frei-sprechen (i), a, o, to acquit

der **Freitag,** –s, –e, Friday

fremd, strange

fressen (i), a, e, to eat (of animals)

die **Freude,** –n, joy

freuen, *wk.*, to please; **sich f.**, to be
pleased (at, über, *w. accus.*)

der **Freund,** –es, –e, friend

freundlich, friendly

frisch, fresh

froh, glad

fröhlich, happy, merry

früh, early

der **Frühling,** –s, –e, spring

das **Frühstück,** –s, –e, breakfast

sich fühlen, *wk.*, to feel

führen, *wk.*, to lead, take

füllen, *wk.*, to fill

die **Füllfeder,** –n, fountain-pen

für, *w. accus.*, for; **was für ein,** what
sort of

fürchten, *wk.*, to fear, be afraid of

der **Fürst,** –en, –en, prince

der **Fuß,** –es, ⸚e, foot; **zu Fuß gehen,**
to walk

füttern, *wk.*, to feed

G

gab . . . auf, *past of* aufgeben

die **Gabe,** –n, gift

die **Gabel,** –n, fork

der **Gang,** –es, ⸚e, course

die **Gans,** ⸚e, goose

ganz, entire, whole

der **Garten,** –s, ⸚, garden

der **Gärtner,** –s, —, gardener

die **Gas'later'ne,** –n, gas street-light

der **Gast,** –es, ⸚e, guest

das **Gasthaus,** –es, ⸚er, tavern

die **Gaststätte,** –n, hotel *or* restaurant

der **Gastwirt,** –s, –e, inn-keeper

das **Gastzimmer,** –s, —, guest-room

das **Gebäu'de,** –s, —, building

geben (i), a, e, to give; **es gibt,** there
is (are)

gebraten, *p.p. of* braten, roast

der **Geburts'tag,** –s, –e, birthday; —s-
kind, b. child; —skuchen, b. cake;
—stisch, b. table

der **Gedan'ke,** –ns, –n, thought

das **Gedicht',** –s, –e, poem

das **Gedrän'ge,** –s, crowding

gefähr'lich, dangerous

gefallen (ä), ie, a, to please (*w. dat.*)

der **Gefan'gene** (*adj. infl.*), prisoner

der **Gefan'genwärter,** –s, —, prison-
keeper

das **Gefäng'nis,** –ses, –se, prison

gegen, *w. accus.*, against

das **Gegenteil,** –s, opposite

gegenü'ber, *w. dat.*, opposite

das **Gehalt',** –s, ⸚er, salary

das **Geheim'nis,** –ses, –se, secret

geheim'nisvoll, mysterious

gehen, *irreg.*, ist gegangen, to go

gehö'ren, *wk.*, to belong; — zu, be
part of

der **Geist,** –es, ⸚er, spirit

geistig, spiritual, mental

das **Geld,** –es, –er, money

der **Gelehr'te** (*adj. infl.*), man of
learning

gelin'gen, a, ist gelungen, to succeed

gelten (i), a, o, to pass, be considered

gemein', common

die **Gemein'de,** –n, community, congregation

das **Gemü'se,** –s, —, green vegetable

der **Gemü'sehändler,** vegetable dealer

gemüt'lich, cozy, comfortable

genug', enough

das **Geräusch',** –es, –e, noise, sound

gern, gladly; *comp.*, lieber

der Geruch', –8, ⁔e, odor

der Gesand'te (adj. infl.), envoy, minister

das Geschäft', –8, –e, shop, business

geschehen (ie), a, ist geschehen, to happen

das Geschenk', –8, –e, present

die Geschich'te, –n, story; history

das Geschirr', –8, dishes

das Geschöpf', –8, –e, creature

gescho'ren, p.p. of scheren, shorn

die Gesell'schaft, –en, company, party

das Gesicht', –8, –er, face

gesinnt', minded, disposed

der Gesin'nungsgenos'se, –n, –n, one sharing a conviction

die Gestalt', –en, form

gestern, yesterday; gestern abend, last night

gesund', healthy, well

die Gewalt', –en, force, violence

gewin'nen, a, o, to gain

gewiß', certain

gewöhn'lich, usual, customary

es gibt, see geben

gießen, o, o, to pour

ging, past of gehen

das Gitter, –8, —, grating

die Gittertür, –en, door in grating

glänzen, wk., to shine

glänzend, brilliant

das Glas, –8, ⁔er, glass

die Glaskugel, –n, glass ball

der Glasschrank, –8, ⁔e, glass cabinet

glauben, wk., to believe (w. dat. of person)

gleich, equal, same; immediately

gleiten, i, ist geglitten, to glide

glitzernd, glistening, glittering

die Glocke, –n, bell

das Glück, –8, luck, good luck, happiness

glücken, wk., ist geglückt, to succeed

glücklich, happy, fortunate

der Glückwunsch, –es, ⁔e, congratulation

die Glühbirne, –n, electric bulb

gnädig, gracious

das Gold, –es, gold

golden, of gold, golden

Gott, –es, ⁔er, God

graben (ä), u, a, to dig

grau, gray

grausam, cruel

greifen, i, i, to seize, resort (to)

die Grenze, –n, border, frontier

groß, large, great; grown-up

die Großeltern, grandparents

die Großmutter, ⁔, grandmother

der Großvater, –8, ⁔, grandfather

grün, green

der Grund, –es, ⁔e, ground; zu Grunde gehen, to perish, go to ruin

grüßen, wk., to greet

günstig, favorable

der Gur'kensalat', –8, cucumber salad

gut, good, well; very well

das Gut, –es, ⁔er, estate

der Gutsbesitzer, –8, —, owner of an estate

H

das Haar, –es, –e, hair

haben, to have

der Hafen, –8, ⁔, harbor

die Hälfte, –n, the half

der Hals, –es, ⁔e, throat, neck

halsbrecherisch, break-neck

hält . . . an, see anhalten

halten (ä), ie, a, to hold, stop; — für, take for

die Hand, ⁔e, hand

handeln, wk., to treat, deal (with)

handfest, stalwart, sturdy

die Handschrift, –en, handwriting

hängen (hangen), i, a, to hang, depend

hart, hard

häßlich, ugly

die Häßlichkeit, ugliness

häufig, frequent

der Haupthafen, –s, ", main harbor

das Haupt'quartier', –s, –e, headquarters

die Hauptstadt, "e, capital (city)

die Hauptstraße, –n, main street

das Haus, –es, "er, house; zu Hause, at home; nach Hause, (toward) home

die Hausfrau, –en, housewife

der Haushalt, –s, household

das Heer, –es, –e army

heilig, holy

das Heim, –es, –e, home. See footnote on p. 194

die Heimat, –en, home

heimlich, secret

der Heimweg, –s, way home

Heinrich Heine, German poet (1797–1856)

heiraten, wk., to marry

heiß, hot

heißen, ie, ei, to be called; mean, be; bid

helfen (i), a, o, to help (w. dat.)

der Helfer, –s, —, helper, accomplice

hell, bright, light

das Hemd, –es, –en, shirt

heraus', out

heraus'helfen (i), a, o, to help to get out (w. dat.)

herein', in, come in

der Herr, –n, –en, gentleman, Mr., master

herrlich, splendid, magnificent

herrschen, wk., to rule, prevail

um . . . herum', around

herun'ter, down

herun'ter=klappen, wk., to let down

herun'ter=kommen, a, ist heruntergekommen, to come down

herun'ter=lassen (ä), ie, a, to let down

das Herz, –ens, –en, heart

herzlich, cordial; heart-felt, sincere

heute, today; heute nacht, to-night

heutzutage, nowadays

hier, here

die Hilfe, help

der Hilferuf, –s, –e, call for help

der Himmel, –s, —, sky, heaven

hinaus', adv., out

hinaus'=sehen (ie), a, e, to look out

hinein', adv., into

hinten, adv., behind, in the stern

hinter, w. dat. or accus., behind

hinzu'=setzen, wk., to add

hoch, comp. höher, sup., höchst, high

das Hoch, cheer

höchst, very, most

die Hochzeit, –en, wedding

der Hochzeitsbrauch, –s, "e, wedding custom; —gabe, wedding gift; —gast, wedding guest; —geschenk', wedding gift; —mahl, wedding feast

der Hof, –es, "e, court, courtyard

hoffen, wk., to hope

hoffentlich, as I (we, etc.) hope

holen, wk., go and get, get, fetch

das Holz, –es, "er, wood

hören, wk., to hear

das Hotel', –s, –s, hotel

hübsch, pretty

das Huhn, –es, "er, chicken, fowl

der Hund, –es, –e, dog

hungrig, hungry

der Hut, –es, "e, hat

J

ich, I

die Idee', –n, idea

ihm, ihn, *dat. and accus. of* er

ihr, *plur. of* du; her; their

Ihr, your

im = in dem

immer, always

im'merhin', after all

im'merzu', all the time

imstan'de sein, to be able to

in, *w. dat. or accus.*, in

indem', while

inner, inner

innerhalb, *w. gen.*, inside of

der Inspek'tor, –s, –to'ren, inspector

interessant', interesting

interessie'ren, *wk.*, to interest

inzwi'schen, meanwhile

iß, *imper. of* essen

(das) Ita'lien, –s, Italy

J

ja, yes; particle, see p. 18, footnote 1

das Jahr, –es, –e, year

das Jahrhun'dert, –s, –e, century

der Jammer, –s, grief

jawohl', yes indeed

das Jawort, –s, consent to marry

jeder, every, each

jedesmal, each time

jemand, –s, somebody

jener, that, that one; former

jenseits, *w. gen.*, on the other side of

jetzt, now

jubeln, *wk.*, to jubilate, shout

jung, young

der Junge, –n, –n, boy

K

der Kaffee, –s, coffee

kahl, bald, bare

das Kalb, –es, –er, calf

kalt, cold; die Kälte, cold

kam, kamen, *past of* kommen

kam . . . an, *past of* an-kommen

der Kamin', –s, –e, fireplace

der Kampf, –es, –e, struggle

kämpfen, *wk.*, to struggle

der Kanal', –s, Channel

er kann, *see* können

die Kanzel, –n, pulpit

der Kapitän', –s, –e, captain (ship)

Karl, –s, Charles

die Karte, –n, card; map

die Kartof'fel, –n, potato

der Käse, –s, —, cheese

der Kasten, –s, –, box

kaufen, *wk.*, to buy

der Käufer, –s, —, customer

das Kaufhaus, –es, –er, department store

der Kaufmann, –s, Kaufleute, business man

kaum, scarcely, hardly

kein, no, none, no one

keinmal, not once, at no time

der Keller, –s, —, cellar

der Kellner, –s, —, waiter

kennen, *irreg.*, to know, be acquainted with

der Kerkermeister, –s, —, jailer

das Kind, –es, –er, child

das Kino, –s, –s, movie

die Kirche, –n, church

kirchlich, *adj.*, church

die Kirchtür, –en, church door

kläglich, pitiful

klar, clear

sich klären, *wk.*, to clear up

die Klasse, –n, class, classroom

das Klavier', –8, –e, piano

das Kleeblatt, –8, ⸚er, clover-leaf; trio

das Kleid, –es, –er, dress, clothing

kleiden, wk., to dress

die Kleidung, clothing

klein, small

die Kleinstadt, ⸚e, small town

klingeln, wk., to ring

klingen, a, u, to sound

klopfen, wk., to knock

klug, clever

der Knabe, –n, –n, boy

knacken, wk., to crack

der Knicks, –es, –e, curtsy

knirschen, wk., to crunch

der Knoten, –8, —, knot

die Köchin, –nen, (female) cook

der Kochofen, –8, ⸚, cook-stove

der Kolle'ge, –n, –n, colleague

Köln, –8, Cologne

Kölner, of Cologne, Cologne

kommen, a, ist gekommen, to come

der Komponist', –en, –en, composer

der König, –8, –e, king

das Königreich, –8, –e, kingdom

können, can

der Kopf, –es, ⸚e, head

das Kopfrechnen, –8, mental arithmetic

der Körper, –8, —, body

körperlich, physical

der Korridor, –8, –e, corridor

kosten, wk., to cost

köstlich, delicious

krachen, wk., to crash

kräftig, nutritious

der Kragen, –8, —, collar

krank, ill, sick

der Kranz, –es, ⸚e, wreath

der Krieg, –es, –e, war

die Küche, –n, kitchen

der Kuchen, –8, —, cake

das Küchenmöbel, –8, —, kitchen furniture

der Kuchenteller, –8, —, cake-plate

die Kuh, ⸚e, cow

kühl, cool

der Kühlschrank, –8, ⸚e, refrigerator

kühn, bold

die Kunst, ⸚e, art

die Kunstgeschichte, history of art

kurz, short; in short

die Kusi'ne, –n, (female) cousin

der Kuß, –es, ⸚e, kiss

küssen, wk., to kiss

die Küste, –n, coast

der Kutscher, –8, —, driver, coachman

L

lächeln, wk., to smile

lachen, wk., to laugh

der Lackschuh, –8, –e, patent-leather shoe

die Ladung, –en, cargo, load

die Lampe, –n, lamp

das Land, –es, ⸚er, land; auf dem Lande, in the country

landen, wk., ist gelandet, to land

die Landleute (plur.), country people

die Landschaft, –en, landscape

die Landstraße, –n, road, highway

lang, long

lange, a long time

langsam, slow

der Lärm, –8, noise, din

lassen (ä), ie, a, to let; have

die Later'ne, –n, lantern; light; street-light

laufen (äu), ie, ist gelaufen, to run

laut, loud, aloud

läuten, wk., to ring

leben, wk., to live

das Leben, –8, life

leben'dig, alive

die Le'benserin'nerungen (*plur.*), memoirs

le'bensläng'lich, for life

der Le'bensun'terhalt, –s, livelihood, support

Lebewohl' sagen, to say goodbye

der Lebkuchen, –s, —, honey-cake

der Leckerbissen, –s, —, tidbit

das Lederpolster, –s, —, leather upholstery

legen, *wk.*, to lay, put

legt . . . ab, *see* ab=legen

der Lehrer, –s, —, teacher

die Lehrerin, –nen, (woman) teacher

leicht, light, easy

leider, unfortunately

leihen, ie, ie, to lend

leise, soft, gentle

lenken, *wk.*, to guide, steer

lernen, *wk.*, to learn

lesen (ie), a, e, to read

der Leser, –s, —, reader

der letzte, the last; zum letztenmal, for the last time

die Leute (*plur.*), people

das Licht, –es, –er, candle

lieb, dear, sweet; lieb=haben, to love

das Liebchen, –s, —, sweetheart

die Liebe, love

lieben, *wk.*, to love

der Lie'besroman', –s, –e, ' love novel,' love story

liebevoll, loving

der Liebling, –s, –e, favorite

das Lied, –es, –er, song

liegen, a, e, to lie

ließ . . . ein, *past of* einlassen

liest, *see* lesen

der Lindenbaum, –s, ⸚e, linden (tree)

link, left

loben, *wk.*, to praise

das Loch, –es, ⸚er, hole

locken, *wk.*, to entice, lure

der Löffel, –s, —, spoon

los; was ist los ? what is going on ?

lösen, *wk.*, to loosen

los=lösen, *wk.*, to loosen

die Lunge, –n, lung

die Lust, ⸚e, desire

lustig, jolly, merry

M

machen, *wk.*, to make; schnell machen, to hurry up

die Macht, ⸚e, power

macht . . . auf, *see* aufmachen

das Mädchen, –s, —, girl; servant-girl

das Maiglöckchen, –s, —, lily of the valley

das Mal, –s, –e, time

mal, *w. imper.*, just

man, one, people, they

manch, many a, some

manchmal, sometimes

der Mann, –es, ⸚er, man, husband

die Männerstimme, –n, male voice

der Mantel, –s, ⸚, cloak

die Mark, —, mark (coin)

der Markt, –es, ⸚e, market

der Marzipan', –s, almond paste, marchpane

die Mauer, –n, (masonry) wall

der Medizi'ner, –s, —, medical student

das Meer, –es, –e, ocean

mehr, more; nicht —, no longer

mehrere, several

die Meile, –n, mile (4½ miles)

mein, my, mine

meinen, *wk.*, to mean, think and say

meinetwegen, so far as I am concerned

Meißner, of Meiszen, in Saxony

meistens, mostly

die Melodie', –n, melody

die Menge, –n, crowd, quantity, number

der Mensch, –en, –en, human being

das Messer, –s, —, knife

mieten, *wk.*, to rent

die Milch, milk

mildern, *wk.*, to make milder, commute

die Million', –en, million

der Millionär', –s, –e, millionaire

die Minu'te, –n, minute

der Minu'tenzeiger, –s, —, minute-hand

mir, *dat. of* ich

mißglü'cken, *wk.*, ist mißglückt, to fail

mit, *w. dat.*, with; along

mit=bringen, *irreg.*, to bring along

mit=fahren (ä), u, ist mitgefahren, to drive along

der Mithelfer, –s, —, accomplice

mit=nehmen (i), a, o, to take along

der Mittag, –s, –e, noon

das Mittagessen, –s, —, dinner

die Mitte, middle, center

mit=teilen, *wk.*, to communicate, tell

die Mitternacht, ̈e, midnight

der Mittwoch, –s, –e, Wednesday

das Möbel, –s, —, piece of furniture

das Mö'belgeschäft', –s, –e, furniture store

ich möchte, I should like to

die Mode, –n, fashion

modern', modern

mögen, may, like

möglich, possible

der Monat, –s, –e, month

der Mönd, –es, –e, moon

der Möntag, –s, –e, Monday

der Morgen, –s, —, morning

morgen, to-morrow; — früh, to-morrow morning

müde, tired

die Mühe, –n, trouble, pains

der Mund, –es, mouth

das Muse'um, –s, –seen, museum

die Musik', music

der Musikant', –en, –en, musician

der Muskel, –s, –n, muscle

ich (er) muß, I (he) must

müssen, must

der Mut, –es, courage

mutig, courageous

die Mutter, ̈, mother

die Mütze, –n, cap

N

na, well, O well

nach, *w. dat.*, after, to

der Nachbar, –s, –n, neighbor

nachdem', *conj.*, after

nach=denken, *irreg.*, to reflect

nach=erzählen, *wk.*, to retell

der Nachmittag, –s, –e, afternoon

die Nachricht, –en, news, message

der Nachschlüssel, –s, —, duplicate key

nächst, next

die Nacht, ̈e, night

nachts, during the night

die Nachtwache, –n, night watch

der Nachtwächter, –s, —, night-watchman

nah, near by

die Nahrung, food, nourishment

der Name(n), –ns, –n, name

namens, by the name of

naß, wet

natür'lich, of course

neben, *w. dat. or accus.*, next to

das Nebenzimmer, –s, —, adjoining room

necken, *wk.*, to tease

der Neffe, –n, –n, nephew

nehmen (i), a, o, to take

nein, no

nennen, *irreg.*, to name

der Nerv (*pron.* –f), –s, –en, nerve
das Nest, –es, –er, nest
nett, nice, pleasant
neu, new, recent
das Neujahr, –s, New Year
neulich, recently, the other day
nicht, not; n. wahr? not so, isn't it?
die Nichte, –n, niece
nichts, nothing; n. als, nothing but
nie, never
sich nieder=legen, *wk.*, to lie down
niedlich, ' cute '
niemand, –s, nobody, no one
noch, still, yet; noch ehe, even before;
noch nicht, not yet; noch nie, never
yet
der Norden, –s, north
die Nordsee, North Sea
die Not, ⸚e, distress, need
der Notfall, –s, ⸚e, case of need
nötig, necessary
null, zero
nun, now; well
nur, only
Nürnberger, *adj.*, Nuremberg
die Nuß, ⸚e, nut
die Nußschale, –n, nutshell

O

O weh', alas, O dear
ob, whether
oben, *adv.*, above, on top
ober, *adj.*, upper
der Ober (= Oberkellner), –s, —,
head waiter
obgleich', although
das Obst, –es, fruit
der Obstbaum, –s, ⸚e, fruit tree
der Obstgarten, –s, ⸚, orchard
obwohl', although
oder, or
der Ofen, –s, ⸚, stove; oven

offen, open
öffnen, *wk.*, to open
oft, often
ohne, *w. accus.*, without
das Ohr, –s, –en, ear
der Onkel, –s, —, uncle
die Operation', –en, operation
die Ordnung, –en, order
die Orgel, –n, organ
der Osten, –s, east

P

das Paar, –es, –e, pair, couple
ein paar, a few
das Pakēt', –s, –e, package
das Papier', –s, paper
der Paß, –es, ⸚e, passport
passen, *wk.*, to fit, suit, match
passie'ren, *wk.*, ist passiert, to happen
paßt . . . auf, *see* aufpassen
das Peitschenknallen, –s, cracking of
whips
persön'lich, personal
der Pfannkuchen, –s, —, cruller, pancake
der Pfarrer, –s, —, parson
die Pfeffernuß, ⸚e, spiced cooky
der Pfennig, $\frac{1}{100}$ of a mark
das Pferd, –es, –e, horse
das Pferderennen, –s, —, horse-race
das Pflaster, –s, —, pavement
die Pflicht, –en, duty
das Pförtchen, –s, —, little door,
wicket
das Pfund, –es, — *or* –e, pound
der Plan, –es, ⸚e, plan, map
der Platz, –es, ⸚e, room, space, place,
square
das Plätzchen, –s, —, cooky
plaudern, *wk.*, to chat
plötzlich, suddenly

der Polizei'beam'te (*adj. infl.*), policeman

der Polterabend, –s, –e, 'polterabend'

das Porzellan', –s, china; Meißner
P., Dresden china

die Post, –en, post, mail; postoffice

praktisch, practical

der Präsident', –en, –en, president

predigen, *wk.*, to preach

der Preis, –es, –e, price

der Preuße, –n, –n, Prussian

(das) Preußen, –s, Prussia

preußisch, Prussian

der Profes'sor, –s, –o'ren, professor

prosit (Latin) Neujahr, Happy New
Year

der Punsch, –es, –e, punch

Q

qualvoll, agonizing

R

das Rad, –es, –er, wheel

das Radies'chen, –s, —, radish

rasseln, *wk.*, to rattle

die Rast, –en, rest

der Rat, –es, advice

raten (ä), ie, a, to advise; guess

der Ratskeller, –s, —, Ratskeller

rauchen, *wk.*, to smoke

der Raum, –es, –e, quarter, hall

die Rechenstunde, –n, arithmetic lesson

rechnen, *wk.*, to figure

recht, right (opposite of *wrong* and
left); recht haben, to be right

das Recht, –s, –e, right

die Rede, –n, speech

reden, *wk.*, to talk, speak

die Redewendung, –en, idiom

redlich, honest, sincere

rege, lively, gay

regie'ren, *wk.*, to rule

die Regie'rung, –en, government

regnen, *wk.*, to rain

reich, rich

das Reich, –es, –e, realm, Reich

der Reichtum, –s, –er, wealth, riches

reif, ripe

die Reise, –n, journey, trip

reisen, *wk.*, ist gereist, to travel

der Reisende (*adj. infl.*), traveler

die Reisetasche, –n, traveling bag

reißen, i, i, to pull

reiten, i, ist geritten, to ride

rennen, *irreg.*, ist gerannt, to run

das Reptil', –s, –e *or* –ien, reptile

retten, *wk.*, to save

die Rettung, –en, rescue

die Revolution', –en, revolution;
—sheer, –s, –e, revolutionary army;
—sjahr, –s, –e, year of revolution

der Rhein, –s, Rhine

richtig, correct, right

die Richtung, –en, direction

riechen, o, o, to smell

der Röntgenstrahl, –s, –en, R. ray

die Rose, –n, rose

rot, red

die Rückfahrt, –en, journey back

die Rückkehr, return

rudern, *wk.*, to row

der Ruf, –es, –e, call, shout

rufen, ie, u, to call, shout

rund, round

der Rundfunk, –s, –e, radio

S

der Saal, –es, Säle, hall, room

die Sache, –n, thing

(das) Sachsen, –s, Saxony

sagen, *wk.*, to say

sah, *past of* sehen

der Salat', –s, –e, salad

ſammeln, *wk.*, to collect

der Samstag, –s, –e, Saturday

der Sand, –es, sand

ſanft, gentle

ſauſen, *wk.*, to rush

es iſt ſchade, it is too bad

ſchaffen, u, a, to create, make

ſchaltet ... ein, *see* einſchalten

das Schaltjahr, –s, –e, leap-year

die Schande, shame, disgrace

der Schatz, –es, –e, treasure, sweet-heart

ſchauen, *wk.*, to see, look

das Schaufenſter, –s, —, shop-window

der Schein, –s, light

ſcheinen, ie, ie, to seem

ſchenken, *wk.*, to present, give

ſcherzen, *wk.*, to jest

ſchicken, *wk.*, to send

das Schickſal, –s, –e, fate, fortune

ſchien(en), *past of* ſcheinen

ſchießen, o, o, to shoot

das Schiff, –es, –e, ship

die Schildwache, –n, sentry

der Schinken, –s, —, ham

ſchlafen (ä), ie, a, to sleep

der Schlag, –es, –e, blow

ſchlagen (ä), u, a, to strike

die Schlagſahne, whipped cream

ſchlank, slender

ſchlecht, bad, poor

der Schleier, –s, —, veil

die Schleppe, –n, train (of dress)

ſchließen, o, o, to close; conclude

ſchließlich, finally

der Schlips, –es, –e, necktie

der Schlittſchuh, –s, –e, skate

das Schloß, –es, –er, lock; castle

der Schluck, –s, –e, swallow, drop

der Schlüſſel, –s, —, key

der Schmerz, –es, –en, pain, grief

ſchmücken, *wk.*, to adorn, trim

der Schnee, –s, snow

ſchneiden, ſchnitt, geſchnitten, to cut

der Schneider, –s, —, tailor

ſchneidern, *wk.*, to make dresses

ſchneidig, dashing, smart

ſchnell, quick, fast

die Schnurre, –n, yarn, funny story

die Schokolade, chocolate

ſchon, already

ſchön, beautiful; very well, all right

die Schönheit, –en, beauty

(das) Schottland, –s, Scotland

der Schrank, –es, –e, cupboard, cabinet

ſchrecklich, terrible

ſchreiben, ie, ie, to write

der Schreibtiſch, –es, –e, writing-desk

ſchriftlich, in writing

der Schuh, –es, –e, shoe

die Schuld, –en, blame, fault; debt

die Schule, –n, school

der Schüler, –s, —, pupil

der Schulkamerad', –en, –en, school-mate, school-chum

die Schüſſel, –n, bowl, dish

ſchützen, *wk.*, to protect

ſchwach, weak

der Schwager, –s, –, brother-in-law

die Schwägerin, –nen, sister-in-law

ſchwanken, *wk.*, to waver

ſchwarz, black

die Schweiz, Switzerland

ſchwellen, *wk.*, to swell

ſchwer, heavy

die Schweſter, –n, sister

die Schwiegermutter, –, mother-in-law

der Schwiegerſohn, –s, –e, son-in-law

die Schwiegertochter, –, daughter-in-law

ſchwierig, difficult

ſchwimmen, a, o, to swim

der See, –s, –n, lake

die See, –n, sea, seaside

das Seebad, -s, "er, seaside resort

seekrank, seasick

das Segel, -s, —, sail

das Segelboot, -s, -e, sailboat

segelfertig, ready to sail

das Segelschiff, -s, -e, sailing vessel

segnen, wk., to bless

sehen (ie) a, e, to see, look at

sehr, very; very much

die Seide, silk

das Seil, -s, -e, rope

sein, his, its, one's

sein, to be

seit, prep. w. dat., since; conj., since

seitdem', conj., since; adv., since then

die Seite, -n, side; page

der Sekretär', -s, -e, secretary

der Sekt, -es, -e, German champagne

die Sekun'de, -n, second

selber, -self, -selves

selbst, -self, -selves; even

die Selbst'biographie', -n, autobiography

der Selbstmord, -s, -e, suicide

senden, irreg., to send

der Sessel, -s, —, arm-chair

setzen, wk., to place, set

sich, himself, herself, themselves

sicher, secure, safe, certain

der Sieg, -es, -e, victory

sieh, imper. of sehen

siehst, sieht, see sehen

silbern, silver, of silver

der Silve'ster, -s, —, day before New Year, New Year's Eve

der Silve'sterabend, -s, -e, New Year's Eve

singen, a, u, to sing

sitzen, saß, gesessen, to sit

so, so, thus, such; so schnell sie konnten, as quickly as they could

sobald', as soon as

das Sofa, -s, -s, sofa

sofort', at once

sogar', even

der Sohn, -es, "e, son

solch, such

der Soldat', -en, -en, soldier

sollen, shall, is to, is said to

der Söller, -s, —, garret

der Sommer, -s, —, summer

das Sommerhäuschen, -s, —, summer cottage

die Sommerreise, -n, summer trip

sondern, but

der Sonnabend, -s, -e, Saturday

die Sonne, -n, sun

der Sonntag, -s, -e, Sunday

sonst, else, otherwise, usually

die Sorge, -n, worry; sich (dat.) Sorgen machen, to worry

sorgen, wk., to care for

soviel, so much

sowie', as well as

(das) Spanien, -s, Spain

spannend, exciting

später, later, afterwards

der Spazier'gang, -s, "e, walk

die Speise, -n, food; dessert

spielen, wk., to play

der Spiel'kamerad', -en, -en, playmate

der Spinat', -s, spinach

die Spitze, -n, top, summit

die Sprache, -n, language

sprechen (i), a, o, to speak

das Sprechzimmer, -s, —, consultation room

sprich, imper. of sprechen

springen, a, ist gesprungen, to jump

der Staat, -es, -en, state

der Stab, -es, "e, stave, bar

die Stadt, "e, city, town

der Stadtrichter, -s, —, city judge

der Stahl, -es, steel

das Stahlmöbel, -s, —, steel furniture

der Stall, -es, ⸚e, stable, barn

das Stamm'lokal', tavern one frequents

das Standesamt, -s, ⸚er, registry office

stark, strong

statt, *w. gen.*, instead of

stattlich, handsome, distinguished

stecken, *wk.*, to stick, slip

stehen, *irreg.*, to stand

stehlen (ie), a, o, to steal

steif, stiff

steigen, ie, ist gestiegen, to climb; get in; get out

die Stelle, -n, place, position

stellen, *wk.*, to place, put; sich stellen, to feign, pretend

sterben (i), a, ist gestorben, to die

der Stern, -es, -e, star

stießen . . . an, *past of* anstoßen

still, silent, quiet

still=liegen, a, e, to lie still, 'lie low'

die Stimme, -n, voice

stimmten . . . ein, *see* ein=stimmen

die Stimmung, -en, mood, atmosphere

das Stockwerk, -s, -e, story (of building)

stolz, proud

stoßen (ö), ie, o, to thrust, knock

die Strafe, -n, punishment, sentence

die Sträflingsjacke, -n, convict's jacket

die Straße, -n, street

der Straßenkampf, -s, ⸚e, street fighting

der Strauch, -es, ⸚er, shrub, bush

die Strecke, -n, stretch, route

der Streifen, -s, —, strip

streiten, i, i, to quarrel, fight

der Strom, -es, ⸚e, large river, current

die Stube, -n, room

das Stück, -es, -e, piece

der Student', -en, -en, student

studie'ren, *wk.*, to study

das Studium, -s, -dien, study

der Stuhl, -es, ⸚e, chair

die Stunde, -n, hour

der Stundenzeiger, -s, —, hour-hand

der Sturm, -es, ⸚e, (wind) storm

stürmen, *wk.*, to storm

stürzen, *wk.*, ist gestürzt, to rush, plunge

die Subaltern'natur', -en, person with a sense of inferiority

suchen, *wk.*, to look for, seek

der Süden, -s, south

die Summe, -n, sum

summen, *wk.*, to hum

die Suppe, -n, soup

süß, sweet

die Süßigkeit, -en, sweets

die Szene, -n, scene

T

der Ta'bak, -s, tobacco

die Tafel, -n, blackboard

die Ta'felmusik', dinner music

der Tag, -es, -e, day; guten T. sagen, to say how do you do

tagelang, for days

der Tagesanbruch, -s, break of day

der Takt, -es, -e, rhythm

das Tal, -es, ⸚er, valley

der Tand, -es, tinsel

die Tankstelle, -n, filling station

der Tannenbaum, -s, ⸚e, spruce

die Tante, -n, aunt

der Tanz, -es, ⸚e, dance

tanzen, *wk.*, to dance

die Tanz'musik', dance music

die Tasche, -n, pocket

das Taschengeld, -s, ⸚er, allowance

die Taffe, –n, cup
die Tat, –en, deed
der Teil, –es, –e, part
teilnahmsvoll, sympathetic
das Telephon', –s, –e, telephone
der Teller, –s, —, plate
der Teppich, –s, –e, rug, carpet
teuer, expensive, dear
tief, deep, far
das Tier, –es, –e, animal
der Tisch, –es, –e, table; bei T., at
    table, at dinner; zu T., to dinner
die Tischrede, –n, after-dinner speech
die Tochter, –, daughter
der Tod, –es, death
die Todesstrafe, –n, death penalty
die Tonne, –n, ton
der Topf, –es, –e, pot
das Tor, –es, –e, gate
der Torweg, –s, –e, gateway
tot, dead
traben, wk., to trot
tragen (ä), u, a, to carry, bear; wear
trauen, wk., unite in marriage;
    trust (w. dat. of person)
die Traurede, –n, marriage sermon
traurig, sad
der Trauring, –s, –e, wedding-ring
die Trauung, –en, marriage ceremony,
    wedding
der Trauzeuge, –n, –n, marriage wit-
    ness
treffen (i), a, o, to hit; meet
treten (i), a, ist getreten, to step,
    enter, tread
treu, faithful, true
trinken, a, u, to drink
tritt, 3d. person sg. of treten
trösten, wk., to console, comfort
trotz, w. gen., in spite of
die Truppe, –n, troops
die Tulpe, –n, tulip
tut, tat, getan, to do

die Tür(e), –en, door
die Türkei', Turkey
der Turm, –es, –e, tower
die Turmuhr, –en, tower-clock
typisch, typical
der Tyrann', –en, –en, tyrant

U

übel, evil, bad; ist dir übel, do you feel
    ill
über, w. dat. or accus., over; w.
    accus., about, across
überall', everywhere
überle'gen, wk., to consider
übernach'ten, wk., to spend the night
der Überrock, –s, –e, overcoat
überset'zen, wk., to translate
die Überset'zung, –en, translation
übertö'nen, wk., to drown, deaden
üblich, customary
übrig, left over
die Übung, –en, exercise
das Ufer, –s, —, bank, shore
die Uhr, –en, timepiece, watch, clock
der Uhrmacher, –s, —, watchmaker
um, w. accus., around, at; um . . .
    herum', around
umar'men, wk., to embrace
umge'ben (i), a, e, to surround
umher'=werfen (i), a, o, to throw
    around
um=kehren, wk., ist umgekehrt, to turn
    back, turn around
um=kippen, wk., ist umgekippt, to tip
    over, capsize
umsonst', in vain
der Umweg, –s, –e, roundabout way
um=werfen (i), a, o, to throw about
der Umzug, –s, –e, the moving
unartig, naughty
unaufhör'lich, incessant
unbekannt, unknown

unbequēm, uncomfortable

unentdeckt, undiscovered

der Unfall, –s, ⸚e, accident

ungeduldig, impatient

ungefähr, about, approximately

unglaub'lich, unbelievable

das Unglück, –s, misfortune, mishap

unglücklich, unfortunate, disastrous; unhappy, distressed

die Universität', –en, university

unmöglich, impossible

unnötig, unnecessary

unpraktisch, impractical

uns, us

unser, our, ours

unten, adv., below

unter, w. dat. or accus., under, among

der Un'terbeam'te (adj. infl.), subordinate official

unterneh'men (i), a, o, to undertake

das Unterneh'men, –s, enterprise

der Un'teroffizier', –s, –e, noncommissioned officer

untersu'chen, wk., to examine

die Untersu'chung, –en, examination

untreu, faithless

unwillkommen, unwelcome

usw. = und so weiter, etc.

B

der Vater, –s, ⸚, father

das Vaterland, –s, native land, ' fatherland '

das Veilchen, –s, —, violet

verab'reden, wk., to agree upon

die Verbeu'gung, –en, bow

verbinden, a, u, to bandage

die Verbindung, –en, connection; in V. treten mit, to get in touch with

der Verbre'cher, –s, —, criminal

verbringen, irreg., to spend, pass

verbüßen, wk., to serve (a sentence)

verdächtig, suspicious, suspected

die Verei'nigten Staaten, United States

verenden, wk., ist verendet, to die, perish

die Verfas'sung, –en, constitution

der Verfol'ger, –s, —, pursuer

vergeben (i), a, e, w. dat. of person, to forgive

vergēb'lich, in vain

vergehen, irreg., to pass

vergessen (i), a, e, to forget

das Vergnü'gen, –s, —, delight, pleasure

vergöl'det, gilt

verhei'ratet, married

verhüten, wk., to prevent, obviate

verkürzen, wk., to shorten, cut down

verlangen, wk., to demand

sich verlassen auf (w. accus.) (ä) ie, a, to rely on

verle'gen, embarrassed

verlieren, o, o, to lose

verlöbt, engaged

die Verlobte (adj. infl.), fiancée

der Verlobungsring, –s, –e, engagement ring

verraten (ä), ie, a, to betray

verschaffen, wk., to procure

verscheuchen, wk., to frighten away

verschlossen, closed, locked

verschwinden, a, ist verschwunden, to disappear

das Verse'hen, –s, —, mistake

die Versor'gung, –en, care, provision

versprechen (i), a, o, to promise

verstehen, irreg., to understand

der Versuch', –s, –e, attempt

versuchen, wk., to attempt, try

vertrauen, wk., to entrust

das Vertrau'en, –s, confidence

verur'teilen, wk., to condemn

verwahren, wk., to guard, secure

der Verwand'te (*adj. infl.*), relative

verwun'det, wounded

der Vetter, –s, –n, (male) cousin

viel, much, many

vielleicht', perhaps

vier, four

das Viertel, (*pron.* ie *as* i), –s, —, quarter

das Vierteljahr', three months

die Viertelstun'de, –n, quarter of an hour

der Vogel, –s, ⸚, bird

die Voka'bel, –n, word (in a foreign word-list)

das Volk, –es, ⸚er, people, nation

vom = von dem

von, *w. dat.*, of, from

vor, *w. dat. or accus.*, before; ago

der Vor'abend, –s, –e, eve

im vor'aus, in advance

vorbei', past; —fahren, drive past; —gehen, go past; —lassen, let pass

die Vor'bereitung, –en, preparation

der Vorfahr, –en, –en, ancestor

die Vorhalle, –n, front hall

vorher', *adv.*, beforehand, before

vorig, last, past, former

vorn, in front

vor=setzen, *wk.*, to place before

die Vorstadt, ⸚e, suburb

vor=stellen, *wk.*, to introduce

W

wach, awake

die Wache, –n, watch

der Wachsabdruck, –s, ⸚e, wax impression

wachsam, watchful

wachsen (ä), u, ist gewachsen, to grow

die Wachskerze, –n, wax candle

die Waffe, –n, arm, weapon

wagen, *wk.*, to risk, dare

der Wagen, –s, —, wagon, carriage, car

der Wahnsinn, –s, insanity

wahr, true; nicht wahr? not so, isn't it (true)?

während, *w. gen.*, during; *conj.*, while

die Waise, –n, orphan

der Wald, –es, ⸚er, woods

der Walzer, –s, —, waltz

die Wand, ⸚e, wall

wandern, *wk.*, ist gewandert, to wander

die Wanduhr, –en, wall-clock

wann, when

warm, warm

warten auf (*w. accus.*), *wk.*, to wait for

der Wärter, –s, —, keeper

warum, why

was, what; that; was für, what sort of

waschen (ä), u, a, to wash

das Wasser, –s, —, water

weder ... noch, neither ... nor

der Weg, –es, –e, way, road

wegen, *w. gen.*, on account of

das Weib, –es, –er, woman

Weihnachten (*plur., w. sing. verb*), Christmas

weihnachtlich, Christmas (-like)

der Weihnachtsbaum, –s, ⸚e, Christmas tree; —einkauf, Christmas purchase; —lied, Christmas song; —punsch, Christmas punch; —tag, Christmas day

weil, because

der Wein, –es, –e, wine

weinen, *wk.*, to cry, weep

weise, wise

die Weise, –n, manner; auf diese W., in this manner

weiß, white

weiß, weißt, *pres. sg. of* wissen

weit, wide, far, distant; von weitem,

from afar; ohne weiteres, without further ado

weiter=geben (i), a, e, to pass on

der Weizen, –s, wheat

welch, which

die Welle, –n, wave

die Welt, –en, world

der Weltkrieg, –s, –e, world war

wem, *dat. of* wer

wenig, little; *plur.*, few

weniger, less, minus

wenn, if, whenever

wer, who, whoever

werden (i), wurde, ist geworden, to become; *fut. aux.*, shall, will; — zu, to become; — aus, to become of

werfen (i), a, o, to throw, cast

das Werk, –es, –e, work; im Werke sein, to be going on

das Wesen, –s, personality, being

wessen, *gen. of* wer

(das) Westfa'len, –s, Westphalia

das Wetter, –s, weather

wichtig, important

sich widmen, *wk.*, to devote o.s. to (*dat.*)

wie, as, how

wieder, again

wie'der=holen, *wk.*, to get again

wiederho'len, *wk.*, to repeat

wieder=kommen, a, ist wiedergekommen, to return

auf Wiedersehen, goodbye

wiegen, *wk.*, to rock, sway

(das) Wien, –s, Vienna

Wiener, Viennese, of Vienna

die Wiese, –n, meadow

wieviel, how much, how many

am wievielten, on what date

willkom'men, welcome

das Willkom'men, –s, welcome

der Wind, –es, –e, wind

winken, *wk.*, to wave, beckon

wirklich, really, actually

das Wirtshaus, –es, ⸚er, village inn

wissen, wußte, gewußt, to know

die Witwe, –n, widow

wo, where

die Woche, –n, week

das Wochenende, –s, –n, week-end

die Woge, –n, (turbulent) wave

wohin', to what place

wohl, probably, I dare say; I wonder, I presume; well

das Wohl, –s, welfare, health

wohnen, *wk.*, to dwell, live

die Wohnstube, –n, living room (*less pretentious than* Wohnzimmer)

die Wohnung, –en, dwelling, house, apartment

das Wohnzimmer, –s, –, living room

die Wolke, –n, cloud

woraus', out of what

das Wort, –es, –e *or* ⸚er, word

die Wunde, –n, wound

das Wunder, –s, –, miracle

wunderschön, wonderful

der Wunsch, –es, ⸚e, wish

wünschen, *wk.*, to wish

die Würde, –n, dignity

der Wurm, –es, ⸚er, worm

die Wurst, ⸚e, sausage

wütend, furious, raging

3

die Zahl, –en, number

zählen, *wk.*, to count

der Zahn, –es, ⸚e, tooth

z.B. = zum Beispiel, e.g.

die Zehnta'lernote, –n, ten taler bill (Taler = 3 marks)

das Zeichen, –s, –, sign, signal

zeigen, *wk.*, to show

der Zeiger, –s, –, hand (of timepiece)

die Zeit, –en, time

die Zeitung, –en, newspaper

das Zeitwort, –s, ⸚er, verb

die Zelle, –n, cell

der Zellenschlüssel, –s, —, key to a cell

zerbrechen (i), ā, ŏ, to break

zerschinden, zerschindete, zerschunden, to skin

zerschmettern, wk., to smash, crush

zerschneiden, i, i, to cut in two

zerstören, wk., to destroy

der Zettel, –s, —, note, piece of paper

ziehen, zog, ist gezogen, to go; tr., to draw

das Ziel, –es, –e, goal

ziemlich, rather, fairly

die Zigarre, –n, cigar

die Zigarrenkiste, –n, cigar-box

das Zimmer, –s, —, room

die Ziviltrauung, –en, civil marriage

zu, to; too; for

das Zuchthaus, –es, ⸚er, penitentiary

zuerst', at first

der Zufluchtsort, –s, –e, place of refuge

zufrie'den, satisfied, content

der Zug, –es, ⸚e, train

die Zukunft, future

zum = zu dem

zu=nähen, wk., to sew up

die Zunge, –n, tongue

zur = zu der

zurück', back, back again

zurück'=fahren, u, ist zurückgefahren, to drive back

zurück'=halten (ä), ie, a, to keep back

zurück'=kehren, wk., ist zurückgekehrt, to return

zurück'=legen, wk., to traverse, put behind one

zusam'men, together

zu=schließen, o, o, to lock

zu=stecken, wk., to slip to

zu=steuern, wk., ist zugesteuert, to steer for, head for

zuviel', too much

die Zwangsarbeit, –en, penal labor

zwar, to be sure

zwei, two

zwischen, w. dat. and accus., between

ENGLISH–GERMAN VOCABULARY

A

able; to be able, imſtan'be ſein; kön=
nen, *modal aux.*

about, über *w. accus.*

acquit, frei=ſprechen (i), a, o

across, über *w. accus.*

in **advance,** im vor'aus

advise, raten (ä), ie, a, *w. dat. of
person*

afraid; to be afraid for, Angſt haben
um

after, *prep.,* nach, *w. dat.; conj.,* nach=
dem'

after-dinner speech, die Tiſchrede, –n

afternoon, der Nachmittag, –s, –e; in
the —, am Nachmittag

again, wieder

against, gegen *w. accus.*

ago; a year ago, vor einem Jahr

alive, am Leben

all, alle; all that, alles, was

all kinds, allerlei'

allow, erlauben, *wk., w. dat. of person*

alone, allein'

already, ſchon

also, auch

altar, der Altar', –s, –e

always, immer

America, (das) Ame'rika, –s

American, der Amerika'ner, –s, —

angry, böſe

answer, antworten, *wk.*

appear, erſcheinen, ie, iſt erſchienen

apple, der Apfel, –s, –

are they not, nicht wahr; doch

arithmetic lesson, die Rechenſtunde, –n

arm, der Arm, –es, –e

arm-chair, der Seſſel, –s, —

around, um *w. accus.*

as if, als ob

ask, fragen, *wk.;* ask for, bitten um,
a, e

at, bei, zu, an, um, in

aunt, die Tante, –n

autobiography, die Selbſt'biogra=
phie', –n

away, (distant) entfernt'

B

baker, der Bäcker, –s, —

ball, der Ball, –es, –e

be, ſein, war, iſt geweſen; es gibt, a, e;
how are you, wie geht es Ihnen?

bear, tragen (ä), u, a

beat, ſchlagen (ä), u, a

beautiful, ſchön

because, weil

become, werden (i), wurde, iſt ge=
worden

bed, das Bett, –es, –en; in bed, im
Bett; go to bed, zu Bett gehen

before, *prep.,* vor, *w. dat. or accus.;
conj.,* bevor', ehe

begin, an=fangen (ä), i, a

behind, hinter, *w. dat. or accus.*

believe, glauben, *wk., w. dat. of
person*

beside, besides, außer, *w. dat.*

best, der beste

betray, verraten (ä), ie, a

better, besser

between, zwischen, *w. dat. or accus.*

big, groß

bird, der Vogel, –s, ⸚

birthday, der Geburts'tag, –s, –e

black, schwarz

bless, segnen, *wk.*

blood, das Blut, –es

bloody, blutig

boat, das Boot, –es, –e

book, das Buch, –es, ⸚er

bookshop, die Buchhandlung, –en

border, die Grenze, –n

both, beide

bowl, die Bowle, –n

box, der Kasten, –s, ⸚

boy, der Junge, –n, –n; der Knabe, –n, –n

bread, das Brot, –es, –e

break, zerbrechen (i), a, o

breathe, ätmen, *wk.*

brew, brauen, *wk.*

bring, bringen, *irreg.;* — along, mitbringen

brother, der Bruder, –s, ⸚; brother-in-law, der Schwager, –s, ⸚

burn, brennen, *irreg.*

business, das Geschäft', –s, –e; — man, der Kaufmann, –s, Kaufleute

busy, beschäf'tigt

but, aber, sondern

buy, kaufen, *wk.*

by; drive by, vorbei=fahren (ä), u, ist vorbeigefahren

C

cabinet, der Schrank, –es, ⸚e

cake, der Kuchen, –s, —

calf, das Kalb, –es, ⸚er

call, rufen, ie, u; call for, abholen, *wk.;* to be called, heißen, ie, ei

can, können, *modal aux.*

cap, die Mütze, –n

capsize, um=kippen, *wk.,* ist umgekippt

car, der Wagen, –s, —

care, sorgen, *wk.;* do not care to, mag nicht

carriage, der Wagen, –s, —

carry, tragen (ä), u, a

castle, das Schloß, –es, ⸚er

catch, fangen (ä), i, a

celebrate, feiern, *wk.*

cell, die Zelle, –n

century, das Jahrhun'dert, –s, –e

ceremony (of marriage), die Trauung, –en

chair, der Stuhl, –es, ⸚e

cheap, billig

chicken, das Huhn, –es, ⸚er

child, das Kind, –es, –er

Christmas, (die) Weihnachten, *plur.,* *w. sing. verb;* — Eve, der Heilige Abend, der Weihnachtsabend; — song, das Weihnachtslied; — shopping, Weihnachtseinkäufe (*plur.*); — tree, der Weihnachtsbaum

church, die Kirche, –n; at church, in der Kirche; *adj.,* kirchlich

cigar, die Zigar're, –n

cigar box, die Zigar'renkiste, –n

city, die Stadt, ⸚e

class, die Klasse, –n

clear, klar

clever, klug

clock, die Uhr, –en

close, schließen, o, o

clothes, Kleider (*plur.*)

clothing, die Kleidung

cloud, die Wolke, –n

coat, der Mantel, –s, ⸚; inside coat-pocket, die Brusttasche, –n

coffee, der Kaffee, –s

cold, kalt

come, kommen, a, ist gekommen

company, der Besuch', –s, –e

consent (to marry), das Jawort,
–s, –e

contented, zufrie'den

cook (woman), die Köchin, –nen

cooky, das Plätzchen, –s, —

cordial, herzlich; most cordially,
aufs herzlichste

corner, die Ecke, –n

cost, kosten, wk.

count, zählen, wk.

country; in the c., auf dem Lande;
to the c., aufs Land

country people, die Landleute

courage, der Mut, –es

courageous, mutig

cousin (male), der Vetter, –s, –n

covered, bedeckt'

cow, die Kuh, ⸚e

cozy, gemüt'lich

creature, das Geschöpf', –s, –e

criminal, der Verbre'cher, –s, —

crowd, die Menge, –n

cruel, grausam

cucumber salad, der Gur'kensalat', –s

cut, schneiden, i, i

D

dance, tanzen, wk.

dare, dürfen, modal aux.

dark, dunkel

dashing, schneidig

daughter, die Tochter, ⸚

day, der Tag, –es, –e

dear, lieb

death, der Tod, –es

decide, beschließen, o, o

delicious, köstlich

demand, verlangen, wk.

devote oneself, sich widmen, wk.

die, sterben (i), a, ist gestorben; —
a slow death, eines langsamen
Todes —

difficult, schwer

dignity, die Würde, –n

dining-room, die Eßstube, –n (small
and unpretentious); das Eßzim=
mer, –s, —; — furniture, die
Eßzimmermöbel (plur.)

dinner; at —, bei Tisch

disgrace, die Schande

dishes, das Geschirr', –s

do, tun, tat, getan; machen, wk.;
how do you do, guten Tag; there
is not much doing, es ist nicht viel
los; it can be done, es geht

doctor, der Arzt, –es, ⸚e; der Dok=
tor, –s, –to'ren; in address, Herr
Doktor

dog, der Hund, –es, –e

door, die Tür, –en

dress; to make dresses, schneidern,
wk.

drink, trinken, a, u

drive, fahren (ä), u, ist gefahren;
— past, vorbei'=fahren

dune, die Düne, –n

duplicate key, der Nachschlüssel, –s, —

during, während, w. gen.

duty, die Pflicht, –en

dwelling, die Wohnung, –en

E

each, jeder

each other, einan'der or plur. pronoun

early, früh

eat, essen (i), a, gegessen

egg, das Ei, –es, –er

eight, acht

either . . . or, entwe'der (or ent'=
weder) . . . oder

electric, elek'trisch

eleven, elf

else, sonst

end, das Ende, –s, –n

engaged, verlobt; — couple, das Brautpaar, –s, –e

English, Englisch (language)

enough, genug'

enter, eintreten (i), a, ist eingetreten

entire, ganz

estate, das Gut, –es, ‑‑er

eve, der Abend, –s, –e

even, sogar'

evening, der Abend, –s, –e; to-morrow —, morgen abend; one —, eines Abends

every, jeder

everything, alles

examination, die Untersu'chung, –en

excite, auf‑regen, wk.

expression, der Ausdruck, –s, ‑‑e

F

face, das Gesicht', –s, –er

faithful, treu

fall, fallen (ä), ie, ist gefallen

family, die Fami'lie, –n

far, weit

fashion, die Mode, –n

fast, schnell

fasten, an‑bringen, irreg.

father, der Vater, –s, ‑‑

favorable, günstig

feel, sich fühlen, wk.

fetch, holen, wk.

few, wenige; a few, ein paar, einige

fiancée, die Braut, ‑‑e

fifteenth, der fünfzehnte

fifth, der fünfte

fight, streiten, i, i

fighter for liberty, der Freiheitskämpfer, –s, —

film, der Film, –es, –e

find, finden, a, u

fine, famos'

finger, der Finger, –s, —

fire, das Feuer, –s, —

first, der erste; adv., zuerst

fit, passen, wk.

five, fünf

flee, fliehen, o, ist geflohen

flight, die Flucht

flow, fließen, o, ist geflossen

flower, die Blume, –n

fly, fliegen, o, ist geflogen

follow, folgen, wk., ist gefolgt

food, das Essen, –s

for, für, w. accus.; for an hour, eine Stunde; for Christmas, zu Weihnachten

force, die Gewalt', –en

forget, vergessen (i), a, e

forgive, vergeben (i), a, e, w. dat. of person

four, vier

France, (das) Frankreich, –s

free, frei

freedom, die Freiheit, –en

friend, der Freund, –es, –e; woman —, die Freundin, –nen

from, von, w. dat.

in front of, vor, w. dat. or accus.

frontier, die Grenze, –n

fruit, das Obst, –es

fugitive, der Flüchtling, –s, –e

fulfil, erfüllen, wk.

funny, lustig

furniture; piece of f., das Möbel, –s, —; furniture, die Möbel (plur.)

G

garden, der Garten, –s, ‑‑

gate, das Tor, –es, –e

gentleman, der Herr, –n, –en

German, beutſch, ber Deutſche (*adj. infl.*)

Germany, (das) Deutſchland, –s

get, werden, (i), wurde, iſt geworden; (go and) get, holen, *wk.*, get into, ſteigen in (*w. accus.*) ie, iſt geſtiegen; get up, auf=ſtehen, *irreg.*, iſt auf= geſtanden

give, geben (i), a, e; (to present), ſchenken, *wk.*

glad; they are glad, ſie freuen ſich

glass, das Glas, –es, ⸚er

glittering, glitzernb

go, gehen, ging, iſt gegangen; fahren (ä), u, iſt gefahren; go by railway, mit der Eiſenbahn fahren

god, Gott, –es, ⸚er

going; what was going on, was im Werke war

golden, gölden

good, gut; a good thing, gut

goodbye, auf Wiederſehen

goose, die Gans, ⸚e

government, die Regie'rung, –en

grandchild, der Enkel, –s, —

gray, grau

great, groß

greet, begrüßen, *wk.;* — each other, ſich begrüßen

grow, wachſen (ä), u, iſt gewachſen

grown-up, groß

guess, raten (ä), ie, a

guest, der Gaſt, –es, ⸚e

'gymnasium,' das Gymna'ſium, –s, –ſien

H

hair, das Haar, –es, –e

half, die Hälfte, –n; half past four, halb fünf

ham, der Schinken, –s, —

hand, die Hand, ⸚e; in our hands, in der Hand

hand over, überge'ben (i), a, e

hang, hängen, i, a

happen, paſſieren, *wk.*, iſt paſſiert; geſchehen (ie) a, iſt geſchehen

happy, glücklich; Happy New Year, proſit (pröſt) Neujahr

harbor, der Hafen, –s, ⸚

hat, der Hut, –es, ⸚e

have, haben; have to, müſſen; has them taken, läßt ſie ... bringen

hear, hören, *wk.*

help, helfen (i), a, o, *w. dat.*

her, *poss. adj.,* ihr

here, hier

herring-salad, der He'ringsſalat', –s

hers, der (die, das) ihrige (ihre)

herself, ſich

high, hoch (hoh–)

his, ſein

history, die Geſchich'te

hold, halten (ä), ie, a

hole, das Loch, –es, ⸚er

home, das Haus, –es, ⸚er; at home, zu Hauſe; to take home, nach Hauſe bringen

homeland, die Heimat, –en

home town, die Heimatſtadt, ⸚e

honest, ehrlich

honesty, die Ehrlichkeit

honor, die Ehre, –n

horse, das Pferd, –es, –e

hospitable, gaſtlich

hot, heiß

hotel, das Hotel', –s, –s

hour, die Stunde, –n

house, das Haus, –es, ⸚er

housewife, die Hausfrau, –en

how, wie

husband, der Mann, –es, ⸚er

hymn, der Choral', –s, ⸚e

I

if, wenn; as if, als ob
impatiently, ungeduldig
in, in, *w. dat. or accus.;* in the afternoon, am Nachmittag; in the country, auf dem Lande
inhabitant, der Einwohner, –s, —
inn, das Wirtshaus, –es, –er
insurgent, der Aufrührer, –s, —
intend, wollen, *modal aux.*
interest, interessie'ren, *wk.*
into, in, *w. accus.*
invitation, die Einladung, –en
it, es (er, sie)

J

Jack, Hans
jolly, lustig

K

keep, halten (ä), ie, a
keeper, der Wärter, –s, —
key, der Schlüssel, –s, —
kind; all kinds of, allerlei'
king, der König, –s, –e
kitchen, die Küche, –n
knife, das Messer, –s, —
knot, der Knoten, –s, —
know, wissen, *irreg.;* kennen, *irreg.;* können, *modal aux.*

L

lady, die Dame, –n; young lady, das Fräulein, –s, —
lake, der See, –s, –n
land, das Land, –es, –er; go on land, an Land gehen
land, landen, *wk.,* ist gelandet
large, groß

last, der letzte; of last year, vom vorigen Jahr
late, spät
latest, der neuste
the latter, dieser
laugh, lachen, *wk.;* — at, lachen über *w. accus.*
lay off, ab=legen, *wk.*
learn, lernen, *wk.*
learned, gelehrt'; a learned man, ein Gelehrter (*adj. infl.*)
leave, der Abschied, –s
lend, leihen, ie, ie
lesson, die Stunde, –n
let, lassen (ä), ie, a; let us talk over, besprechen wir; — down, herun'ter= lassen
letter, der Brief, –es, –e
liberation, die Befrei'ung, –en
lie, liegen, a, e
life, das Leben, –s
light, das Licht, –es, –er
like; how do you —, wie findet ihr; would like, möchte; likes to sit, sitzt gern
like (as), wie
lilac, der Flieder, –s
little, klein
live, leben, *wk.,* wohnen, *wk.*
living; to make one's —, sich ernäh= ren, *wk.*
lock, zu=schließen, o, o
long, *adv.,* lange
look for, suchen, *wk.;* look out upon, hinaus=sehen auf *w. accus.,* (ie), a, e
loosen, lösen, *wk.*
lose, verlieren, o, o
loud(ly), laut

M

make, machen, *wk.;* — a speech, eine Rede halten

man, der Mann, –es, ⸚er
many, viele; many a, manch
map, der Plan, –es, ⸚e; die Karte, –n
mark (coin), die Mark, —
market, der Markt, –es, ⸚e
married, verhei'ratet
marry, heiraten, wk.
matinée idol, der Filmheld, –en, –en
meat, das Fleisch, –es
meet, treffen (i), a, o, w. accus.
mentally, geistig
merrily, lustig
merry Christmas, fröhliche Weih=
    nachten
midnight, die Mitternacht, ⸚e
million, die Million', –en
millionaire, der Millionär', –s, –e
mine, das (der, die) meinige (meine);
    meiner, meine, meins
miserable, elend
money, das Geld, –es, –er
more, mehr
morning, der Morgen, –s, —; in the
    —, am M.
most, der (die, das) meiste; adv., am
    meisten, am besten
mother, die Mutter, ⸚
mountain, der Berg, –es, –e
move, ziehen, o, ist gezogen
Mr., Herr
Mrs., Frau
much, viel; how much, wieviel
multiplication table, das Einmaleins'
music, die Musik'
musician, der Musikant', –en, –en
must, müssen, modal aux.
my, mein
mysterious, geheim'nisvoll

N

naughty, unartig
nearer, näher

necessary, nötig
need, brauchen, wk.
neighbor, der Nachbar, –s, –n
neither . . . nor, weder . . . noch
nephew, der Neffe, –n, –n
nest, das Nest, –es, –er
never, nie
new, neu; New Year, das Neujahr, –s
newspaper, die Zeitung, –en
New York, adj., New Yorker
next, der nächste
nice, schön
niece, die Nichte, –n
night, die Nacht, ⸚e
nine, neun
nineteenth, der neunzehnte
no, nein; kein
no one, niemand, –s
noble, edel
nobody, niemand, –s
noise, der Lärm, –s; (sound) das
    Geräusch', –es, –e
none, kein
not, nicht
note, der Zettel, –s, —
nothing, nichts; nothing that, nichts,
    was
November, der Novem'ber, –s, —
now, jetzt
Nuremberg, (das) Nürnberg, –s
nutshell, die Nußschale, –n

O

observation, die Beob'achtung, –en
obtain, bekommen, a, o
occupy, beschäftigen, wk.
October, der Okto'ber, –s, —; in —,
    im Oktober
odor, der Geruch', –s, ⸚e
of, use genitive; (made of) aus;
    von
offer, bieten, o, o

official, der Beam'te (adj. infl.);
     lower o., der Unterbeamte
often, oft
old, alt
old-fashioned, altmodisch
on, an; auf
once, einmal; once more, noch einmal
one, ein; einer, etc.; man
only, nur
open, öffnen, wk.
or, oder
orchard, der Obstgarten, -s, ⸚
order, bestellen, wk.
in order to, um zu
other, ander
ought, sollte, etc.
our, ours, unser, der (die, das) unsrige
out, hinaus'
outdoors, draußen
outside, außerhalb w. gen.
oven, der Ofen, -s, ⸚
over, prep., über, w. dat. or accus.;
     adv., vorbei', aus

P

package, das Paket', -s, -e
parachute, der Fallschirm, -s, -e
pardon, begnadigen, wk.
parents, die Eltern
Paris, adj., Pari'ser
pass, see past
passport, der Paß, -es, ⸚e
past, vorbei'; go —, vorbei=gehen,
     irreg., ist vorbeigegangen
pastor, der Pfarrer, -s, —
patent-leather shoe, der Lackschuh,
     -s, -e
pay, bezahlen, wk.
penal labor, die Zwangsarbeit, -en
people, Leute (plur.); der Mensch, -en,
     -en; das Volk, -es, ⸚er
perhaps, vielleicht'

personality, das Wesen, -s
personally, persön'lich
pfennig (coin), der Pfennig, -s, — or
     -e
physically, körperlich
physician, der Arzt, -es, ⸚e; der
     Doktor, -s, -to'ren
picture, das Bild, -es, -er; — post
     card, die Ansichtskarte, -n
piece, das Stück, -es, -e; — of paper,
     der Zettel, -s, —
plate, der Teller, -s, —
play, spielen, wk.
playmate, der Spiel'kamerad', -en, -en
please, interj., bitte
please; it pleases her, es gefällt
     ihr
pleasure, das Vergnügen, -s, —
pocket, die Tasche, -n
policeman, der Polizei'beam'te, (adj.
     infl.)
polka, die Polka, -s
poor, arm
position, die Stelle, -n
practical, praktisch
preach, predigen, wk.; halten (Trau=
     rede)
present, das Geschenk', -s, -e
be present, dabei' sein
pretty, hübsch
price, der Preis, -es, -e
prince, der Fürst, -en, -en
prison; in —, im Gefängnis
prisoner, der Gefangene (adj. infl.)
promise, versprechen (i), a, o
promise, das Versprechen, -s, —
prove, beweisen, ie, ie
Prussian, adj., preußisch
punch, der Punsch, -es, ⸚e
punishment, die Strafe, -n
pupil, der Schüler, -s, —
pursuer, der Verfolger, -s, —
put on, an=ziehen, zog an, angezogen

Q

question, die Frage, –n
quiet, still
quite, ganz

R

radio, der Rundfunk, –s, –e
railway, die Eisenbahn, –en
raise, erheben, o, o
reach, erreichen, wk.
read, lesen (ie), a, e
ready (done), fertig; (ready for), bereit'
really, wirklich
receive, erhalten (ä), ie, a
recuperate, sich erholen, wk.
red, rot
refrigerator, der Kühlschrank, –s, ⸚e
rejoice, sich freuen, wk.
relative, der Verwand'te (adj. infl.)
rely, sich verlassen (ä), ie, a (auf w. accus.)
remain, bleiben, ie, ist geblieben
remember, sich erinnern an, w. accus.; — me to, grüßen Sie . . . von mir
rent, mieten, wk.
resemble, einem ähnlich sehen (ie), a, e
return, zurück-kehren, wk., ist zurückgekehrt
rich, reich
ride, fahren (ä), u, ist gefahren
right, das Recht, –es, –e
right (not left), recht; (not wrong), recht, richtig
ripe, reif
road, die Landstraße, –n
roast, gebraten
roof, das Dach, –es, ⸚er
room, das Zimmer, –s, —; (less pretentious) die Stube, –n; (space) Platz

room, wohnen, wk.
rope, das Seil, –s, –e
rose, die Rose, –n
round, rund
row, rudern, wk.
rule, die Regie'rung, –en
run, laufen (äu), ie, ist gelaufen
rush, stürzen, wk., ist gestürzt

S

sake; for the sake of, um . . . willen
salad, der Salat', –s, –e
salary, das Gehalt', –s, ⸚er
say, sagen, wk.
school, die Schule, –n
school-chum, der Schulkamerad, –en, –en
seaside resort, das Seebad, –s, ⸚er
secret, das Geheimnis, –ses, –se
see, sehen (ie), a, e; see again, wieder=sehen
send, schicken, wk.
servant-girl, das Dienstmädchen, –s, —
seven, sieben
several, mehrere
sew up, zu=nähen, wk.
shall, (future) werden
shoe, der Schuh, –es, –e
shoot, schießen, o, o
shop, das Geschäft, –s, –e; der Laden, –s, ⸚
shopping; do —, Einkäufe machen, wk.
shortly, kurz
should, sollte, etc.
shout, rufen, ie, u
show, zeigen, wk.
shrub, der Strauch, –es, ⸚er
sick, krank
side, die Seite, –n
silent; to be silent, schweigen, ie, ie
silk, die Seide
sing, singen, a, u

sister, die Schwester, –n

sit, sitzen, saß, gesessen

six, sechs

sky, der Himmel, –s, —

sleep, schlafen (ä), ie, a

slow, langsam

small, klein

smile, lächeln, *wk.*

smoke, rauchen, *wk.*

so, so

soldier, der Soldat', –en, –en

some, einige, manche

some one, jemand, –s

something, etwas

son, der Sohn, –es, ⸚e; little son, das Söhnchen, –s, —

son-in-law, der Schwiegersohn, –s, ⸚e

soon, bald

as soon as, sobald'

speak, sprechen (i), a, o

speech, die Rede, –n; make a —, eine Rede halten (ä), ie, a

spend (time), verbringen, *irreg.*

spinach, der Spinat', –s

in spite of, trotz *w. gen.*

splendid, herrlich

spring, der Frühling, –s, –e

stand, stehen, *irreg.*

star, der Stern, –es, –e

start on, an=treten (i), a, e

station, der Bahnhof, –s, ⸚e; at the —, am Bahnhof

stay, bleiben, ie, ist geblieben; wohnen, *wk.*

steal, stehlen (ie), a, o

steel furniture, die Stahlmöbel (*plur.*)

still, noch

storm, stürmen, *wk.*

story, die Geschich'te, –n

stranger, der Fremde (*adj. infl.*)

street, die Straße, –n

strong, stark

style, der Stil, –s, –e

succeed; he will not —, es wird ihm nicht gelingen (glücken)

such, solch, so

suffer, leiden, litt, gelitten

suit, der Anzug, –s, ⸚e

sum, die Summe, –n

support o.s., sich ernähren, *wk.*

sweets, die Süßigkeiten (*plur.*)

swim, schwimmen, a, o

Switzerland, die Schweiz

T

table, der Tisch, –es, –e

take, nehmen (i), a, o; bringen, *irreg.*

talk, reden, *wk.*; talk over, besprechen (i), a, o

tanned, braun

tavern, das Wirtshaus, –es, ⸚er

teacher, der Lehrer, –s, —; (woman) t., die Lehrerin, –nen

tell, erzählen, *wk.*

terrible, schrecklich

than, als

thank, danken, *wk.*, *w. dat. of person*

many thanks, danke schön; vielen Dank

that, *conj.*, daß

that, *dem. pro. or adj.*, das, jener

that, *rel.*, der; nothing that, nichts, was

their, ihr

then, da

there are, es gibt; es sind

they, sie; man

think, denken, *irreg.*; — of, — an *w. accus.*; — over, überle'gen, *wk.*

third, der dritte

this, dieser

thought, der Gedanke, –ns, –n

three, drei

through, durch, *w. accus.*

throw about, umher'=werfen (i), a, o

tile, der Ziegel, –s, —; der Dachziegel

time, die Zeit, –en; at that time, damals; three times, dreimal

tinsel, der Tand, –es

tired, müde (of, *gen.*)

to, zu; nach; um . . . zu

today, heute

to-morrow evening, morgen abend

to-night, heute abend

too (excessively), zu

top, die Spitze, –n

touch glasses, an=stoßen (ö) ie, o

tower, der Turm, –es, ⸚e

town, die Stadt, ⸚e

train, die Eisenbahn, –en; on the —, mit der Eisenbahn

train (of dress), die Schleppe, –n

travel, reisen, *wk.*, ist gereist

tree, der Baum, –es, ⸚e

trim, schmücken, *wk.*

troop, die Truppe, –n

true, treu; wahr

trust, trauen, *wk., w. dat.*

tulip, die Tulpe, –n

Turkey, die Türkei'

turn (become), werden (i), wurde, ist geworden

twelve, zwölf

twenty, zwanzig

two, zwei; the two, die beiden

typical, typisch

U

uncle, der Onkel, –s, —

under, unter *w. dat. or accus.*

unhappy, unglücklich

university, die Universität', –en

unlock, aufschließen, o, o

unnecessary, unnötig

until, *prep.*, bis *or* bis um; *conj.*, bis

use, gebrauchen, *wk.*

V

vacation, die Ferien (*plur.*)

vegetable, (green), das Gemü'se, –s, —

vegetable dealer, der Gemü'sehänd=ler, –s, —

veil, der Schleier, –s, —

veranda, die Veran'da, *plur.*, Veran=den

very much, very, sehr

victory, der Sieg, –es, –e

village, das Dorf, –es, ⸚er

violet, das Veilchen, –s, —

W

wait, warten, *wk.*

waiter, der Kellner, –s, —

walk, zu Fuß gehen

wall, die Wand, ⸚e

wallet, die Brieftasche, –n

waltz, der Walzer, –s, —

wander, wandern, *wk.*, ist gewandert

want, wollen; one wants, man will

warm, warm

wash, waschen, sich waschen (ä), u, a

watch, die Uhr, –en

watchful, wachsam

water, das Wasser, –s, —

wave, winken, *wk.*

wax candle, die Wachskerze, –n

way, der Weg, –es, –e

wear, tragen (ä), u, a

weather, das Wetter, –s

wedding, die Hochzeit, –en; w.-dress, das Brautkleid; w.-ring, der Trau=ring, –s, –e; w. sermon, die Trau=rede

week, die Woche, –n; two weeks, vierzehn Tage

well, gut; wohl, gesund' (healthy)

wet, naß

what, welch

when, als, wenn, wann
whenever, wenn
where, wo
whether, ob
which? welcher? *rel.*, der, die, das;
   wo-compounds
while, *conj.*, während
white, weiß
who? wer? he who, wer; *rel.*, der
whole, ganz
whose, *rel.*, dessen, deren; *interr.*,
   wessen
why, warum′
widow, die Witwe, –n
wife, die Frau, –en
will, (*future*), werden
wind, der Wind, –es, –e
window, das Fenster, –s, —
wish, wünschen, *wk.*
with, mit, *w. dat.*
within, innerhalb, *w. gen.*
without, ohne, *w. accus.*
woman, die Frau, –en
wonderful, wunderschön

wood, der Wald, –es, ⸚er; das Holz,
   –es, ⸚er
word, das Wort, –es, ⸚er *or* –e
work, die Arbeit, –en
work, arbeiten, *wk.*
wound, die Wunde, –n
write, schreiben, ie, ie

X

X-ray, der Röntgenstrahl, –s, –en

Y

yacht, die Jacht, –en
year, das Jahr, –es, –e
yes, ja
yesterday, gestern
you, du, Sie, ihr
young, jung; young lady, das Fräulein, –s, —
your, dein, Ihr, euer
yourself; you must read it —, Sie
   müssen es selber lesen

INDEX